HARBRACE
COLLEGE
WORKBOOK
FORM 11A

INSTRUCTOR'S EDITION

Larry G. Mapp
Middle Tennessee State University

HARCOURT BRACE JOVANOVICH
San Diego   New York   Chicago   Austin   Washington, D.C.
London   Sydney   Tokyo   Toronto

TO THE INSTRUCTOR

The two forms of the *Harbrace College Workbook* are designed to be used either independently or in conjunction with the Eleventh Edition of the *Harbrace College Handbook*. Each form is unique, however, because each develops a particular theme throughout its examples and exercises. Form 11A examines the cosmos, and Form 11C focuses on writing for the world of work. For Form 11A, all of the explanations in the previous edition have been examined and, at least in part, rewritten; nearly all of the exercises have been completely rewritten.

Arrangement   The materials in Form 11A are arranged in sections that parallel the sections in the *Harbrace College Handbook*, Eleventh Edition. The numbers and letters denoting subdivisions within the sections also correspond to those of the *Handbook*.

Section **1** of Form 11A covers the main points of grammar and punctuation; it is, in other words, a practical minicourse in the grammar and punctuation of sentences. Some students may be able to move directly from **section 1** to the later sections that treat word choice and sentence effectiveness (**sections 20** through **30**) or even to sections that go beyond the sentence to longer units of composition (**sections 31** through **33**). Other students will need additional review of basic areas—such as agreement, tense, and the uses of the comma and apostrophe—that is supplied in the intervening sections (**2** through **19**). Of course, the needs of the class or the individual student will determine how much time is devoted to **sections 2** through **19** and how many of the exercises in each section are assigned.

Exercises   The subject matter of the exercises and examples is the cosmos, or, more accurately, our effort as human beings to understand the cosmos. The exercises and examples cover not only contemporary explorations with the space shuttle, complex unmanned spacecraft, and the most advanced telescopes, but also the attempts of our forebears to clarify their relationship with the vast world beyond their own. While students work to improve their writing skills they also learn about the ancient observations of the Crab Nebula by Chinese astronomers; the struggles of Galileo, Copernicus, Lowell, Einstein, and Hawking; the various theories of the beginnings of the cosmos, our solar system, our planet; and the ends of things—the deaths of stars, the disappearances of comets, the extinction of stars. I have tried to make Form 11A an interesting and readable text because I believe that a student who becomes involved in the content of reading material ultimately will become more involved in the language being used. The exercises and examples will have added life and meaning for that student.

Writing   Form 11A includes sections on writing paragraphs (**32**) and essays (**33**). There is enough material in the examples and exercises within each of the chapters to provide a starting point for student writing. Students might be asked to respond to particular questions raised by their reading, perhaps even doing parallel reading in other sources to gather extra material; or they could be encouraged to respond to what they have read in less structured, more expressive writing.

The Dictionary   Use of the dictionary is stressed throughout Form 11A: in the study of nouns, adjectives, adverbs, and verbs, and in the sections on capitalization, abbreviations, italics, and numbers. Unless each member of the class is already familiar with the dictionary, the best place to begin teaching and learning dictionary skills might be **section 19**, "Good Usage and the Dictionary."

Spelling   Although most students receive little formal instruction in spelling after elementary school, correct spelling is important to success in college and in other work. Form 11A does not presume to be a complete spelling manual, but it does emphasize throughout the use of the dictionary to avoid various kinds of misspellings, and it covers all major spelling rules. In addition, it presents a list of words that are frequently misspelled in professional writing. Perhaps even more important, the "Individual Spelling List" at the end of the *Workbook* offers a chart on which students can record the words they misspell in their writing assignments and the reasons for the misspellings.

Note: Each of the forms of the *Harbrace College Workbook* is available in an Instructor's Edition as well as a Student Edition. The Instructor's Edition is an exact replica of the Student Edition, with answers to all exercises overprinted in red.

Acknowledgments   I am grateful to the staff of Harcourt Brace Jovanovich for helping with this book: Stuart Miller, acquisitions editor; Sarah Helyar Smith, manuscript editor; Lisa Werries, production editor; Don Fujimoto, designer; and Lynne Bush, production manager.

I offer special thanks to Jennifer Jordan-Henley and to Cynthia Duke for help in preparing the manuscript.

Finally, my thanks to my wife Ann and to our daughters Anna and Sarah. They are constant and loving supporters of everything I do.

Larry G. Mapp

TO THE STUDENT

You learn how to write chiefly by revising your own work. Corrections made for you are of comparatively little value. Therefore the instructor points out the problem but allows you to make the actual revision for yourself. The instructor usually indicates a necessary correction by a number (or a symbol) marked in the margin of your paper opposite the error. If a word is misspelled, the number **18** (or the symbol **sp**) will be used; if there is a sentence fragment, the number **2** (or the symbol **frag**); if there is a faulty reference of a pronoun, the number **28** (or the symbol **ref**). Consult the text (see the guides on the inside covers), master the principle underlying each correction, and make the necessary revisions in red. Draw one red line through words to be deleted, but allow such words to remain legible in order that the instructor may compare the revised form with the original.

The Comma   After the number **12** in the margin you should take special care to supply the appropriate letter (**a, b, c, d,** or **e**) from the explanatory sections on the comma to show why the comma is needed. Simply inserting a comma teaches little; understanding why it is required in a particular situation is a definite step toward mastery of the comma. (Your instructor may require that you pinpoint each of your errors by supplying the appropriate letter after every number written in the margin.)

Specimen Paragraph from a Student Theme

Marked by the Instructor with Numbers

3   Taking photographs for newspapers is hard work, it is not the

12   romantic carefree adventure glorified in motion pictures and novels. For

18   every great moment recorded by the stareing eye of the camera, there are

twenty routine assignments that must be handled in the same efficient

28   manner. They must often overcome great hardships. The work continues

24   for long hours. It must meet deadlines. At times they are called on to

2   risk their lives to obtain a picture. To the newspaper photographer, get-

ting a good picture being the most important task.

Marked by the Instructor with Symbols

cs   Taking photographs for newspapers is hard work, it is not the

,/   romantic carefree adventure glorified in motion pictures and novels. For

sp   every great moment recorded by the stareing eye of the camera, there are

twenty routine assignments that must be handled in the same efficient

ref   manner. They must often overcome great hardships. The work continues

sub for long hours. It must meet deadlines. At times they are called on to

risk their lives to obtain a picture. To the newspaper photographer, get-

frag ting a good picture being the most important task.

Corrected by the Student

3   Taking photographs for newspapers is hard work; it is not the

12 C romantic, carefree adventure glorified in motion pictures and novels. For

18   every great moment recorded by the ~~stareing~~ *staring* eye of the camera, there are

twenty routine assignments that must be handled in the same efficient

28   manner. ~~They must often overcome great hardships. The work continues~~ *newspaper photographers must often*

24 *overcome great hardships and work long hours to* ~~for long hours. It must meet deadlines.~~ At times they are called on to *meet deadlines.*

risk their lives to obtain a picture. To the newspaper photographer, get-

2   ting a good picture ~~being~~ *is* the most important task.

CONTENTS

GRAMMAR

MECHANICS

PUNCTUATION

SPELLING AND DICTION

EFFECTIVE SENTENCES

EFFECTIVE WRITING

SENTENCE SENSE

1

Develop your sentence sense.

You probably have more sentence sense than you realize. As proof, what is your response to this group of words?

> When the people of Tunguska, Siberia, awoke on June 30, 1908.

Probably you will say, almost without thinking, that something is missing from the sentence.

What would you write instead of "When the people of Tunguska, Siberia, awoke on June 30, 1908"? Maybe you would add words.

> When the people of Tunguska, Siberia, awoke on June 30, 1908, they saw a huge fireball in the morning sky.

In that case your sentence sense tells you to add another subject (*they*) and another verb (*saw*). Or maybe you would simply omit a word.

> The people of Tunguska, Siberia, awoke on June 30, 1908.

Your instinct tells you that without the word *when*, a subordinator, the group of words is a sentence. Whether you add another subject and verb or omit the subordinator, you are responding to your sense of what is needed to make the group of words into a complete thought.

As you have learned to speak and write, you have become aware of what a sentence is. But to develop this awareness fully, you must know the basic parts of a sentence and how they can be put together in clear and varied patterns. An understanding of this section, then, is necessary to the study of almost all the other parts of this text.

Almost all sentences have a *subject*, someone or something spoken about, and a *predicate*, something said (predicated) about the subject.

> SUBJECT + PREDICATE
> The bright blue light + sped across the morning sky.

The predicate may be subdivided into two parts: the *verb* and the *complement*. The verb states an action, an occurrence, or a state of being; and the complement receives the action of the verb or expresses something about the subject.

> SUBJECT + VERB + COMPLEMENT
> An explosion + shattered + the peaceful morning.
> [The complement receives the action of the verb.]
>
> The explosion + was + deafening.
> [The complement expresses something about the subject.]

Most of the sentences that we write have all three of these basic parts: Subject–Verb–Complement (S–V–C). In the examples that follow, the subject is underlined once, the verb twice, and the complement three times. (This is the pattern that you will be asked to follow when working the exercises in this section of the *Workbook*.)

S–V–C   We studied the explosion.

But some sentences have only the subject and the verb.

S–V   Shock waves rippled across the countryside.

To write clearly and simply, we make most of our sentence patterns follow the normal order—that is, Subject–Verb–Complement or Subject–Verb. But sometimes, for variety or for emphasis, we vary from the usual order.

NORMAL ORDER
S–V–C   The size of the explosion was unprecedented.

EMPHATIC ORDER
C–V–S   Unprecedented was the size of the explosion.

We also vary from normal order when we write most questions.

V–S–V–C   How can I describe the sound of the explosion?

C–V–S–V   How much sound does a nuclear bomb make?

And we vary from normal order when we write a sentence that begins with *there* or *it*.

V–S   There was evidence of the explosion all around the planet.

V–S   It is not surprising that the explosion is still being studied.

[When *it* introduces a sentence, the subject is usually more than one word. Here the subject is a clause, a structure discussed in **1b** and **1c**.]

Each of these basic sentence parts, along with the modifiers that may accompany them, is fully discussed in the following pages.

Deduct 5 for each blank correctly filled.

Basic Sentence Parts

Exercise 1-1

NAME _____ SCORE _____

DIRECTIONS   In the following sentences, the subject is underlined with one line, the verb with two lines, and the complement, when there is one, with three lines. Decide whether or not the sentence parts follow normal order. Write 1 in the blank if they do and 2 if they do not. When you have finished, try rewriting in normal order three of the sentences that you have labeled 2. (To do so, you will have to change a question into a statement or omit a "there.")

EXAMPLES

The Tunguska explosion destroyed a huge forested area.   *1*

Can you guess the cause of the explosion?   *2*

1. A comet caused the explosion at Tunguska.   *1*

2. There is only a very slight chance of a comet colliding with Earth.   *2*

3. However, a piece of Comet Encke probably caused the Tunguska event.   *1*

4. The comet was traveling in a direction opposite to that of Earth.   *1*

5. There was a head-on collision at very great speed.   *2*

6. The comet exploded and disintegrated.   *1*

7. There was no crater at the site of the explosion.   *2*

8. What does that mean?   *2*

9. The comet exploded about 8.5 kilometers above the ground.   *1*

10. Subsequently there were great forest fires and huge areas of destroyed timber.   *2*

11. Native hunters were the first to enter the disaster area.   *1*

12. Systematic investigation began two decades later.   *1*

13. What did the first scientists discover?   *2*

14. They discovered a burned area of about 2,000 square kilometers.   *1*

15. There was evidence of scorching over an area of 18 kilometers in diameter.   *2*

16. Leonard Kulik was the leader of the Soviet scientists.   *1*

17. Kulik directed the scientists to search for signs of a disintegrat-

    ing meteorite.   *1*

18. There were no meteorite fragments to be found.   *2*

19. Did the scientists find any physical remnants of the comet?   *2*

20. They found black glossy objects created by the explosion.   *1*

REVISIONS

1.

2.

3.

1a Learn to recognize verbs.

Although the verb is usually the second main part of the sentence, you should master it first because the verb is the heart of the sentence. It is the one part that no sentence can do without. Remember that a trainer can communicate with a dog using only verbs: *Sit. Stay. Fetch.*

Function   The verb, as the heart of the sentence, says something about the subject; it expresses an action, an occurrence, or a state of being.

> ACTION   Meteorites *flash* across the sky.
>
> OCCURRENCE   Some people *consider* meteorites to be signs of good fortune.
>
> STATE OF BEING   Meteorites *look* like rocks.

The verb also determines what kind of complement the sentence will have: either a word or words that will receive the action of the verb or a word or words that will point back to the subject in some way. If the verb is *transitive*, it transfers or passes along its action to a complement called a *direct object*.

> TRANSITIVE   Scientists keep careful records of meteorite showers.
>
> [The transitive verb *keep* passes its action along to its complement, the direct object *records*.]

If the verb is *intransitive*, it does not pass its action along to a complement. One kind of intransitive verb is complete in itself; it has no complement.

> INTRANSITIVE   The meteorite plummeted.
>
> [The verb *plummeted* is complete in itself; it does not need a complement.]

Another type of intransitive verb is the *linking verb*, which links the subject with a complement that refers back to the subject. The most common linking verbs are *be* (*is, are, was, were, has been, have been, will be*, and so on), *seem*, and *appear*, as well as those that are related to the senses, such as *feel, look*, and *taste*.

> INTRANSITIVE   The astronomer seems awestruck.
>
> [The linking verb *seems* calls for a complement that refers back to the subject.]

Position   The verb (underlined twice) is usually the second main part of the sentence, but in questions, emphatic sentences, and sentences that begin with *there* or *it*, the verb may come first or before the subject (underlined once).

USUAL ORDER   Scientists can predict some meteorite showers.

QUESTION   Can scientists predict meteorite showers?

EMPHATIC   Rare is a large meteorite.

THERE   There are physical similarities between meteorites and asteroids.

Always look for the verb first when you are trying to match it with its subject. This practice will help you to avoid agreement errors (the use of a plural verb with a singular subject and vice versa). If you look for the subject first, you may easily choose the wrong word in a sentence like this: "The scientists in the research institute (is, are) studying the moon." You are much less likely to choose "institute" as the subject if you first locate the verb (*is, are*) *studying* and then determine who or what the verb is speaking about: the institute is not studying; the *scientists* are studying.

Form   The verb may be recognized not only by its function and its position but also by its endings in the third person. Verbs ending in *-s* or *-es* are singular in number: he tries, she jumps, it requires. Verbs ending in *-d* or *-ed* are in the past tense: he tried, she jumped, it required. (Sometimes, however, the verb changes its form altogether in the past tense: he rides, he rode; she lies down, she lay down; it comes, it came.)

Auxiliaries (Helping Verbs)   The verb may be one word or several words. The main part of the verb—the word that actually expresses the action, occurrence, or state of being—may be accompanied by *auxiliaries* or *helping verbs*—words like *has, have, should,* and *can* and forms of *be* (see the Appendix for a list of auxiliary verbs). This cluster of verbs is referred to as a *verb phrase.* Often the parts of the verb phrase are separated.

Most meteorites do not survive passage through the atmosphere.

[*Not* often comes between the auxiliary and the main verb; it is a modifier, not a part of the verb, even when it appears in contractions like *don't.*]

Have you seen a shower of meteorites?

[In a question the parts of the verb phrase are usually separated.]

Phrasal Verbs   The main verb may also be accompanied by a word like *up, down,* or *in* that functions as a part of the verb. This part of the verb is called a *particle;* the particle usually changes or adds to the meaning of the main verb.

VERB   I passed a meteorite display in the museum.

VERB WITH I passed up a good opportunity to photograph a meteorite display in
   PARTICLE

the museum.

The particle ordinarily follows immediately after the main verb, but it may sometimes be separated from the main verb.

I passed the opportunity up.

SUMMARY

Function The verb expresses an action (*throw, run, talk*), an occurrence (*prevent, criticize, modify*), or a state of being (*be, seem, appear, become*).

Position The verb is usually the second main part of the sentence ("We *photographed* a meteorite shower."), but it may come elsewhere, especially in questions ("*Can* you *photograph* a meteorite shower?").

Form In the third person (*he, she it*), the verb shows singular number by an *-s* or *-es* ending (feed*s*, come*s*, carri*es*) and past tense by a *-d* or *-ed* ending (solve*d*, walk*ed*, carri*ed*). Sometimes, however, the verb changes form completely in the past tense: *run, ran; buy, bought; choose, chose*. The verb may be only one word (*turned*) or several words (*has turned, will be turning, should turn in*).

Deduct 5 for each blank incorrectly filled.

Verbs in Simple Sentences

Exercise 1–2

NAME _____ SCORE _____

DIRECTIONS   In the following sentences the subject, which is usually the first main part of the sentence, is underlined once. Underline the verb twice and enter the word or words that make up the verb in the blank. Notice that a singular verb is used with a singular subject and a plural verb with a plural subject.

EXAMPLE
Many people recall making a wish after seeing a "falling
star."   *recall*

1. The term "falling star" refers to a meteorite.   *refers*

2. Meteorites usually are composed of stones, iron, or
   a combination of these materials.   *are composed*

3. After entering the Earth's atmosphere, meteorites
   begin to burn.   *begin*

4. The heat from entry into the atmosphere actually
   vaporizes the meteorites.   *vaporizes*

5. This vaporizing process is called "ablation."   *is called*

6. A few meteorites do survive ablation.   *do survive*

7. Most of the meteorites reach the Earth only peb-
   bles in size.   *reach*

8. These surviving pebbles are usually too small to
   find.   *are*

9. Scientists have long wished to find more of these
   surviving pebbles.   *have wished*

10. In recent years they have begun to search Antarc-
    tica for meteorites.   *have begun*

11. In ice and snow even the smallest meteorites are
    easily detected.   *are detected*

12. Scientists also rely on the glacial flow to uncover
    meteorites.   *rely*

13. Glacial flow very slowly alters the margins of Ant-
arctica.

    alters

14. By examining the leading edges of the glacial flow,
scientists discover the embedded meteorites.

    discover

15. Only rarely do large meteorites survive ablation.

    do survive

16. After fragmenting during entry into the atmosphere, large meteorites burst into a shower.

    burst

17. Scientists label all the fragments in a shower with
one name.

    label

18. During the night of February 9, 1969, a meteorite
shower lighted the sky over a small Mexican town.

    lighted

19. Researchers later gathered nearly two tons of speci-
mens from the villagers' farmlands.

    gathered

20. The largest specimen weighed 110 kilograms.

    weighed

Deduct 3 4/5 for each blank incorrectly filled and 3 4/5 for each word incorrectly underlined.

Verbs in Simple Sentences

Exercise 1–3

NAME _____ SCORE _____

DIRECTIONS   Fill in the blank with one of the verbs listed before the exercise. If the verb that you fill in has an auxiliary (helping verb) or a particle already as a part of the sentence, underline that word or words. Then write the complete verb in the blank at the right.

EXAMPLE
Hikers occasionally _____*find*_____ meteorites lying on a trail.

pelted	referred	describe	look	were
exploded	see	discover	understand	split
began	disappeared	left	find	lighted

1. How many "falling" or "shooting stars" <u>did</u> you _____*see*_____ last night?   _*did see*_

2. Often falling in clusters, they ___*left*___ bright streaks in the night sky.   _*left*_

3. Most of them abruptly _*disappeared*_ before reaching the ground.   _*disappeared*_

4. ___*Look*___ up the words "meteor" and "meteorite" in your dictionary.   _*Look up*_

5. We occasionally ___*describe*___ people as experiencing a "meteoric rise to success."   _*describe*_

6. <u>Do</u> you _*understand*_ the description?   _*do understand*_

7. Why <u>do</u> we _*discover*_ relatively few meteorites on Earth?   _*do discover*_

8. On the Moon's surface would you __*find*__ more meteorites than on Earth?   _*would find*_

9. All the fragments at the landing site of a meteor shower <u>are</u> _*referred*_ to with the same name.   _*are referred (to)*_

10. The famous Allende meteorite _*lighted*_ a night sky in Mexico in February 1969.   _*lighted*_

11. Observers ___began___ running from the brilliant fireball with a glowing trail.

___began___

12. The fireball ___split___ into two parts.

___split___

13. Each fireball then ___exploded___ on impact.

___exploded___

14. People ___were___ able to hear the explosion hundreds of miles away.

___were___

15. Thousands of pebbles, as well as larger fragments, ___pelted___ the earth.

___pelted___

1b(1) Learn to recognize subjects of verbs.

All sentences except those that issue commands have a stated subject. And even in a command, the subject—*you*—is understood.

[You] Write a paper about the source of meteorites.

Function   The subject is who or what the sentence is about. Once you have located the verb in the sentence, you need only to ask who or what is *doing, occurring,* or *being*. Your answer will be the complete subject. To find the simple subject, ask specifically who or what the verb is talking about.

Everyone in our class is writing a paper about the source of meteorites.

[Who is writing? *Everyone in our class.* Who specifically is writing? Not *in our class* but *everyone*.]

My topic, unlike the others, has been assigned by the instructor.

[What has been assigned? *My topic, unlike the others.* What specifically has been assigned? Not *my* or *unlike the others* but *topic*.]

As in these examples, a word or a group of words usually comes before and/ or after the simple subject. Do not confuse one of these other words with the subject. If you do, you may fail to make the subject and the verb work together well; you may use a singular subject with a plural verb or vice versa. As was suggested in the discussion of verbs, always identify the verb before you try to locate the subject to avoid this kind of agreement mistake.

The students in our class are studying the source of meteorites.

[The verb, *are studying*, is plural; therefore the subject must be plural too. *Students*, not *class*, is the plural subject; it is the word that answers the question "Who is studying?"]

Position   In most sentences the subject is the first main part of the sentence. But in questions, emphatic sentences, and sentences that begin with *it* or *there*, the subject follows the verb or comes in the middle of the verb phrase.

USUAL ORDER	Scientists carefully catalog meteorite landing sites.
QUESTION	Do scientists keep records of meteorites?
EMPHATIC	Careful and detailed are a scientist's records.
THERE	There are careful scientific records of meteorite landing sites.

Form   Because the subject tells who or what the sentence is about, it must be either a *noun* or a *pronoun*—the two parts of speech that name people and things—or a cluster of words that functions as a noun or pronoun. (Word clusters that may be substituted for a noun or pronoun are explained in section **1d**.)

Nouns are words that name individuals or classes of people (*Charles Dean, tribe, jury*), places (*New Zealand, parks, Earth*), things (*Kleenex, candy, watch*), activities (*Little League, basketball, festival*), and concepts (*divine right of kings, endurance, conclusion*). Pronouns are words used in the place of nouns; they take their meaning from the nouns that they replace.

> NOUNS   *Astronauts* brought meteorite *fragments* from the *moon*.

> PRONOUNS   *They* brought *them* from *it*.   [*They* replaces *astronauts*; *them* replaces *fragments*; *it* replaces *moon*.]

Some pronouns—such as *we*, *he*, and *who*—refer only to people; some—such as *it*, *something*, and *which*—refer only to things; and some—such as *each*, *many*, and *some*—refer to either people or things.

Like verbs, nouns have certain endings that help you to identify them. But unlike verbs, nouns show the plural by an *-s* or an *-es* ending (keys, caves, tomato*es*). Some nouns completely change their form when they are made plural (*man→men; leaf→leaves; child→children*). Nouns may also be recognized by the articles that frequently accompany them (*a* chair, *an* error, *the* person) and by their ability to form the possessive (child*'s* shoe, people*'s* choice, boys*'* dates).

Somewhat like verbs, nouns may consist of more than one word, but all the words are necessary to name the person, place, or thing being spoken of: *space shuttle, Luke Skywalker, Peck Hall*.

SUMMARY

Function   The subject is who or what the sentence is about. Thus when we ask who or what specifically is responsible for the action, the occurrence, or the state of being that the verb expresses, the answer will be the simple subject.

Position   The subject is usually the first main part of the sentence (*Sally Ride* was the first American woman in space.); however, in questions, emphatic sentences, and sentences that begin with *there* or *it*, it may come after the verb or in the middle of the verb phrase (When did *Sally Ride* first fly in space?).

Form   Most nouns and pronouns that function as subjects undergo various changes to show plural number (*hurdle→hurdles; woman→women; I→we*). Noun subjects are frequently preceded by articles (*a* stone, *an* orbit, *the* cosmonauts), and both noun and pronoun subjects are often followed by words that limit their meaning (a planet *without a moon;* each *of the cosmonauts;* someone *in our class*). A noun subject is often made up of more than one word, especially if the noun is naming a particular person, place, or thing (Edmund Halley, Cape Kennedy, Comet Kahoutek).

Deduct 5 for each blank incorrectly filled.

Subjects in Simple Sentences

Exercise 1–4

NAME _____ SCORE _____

DIRECTIONS   In the following sentences the verb is underlined twice. Underline the subject once and write the word or words you have underlined in the blank at the right. (Remember that a simple subject is sometimes made up of two or more words, which are usually capitalized, such as *Mr. Alfredo*, *Cape Kennedy*, or *Fourth of July*.)

EXAMPLE
In 1932 Ernest Öpik advanced a theory of the origin of comets.

Ernest Öpik

1. He imagined an invisible cloud of comets and meteorites orbiting the Sun at great distances.

He

2. Twenty years later another scientist expanded on Öpik's idea.

scientist

3. Jan Oort hypothesized comets and meteorites being jolted from the cloud by a passing star.

Jan Oort

4. Does your dictionary give a good definition of "hypothesis"?

dictionary

5. You still should think of the Öpik-Oort cloud as a hypothesis.

You

6. The cloud is too far away to be visible.

cloud

7. Many years of travel aboard a star ship would bring it into sight.

years

8. For the moment we will assume its existence.

we

9. The cloud of comets and meteorites is disrupted by a passing star.

cloud

10. The star bumps some of the comets and meteorites free of the cloud and free of the Sun's gravity.

star

11. They fall through the solar system closer to orbiting planets.

They

12. The Sun's gravity helps to pull them into the solar system.

gravity

13. Inevitably, there are some collisions.   *collisions*

14. Some of the comets and meteorites are flung by the
    gravity fields of planets towards the Sun.   *Some*

15. After surviving the encounters with planets, many
    of the comets and meteorites fall into the Sun.   *many*

16. The few survivors establish orbits around the Sun.   *survivors*

17. Periodically, the orbits of the planets intersect the
    orbits of the comets and meteorites.   *orbits*

18. After passing near the sun or any planet comets or
    meteors may change their orbit.   *comets, meteors*

19. Our sightings of comets and meteorites come with
    Earth's intersection with their orbits.   *sightings*

20. Comet Brooks 2 altered its orbit from twenty-nine
    to seven years after a near collision with Jupiter.   *Comet Brooks 2*

Deduct 10 for each incorrect revision.

Subjects and Verbs in Simple Sentences   Exercise 1–5

NAME _____ SCORE _____

DIRECTIONS   Here are ten sentences about comets written without people-related subjects. Rewrite each sentence with a person or people (or a personal pronoun like *he, she,*
or *they*) as the subject. Underline the subject of your revised sentence with one line and
the verb with two lines. When you have finished revising the sentences, decide which
version you think is easier and more interesting to read.

EXAMPLE
One cause of some of the Earth's catastrophes has been identified by some scientists
    as the Öpik-Oort cloud.

Some <u>scientists</u> <u>identify</u> the Öpik-Oort cloud as one
cause of some of the Earth's catastrophes.

1. According to the hypothesis our solar system moves slowly within the Milky
   Way.

   <u>They</u> <u>hypothesize</u> that our solar system moves
   slowly within the Milky Way.

2. In this hypothesis the Öpik-Oort cloud occasionally contacts a star.

   <u>Scientists</u> <u>explain</u> that the Öpik-Oort cloud
   occasionally contacts a star.

3. A particular star has been named as the likely influence on the cloud.

   <u>They</u> <u>believe</u> that a particular star is the likely
   influence on the cloud.

4. It has been named Nemesis.

   <u>They</u> <u>have named</u> it Nemesis.

5. In the news media it is referred to as the "death star."

   <u>Some</u> <u>reporters</u> <u>refer</u> to it as the "death star."

6. Nemesis disturbs the cloud at 28-million-year intervals.

   <u>Scientists</u> <u>believe</u> that Nemesis disturbs the cloud at 28-million-year intervals.

7. A resulting shower of comets is theorized by scientists.

   <u>Scientists</u> <u>theorize</u> that a shower of comets results.

8. According to their theory one large comet may hit the Earth after each disturbance.

   After each disturbance, <u>they</u> <u>say,</u> one large comet may hit the Earth.

9. The resulting collision is hypothesized as resembling a nuclear explosion.

   <u>They</u> <u>describe</u> the resulting collision as resembling a nuclear explosion.

10. These regular collisions may result in mass extinctions of plants and animals according to Nobel Prize winner Harold Urey.

    Nobel Prize winner <u>Harold Urey</u> <u>believes</u> regular collisions may cause mass extinctions of plants and animals.

1b(2) Learn to recognize objects and other kinds of complements.

Not every sentence has a complement.

> The dinosaurs abruptly disappeared.

> Dinosaur fossils simply vanished.

Sometimes a complement is possible even if none is stated.

> The public applauded.

> [A complement, though it is not stated, may be added because the verb, *applauded*, is a transitive verb: "The public applauded Kenneth Hsü's book, *The Great Dying*."

If the sentence has a complement, it can be found by following the subject and verb with "who," "whom," or "what."

> The book was a success.   [The book was what? *Success* is the complement.]

> It explained the fate of dinosaurs.   [It explained what? *Fate* is the complement.]

> The author examined dinosaur fossils.   [The author examined what? *Fossils* is the
>
> complement.]

> The era of dinosaurs ended about 65 million years ago.   [There is no word to an-
>
> swer the "Who?" "Whom?" or "What?" Thus the sentence has no complement.]

Function   Following a transitive verb, a complement (or complements) is a word (or words) to which the action of the verb is transferred or passed along. Three types of complements may follow transitive verbs: *direct objects, indirect objects,* and *object complements.* The direct object is the most common type of complement following a transitive verb. Sometimes it is accompanied by either an indirect object, which precedes it, or an object complement, which follows it.

> DIRECT OBJECT   The archaeologist examined the evidence of dinosaurs' ex-
>
> tinction.
>
> [The action of the verb is passed along to the direct object, *evidence.*]

21

INDIRECT OBJECT AND DIRECT OBJECT	The evidence gave archaeologists good ideas about dinosaurs' extinction.

[The action of the verb is passed along to both the indirect object, *archaeologists*, and the direct object, *ideas*. An indirect object follows a verb like *give*, *send*, *bring*, *buy*, *sell* and shows to whom or for whom the verb is doing something.]

DIRECT OBJECT AND OBJECT COMPLEMENT	Hsü called the event a catastrophe.

[The object complement, *catastrophe*, is another name for the direct object, *event*. An object complement follows a verb like *name*, *elect*, *make*, or *consider*.]

DIRECT OBJECT AND OBJECT COMPLEMENT	Most scientists considered the event catastrophic.

[Here the object complement, *catastrophic*, is an adjective that describes the direct object, *event*.]

Note: One test for a direct object is to make the active verb passive—that is, to add a form of *be* to the main verb. The word that is the object of the active verb then becomes the subject of the passive verb.

ACTIVE Scientists identified three causes of the catastrophe.

PASSIVE Three causes of the catastrophe were identified by scientists.

[Note that *scientists*, the subject of the active verb, now follows the passive verb and is the object of the preposition *by*.]

ACTIVE At first, the data gave scientists reasons to suspect an exploding star.

PASSIVE At first, scientists, were given reasons by their data to suspect an exploding star.

[*Data*, the subject of the active verb *gave*, now follows the passive verb and is the object of the preposition *by*.]

A complement (or complements) following a linking verb (forms of *be* and verbs like *seem*, *feel*, *appear*, and *look*) points back to the subject of the sentence; it either describes the subject or renames it in some way. Such complements are called *subject complements*. A complement that renames the subject is either a noun or a pronoun; it is often referred to as a *predicate nominative* or a *predicate noun*. A complement that describes the subject is an adjective; it is often referred to as a *predicate adjective*.

PREDICATE NOMINATIVE	Walter Alvarez was the discoverer.
	[The subject complement, *discoverer*, more or less renames the subject; the discoverer is the same person as Walter Alvarez.]
PREDICATE ADJECTIVE	Alvarez seemed obsessed.
	[The subject complement, *obsessed*, describes something about the subject, *Alvarez*.]

Position   The complement is usually the third main part of the sentence, but it may appear first in a question or in an emphatic sentence. There is no complement in a sentence that begins with the expletive *there* or *it*.

USUAL ORDER	Alvarez is the son of a Nobel Prize winner.
QUESTION	What discoveries did Alvarez make?
EMPHATIC	Intrigued indeed was Alvarez.

Form   The form of the noun complement, whether it is an object or a subject complement, is the same as the form of the subject. It can be distinguished from the subject only by its position in the sentence as the third main part of the basic formula.

SUBJECT	*Dinosaurs* dominated this environment.
OBJECT	Their environment dominated the *dinosaurs*.

Pronoun subject complements have the same form as pronoun subjects: *I*, *he*, *she*, *we*, *they*, and *who*. However, many pronouns used as objects have distinct forms: *me*, *him*, *us*, *them*, and *whom*.

SUBJECT COMPLEMENT	The geologist is he.
	[Compare "*He* is the geologist." The subject complement has the same form that the subject would have.]
OBJECT	No one ignored her.
	[Compare "*She* ignored everyone." The object differs in form from the subject.]

Some pronouns, like nouns, have the same form whether they are subject complements or objects—for example, *you, it, each, some, many,* and *one.*

SUBJECT
COMPLEMENT   The last person to sight the dinosaur was *you.*

OBJECT   The others beat *you.*

Adjectives have the same form whether they are subject complements or object complements.

SUBJECT COMPLEMENT   Jennifer was *lucky.*

OBJECT COMPLEMENT   Jennifer considered herself *lucky.*

SUMMARY

Function   Asking the question "Who?" "Whom?" or "What?" of the subject and its verb reveals whether or not a sentence has a complement. Complements function either as objects—direct or indirect—or object complements that receive the action of transitive verbs ("She sighted the *comet.*") or as subject complements that rename or describe the subjects of linking verbs ("The winner was *she.*").

Position   The complement is usually the third main part of the sentence ("Jennifer was *lucky.*"), but in questions and emphatic sentences the complement may be stated first ("*Lucky* was Jennifer.").

Form   Nouns have the same form whether they are used as subjects, as objects, or as subject complements. Most personal pronouns have different forms as objects (*me, him, her, us, them, whom*) than they do as subject complements (*I, he, she, we, they, who*). Some pronouns have the same form whether they are used as objects or as subject complements (*you, it, each, one, some, many,* for example). Adjectives have the same form whether they are used as subject complements ("Kahoutek was *dull.*") or as object complements ("The announcer called Kahoutek *dull.*").

Deduct 2 1/2 for an error in underlining and 2 1/2 for each blank incorrectly filled.

Subjects, Verbs, and Complements
in Simple Sentences

Exercise 1–6

NAME _____ SCORE _____

DIRECTIONS   In the following sentences underline the simple subject once, the verb twice, and the simple complement or complements three times. Write *subject* in the blank if the complement (or complements) refers back to the subject; write *object* if the complement (or complements) receives the action of the verb. If there is no complement, leave the blank empty.

EXAMPLE

Scientists describe the result of a collision between Earth and a large asteroid or comet nucleus as a "nuclear winter."   *object*

1. A collision with Earth by a large asteroid or comet nucleus would create a crater about 200 km in diameter.   *object*

2. The collision would explode dust and debris into the atmosphere.   *object*

3. An impact in the ocean would create huge and destructive waves.   *object*

4. Such a collision may have occurred about 65 million years ago.   _____

5. Fossils from that age are unusual.   *subject*

6. They do not reveal a natural evolution of species.   *object*

7. Instead they suggest a sudden mass extinction of many species of flora and fauna.   *object*

8. Perhaps the asteroid or comet hit on land.   _____

9. The explosion would create a huge dust cloud.   *object*

10. The cloud would block the Sun's rays.   *object*

11. Without the Sun plants soon would die.   _____

12. Deprived of food many animals would die.   _____

13. Perhaps the event has another explanation.   *object*

14. Perhaps the <u>collision</u> <u>occurred</u> in the ocean. _____

15. Water <u>vapor</u> in huge clouds <u>would saturate</u> the at-
    mosphere.   _____*object*_____

16. <u>Scientists</u> <u>call</u> <u>this</u> the "greenhouse effect."   _____*object*_____

17. One <u>effect</u> <u>would be</u> sharp <u>rises</u> in temperature.   _____*subject*_____

18. Another <u>effect</u> <u>would be</u> the <u>deaths</u> of certain spe-
    cies.   _____*subject*_____

19. Some <u>species</u> (protected deep in the oceans or at
    high altitudes) <u>would survive</u> the climate <u>changes</u>.   _____*object*_____

20. Interestingly, the most adaptable <u>creatures</u> <u>would</u>
    <u>survive</u> either <u>scenario</u>.   _____*object*_____

1c Learn to recognize the parts of speech.

Now that you have learned about the basic structure of a sentence, you are ready to begin working with all of the elements that combine to give a sentence its meaning. The following chart lists the various functions words can perform in a sentence and the types of words that perform each function.

Function	Kinds of Words
Naming	Nouns and Pronouns
Predicating (stating or asserting)	Verbs
Modifying	Adjectives and Adverbs
Connecting	Prepositions and Conjunctions

The next chart summarizes the parts of speech that you will study in detail in the rest of this section (except for interjections).

Parts of Speech	Uses of Sentences	Examples
1. Verbs	Indicators of action, occurrence, or state of being	Tom *wrote* the report. Mary *studied* the maps. They *are* astronomers.
2. Nouns	Subjects and objects	*Kay* gave *Ron* the *list* of *planets.*
3. Pronouns	Substitutes for nouns	*He* will return *it* to *her* later.
4. Adjectives	Modifiers of nouns and pronouns	The *detailed* star map is the *interesting* one.
5. Adverbs	Modifiers of verbs, adjectives, other adverbs, or whole clauses	presented *clearly* a *very* interesting study *entirely* too long *Indeed,* we are ready.

Parts of Speech	Uses in Sentences	Examples
6. Prepositions	Words used before nouns and pronouns to relate them to other words in the sentence	*in* a hurry *with* no thought *to* them
7. Conjunctions	Connectors of words, phrases, or clauses; may be either coordinating or subordinating	black holes *or* shadow matter before the explosion *and* after it *since* the sighting of the comet
8. Interjections	Expressions of emotion (unrelated grammatically to the rest of the sentence)	*Good grief!* *Ouch!* *Well*, we tried.

1d Learn to recognize phrases and subordinate clauses.

A phrase is a series of related words (words grouped together) that lacks either a subject or a verb or both. You are already familiar with phrases that may function as the verb of a sentence—the main verb with one or more auxiliaries (*will be writing*) and the verb with a particle (*put up with* (**1a**)). Other phrases may function as the subject or object (**1d(1)** below) or as modifiers (**1d(2)**).

1d(1) Learn to recognize phrases and subordinate clauses used as subjects and objects.

The main types of word groups that function as subjects and as objects are verbal phrases and noun clauses.

Verbal Phrases   The verbal phrase is the kind of phrase that most frequently functions as a subject or object. The main part of the verbal phrase is the verbal itself—a word that shows action, occurrence, or a state of being as a verb does but that cannot function as the verb of a sentence.

    VERB   Galileo *discovered* Jupiter's moons in 1610.

    VERBALS   *discovering, to discover, having discovered*

Notice that none of these verbals can substitute for the verb *discovered* in a sentence.

Galileo *discovering* Jupiter's moons in 1610   [a fragment]
Galileo *to discover* Jupiter's moons in 1610   [a fragment]
Galileo *having discovered* Jupiter's moons in 1610   [a fragment]

But such verbals, alone or with other words in verbal phrases, can function as subjects or objects just as individual nouns or pronouns can.

NOUN   The *history of astronomy* reveals some surprising facts.   [subject]

VERBAL PHRASE *Studying the history of astronomy* reveals some surprising facts. [subject]

VERBAL PHRASE *To study the history of astronomy* is a worthy goal.   [subject]

VERBAL PHRASE *Having studied the history of astronomy* makes one more appreciative of science in general.   [subject]

NOUN   I enjoy the *history of astronomy*.   [object]

VERBAL PHRASE I enjoy *studying the history of astronomy*.   [object]

VERBAL PHRASE I plan *to study the history of astronomy*.   [object]

VERBAL PHRASE I will never regret *having studied the history of astronomy*.   [object]

Noun Clauses   A clause is a series of related words (words grouped together) that has both a subject and a verb. One kind of clause, referred to as a *main clause* or *independent clause*, can stand alone as a sentence. The other, called a *subordinate clause* or *dependent clause*, may function as a noun—either a subject or object—or as a modifier in a sentence. (**1d(2)**) discusses the use of phrases and subordinate clauses as modifiers. In fact, they are more commonly used as modifiers than as subjects or objects.) As nouns, subordinate clauses usually are introduced by one of these words: *who, whom, whose, which, that, whoever, whomever, what, whether, how, why,* or *where*. These introductory words are clause markers; they are printed in boldface in the following examples.

NOUN   Our *discovery* surprised us.   [subject]

NOUN CLAUSE   **What** *we discovered about asteroids* surprised us.   [subject]

NOUN   We reported our *discovery*.   [object]

NOUN CLAUSE   We reported **what** *we discovered about asteroids*.   [object]

NOUN CLAUSES   **Whoever** *studies asteroids* will learn **that** *fragments of asteroids enter Earth's atmosphere as meteorites*.   [subject and object]

Verbal Phrases and Noun Clauses as Subject Complements   Verbal phrases and noun clauses can replace nouns and pronouns not only as subjects and objects but also as subject complements.

NOUN His passion was *astronomy.*

VERBAL PHRASE His passion was *studying astronomy.*

VERBAL PHRASE His ambition was *to study astronomy.*

NOUN CLAUSE His opinion was *that everyone should study astronomy.*

Deduct 2 1/2 for each error in underlining and 2 1/2 for each blank incorrectly filled.

Verbal Phrases and Noun Clauses as Subjects, Direct Objects, and Subject Complements

Exercise 1-7

NAME _____ SCORE _____

DIRECTIONS   Each of the following sentences contains one or more verbal phrases or noun clauses functioning as subject, direct object, or subject complement. First, underline such verbal phrases and/or noun clauses. Then write in the blank (1) *S* for a phrase or clause functioning as the subject of the sentence, (2) *DO* for a phrase or clause functioning as a direct object, (3) *SC* for a phrase or clause functioning as a subject complement. If you write two or more things in the blank, use dashes between them. (Be sure to look for the main verb of the sentence before you try to identify the subject, direct object, and subject complement.)

EXAMPLE
We hope to explain the origins and compositions of asteroids.   *DO*

1. That asteroids are merely uninteresting cosmic debris is a common misconception.   *S*

2. Now we realize that the history of the Solar System may be concealed in asteroids.   *DO*

3. Recent "disaster movies" demonstrate that the public is curious about asteroids.   *DO*

4. That most asteroids once were parts of larger asteroids is a common hypothesis.   *S*

5. Something seems to have disturbed the early asteroids' orbit.   *SC*

6. The gravity of a large planet like Jupiter or Mars probably caused the deflecting of asteroids into elongated, tilted orbits.   *DO*

7. The asteroids began to collide in the new and crowded orbits.   *DO*

8. Scientists believe that the collisions resulted in the asteroids' being pulverized or expelled into space.   *DO*

9. Scientists now would like to explore the remaining asteroids.   *DO*

10. To send an unmanned spacecraft to an asteroid is now the plan.   *S*

11. To send a spacecraft into the asteroid belt is to risk nearly certain destruction.   *S-SC*

12. To intercept an asteroid nearer the Earth seems a more sensible plan. ___S___

13. Scientists plan to discover the composition and history of that asteroid. ___DO___

14. Scientists hope eventually to mine materials from asteroids. ___DO___

15. Mining asteroids could provide materials for long-term living and construction in space. ___S___

1d(2) **Learn to recognize words, phrases, and subordinate clauses used as modifiers.**

A modifier is a word or word cluster that describes, limits, or qualifies another, thus expanding the meaning of the sentence. Adjectives are the modifiers of nouns or pronouns; adverbs are the modifiers of verbs, adjectives, other adverbs, and sometimes whole sentences. The function of an adjective or an adverb can be fulfilled by a single word, a phrase, or a subordinate clause, as the following sentences demonstrate.

            1   2   3
ADJECTIVES   *One* kind *of meteor that we know much about* is the remnant of a

comet.

[All three adjectival modifiers (a word, a prepositional phrase, and a subordinate clause, in that order) qualify the subject *kind.*]

             1   2
ADVERBS   *On November 12, 1833,* tens of thousands of meteors *unexpectedly*

flashed *into view while observers struggled to understand what was*

happening.

[The first adverbial modifier (a prepositional phrase) qualifies the whole sentence. The second (a word), third (another prepositional phrase), and fourth (a subordinate clause) all modify the verb *flashed.*]

Single-Word Modifiers   Some authorities consider articles (*a, an,* and *the*), number words (*some, few, many,* and so on), and possessive pronouns (*my, its, your,* and so on) to be modifiers, while others call these words "noun determiners." Clearly, all three normally signal that a noun is to follow.

The meteor shower made *its* next visit in 1866 just as *some* astronomers had

predicted.

Other single-word modifiers describe some quality of or set some kind of limitation on the words they refer to.

In the same year astronomers *suddenly* realized that the orbit of Comet Temple, a

small and *undistinguished* comet, was *nearly* identical to the orbit of the meteors.

[*Suddenly* tells how they realized, *small* and *undistinguished* describe the comet, and *nearly* qualifies *identical.*]

Except when they are used as subject complements, adjective modifiers, by their very nature, are almost always found near the nouns or pronouns that they refer to. In emphatic word order, an adjective modifier may follow the noun or pronoun that it qualifies, but in usual word order the adjective precedes the word that it modifies.

USUAL ORDER   The *persistent, meticulous* astronomers were rewarded.

EMPHATIC   The astronomers, *persistent* and *meticulous*, were rewarded.

Adverb modifiers usually are not so clearly tied to the words that they modify and may move around more freely in the sentence, as long as their location does not cause awkward or difficult reading.

Undeniably, the research was worthwhile.
The research, *undeniably,* was worthwhile.
The research was *undeniably* worthwhile.
The research was worthwhile, *undeniably.*

Phrases as Modifiers   A phrase, as you may remember, is a word cluster that lacks either a subject or a verb or both. The two types of phrases that function as modifiers are verbal phrases and prepositional phrases.

Verbal Phrases   The key word in the verbal phrase is the verbal itself (see **1d(1)**). Participles, which usually end in *-ing, -ed,* or *-en* and are often preceded by *having,* can function only as adjective modifiers.

The participial phrase, which consists of the participle and sometimes a modifier and an object that are part of the participle's word cluster, is frequently used to expand the basic formula of a sentence. The use of a participial phrase often avoids a series of short, choppy sentences.

SHORT, CHOPPY   Comet Temple was slowly disintegrating. It created the Leonid meteor shower.

PARTICIPIAL   *Slowly disintegrating,* Comet Temple created the Leonid meteor
PHRASE   shower.
OR
Comet Temple, *slowly disintegrating,* created the Leonid meteor shower.

An infinitive phrase may function as a modifier too. Unlike a participial phrase, however, it may be used as either an adjective or an adverb.

ADJECTIVAL   The tendency *to produce meteor showers* has made many small comets famous.   [The infinitive phrase modifies the subject *tendency.*]

ADVERBIAL   Not every comet is able *to produce meteor showers.*   [The infinitive phrase modifies the predicate adjective (subject complement) *able.*]

Sometimes the verbal has its own subject. It is then called an *absolute phrase* because it does not modify a single word in the sentence but rather the entire sentence (see also **12d**). Although an absolute phrase is not a sentence, it does have a greater degree of independence from the sentence than an ordinary verbal phrase does.

PARTICIPIAL PHRASE	The Leonid meteors, *deflected by Jupiter's gravity,* disappeared from Earth. [The verbal, *deflected,* modifies the subject, *meteors,* and must stand near it in the sentence.]
ABSOLUTE PHRASE	*Their orbits disturbed by Jupiter,* the Leonid meteors disappeared from Earth. [The verbal, *disturbed,* has its own subject, *orbits;* thus the meaning of the phrase is clear wherever it is placed in the sentence.]

Like a participial phrase, an absolute phrase can be used effectively to combine short, choppy sentences.

SHORT, CHOPPY	The meteor shower's orbit was changed by Jupiter's gravity. The shower disappeared until 1966.
ABSOLUTE PHRASE	*Its orbit having been changed by Jupiter's gravity,* the meteor shower disappeared until 1966.

Prepositional Phrases A prepositional phrase begins with a *preposition*—a word like *in, of, to,* or *with*—and ends with an object, either a noun or a pronoun. The preposition is the word that connects the whole phrase to one of the main parts of the sentence, to another modifier, or to the object of another prepositional phrase. (A prepositional phrase often rides piggyback on a preceding prepositional phrase.)

                             1   **2**   **3**

Meteor showers generated *by comets* are not the only examples *of meteors in Earth's*

                 4   **5**

atmosphere. A cloud *of meteors with an unpredictable orbit* regularly collides

6

with Earth's atmosphere and produces what astronomers call "sporadic meteors."

[The first prepositional phrase (adverbial) explains the participle, *generated;* the second (adjectival) modifies the subject complement, *examples;* the third (also adjectival) modifies the object of the preceding phrase, *meteors.* In the second sentence, the fourth and fifth phrases (both adjectival) modify the subject, *clouds;* and the sixth (adverbial) modifies the verb, *collide.*]

Often, as in the case of *with an unpredictable orbit,* the prepositional phrase does not immediately follow the word it modifies. When you see a preposition (such as *with*), you know that an object ("with fine *dust*") and perhaps a modifier of the object ("with *fine* dust") follow.

There are so few prepositions that you can easily memorize a list of the most common ones (see the Appendix). But the prepositions that we do have we use again and again. We write few sentences that do not include at least one prepositional phrase. Notice how incomplete the meaning of the following sentences would be without the prepositional phrases that qualify the meanings of the words they modify.

The dust *from disintegrated meteors* sinks earthward.

[Without the prepositional phrase, the sentence reads "The dust sinks earthward."]

The best conditions *for seeing this phenomenon* occur *in northern Sweden during*

the summer months.

[Without the prepositional phrases the sentence reads "The best conditions occur."]

Deduct 2 1/2 for each incorrect underlining and 2 1/2 for each blank incorrectly filled.

Word and Phrase Modifiers:
Adjectives and Adverbs   Exercise 1–8

NAME _____ SCORE _____

DIRECTIONS   In each of the following sentences, the word in italics is qualified by one or more single-word and/or phrase modifiers. First underline these modifiers; then draw an arrow from each one to the italicized word. Do not underline or draw an arrow from the articles—*a, an,* and *the.* Write *adj.* in the blank if the modifier or modifiers are functioning as adjectives and *adv.* if the modifier or modifiers are functioning as adverbs. Notice how the modifiers make the italicized words more exact in meaning.

EXAMPLES

The most accurate *measurement* of great distance uses light.   *adj.*

Scientists simply *measure* the time necessary for light to cover a dis-

tance.   *adv.*

1. On the scale the *Moon* is only 1.28 seconds away.   *adj.*

2. Light *travels* from Earth to Pluto in just over five hours.   *adv.*

3. We *see* Pluto not as it is but as it was over five hours ago.   *adv.*

4. *Think* now about the sizes of the planets.   *adv.*

5. *Most* of the planets are immense compared with the Earth.   *adj.*

6. *Jupiter* is 11 times larger in diameter than Earth.   *adj.*

7. Jupiter could contain 1,323 *Earths* packed inside it.   *adj.*

8. However, 1,300,000 Earths *would fit* snugly inside the Sun.   *adv.*

9. *Traveling* at the speed of light, we could pass Pluto in $5\frac{1}{2}$ hours

   and still be in the solar system.   *adv.*

10. We would then enter the imagined *Öpik-Oort cloud* in which

    comets are born.   *adj.*

11. We *would leave* the solar system after $1\frac{1}{2}$ years of travel at the

    speed of light and after covering 15 million million kilometers.   *adv.*

12. Looking behind us we would see our *Sun*, a dwindling but
    still bright star.   *adj.*

13. After traveling another 26 million million kilometers, we
    would approach another star.   *adv.*

14. Our *travel* beyond the solar systems would be in bleak isola-
    tion.   *adj.*

15. The triple star Alpha Centauri *would be* our destination after
    a voyage of four years and four months.   *adv.*

Subordinate Clauses   In **1d(1)** you studied one kind of subordinate clause—the noun clause, which can function as a subject or object. (As you may remember, a subordinate clause contains both a subject and a verb, but, unlike a main clause, cannot stand by itself as a sentence because of the subordinator that introduces it.) Other kinds of subordinate clauses—the adjective clause and the adverb clause—act as modifiers.

Adjective Clauses   Adjective clauses are introduced by a subordinator such as *who, whom, that, which,* or *whose*—often referred to as *relative pronouns.* A relative pronoun relates the rest of the words in its clause to a word in the main clause, and, as a pronoun, also serves some noun function in its own clause, often as the subject. (Remember that a clause, unlike a phrase, has both a subject and a verb.)

G. E. D. Adcock, *who* had memorized the position of nearly 10,000 telescopic

stars, discovered two new comets within a week.

[The relative pronoun *who* relates the subordinate clause to the subject of the main clause, G. E. D. Adcock, and also serves as subject of the verb, *had memorized,* in its own clause.]

An adjective clause follows the noun or pronoun that it modifies. It cannot be moved elsewhere without confusing either the meaning or the structure of the sentence.

CORRECT PLACEMENT   A comet *that has been discovered,* lost, and then rediscovered after some years receives a hyphenated name.

INCORRECT PLACEMENT   A comet receives a hyphenated name *that has been discovered,* then lost, and rediscovered after some years.

Sometimes the relative pronoun is omitted when the clause is short and no misreading could result.

WITH SUBORDINATOR   Halley is the one astronomer *whom* almost everyone recognizes.

WITHOUT SUBORDINATOR   Halley is the one astronomer almost every one recognizes.

Adverb Clauses   An adverb clause is introduced by a subordinator such as *since, when, if, because, although,* or *so that* (see the Appendix for a list of the most commonly used subordinators). Like the adjective clause, the adverb clause adds another subject and verb (and sometimes other elements) to the sentence. But unlike the relative pronoun that introduces the adjective clause, the subordinator of an adverb clause does not function as a main part of its own clause. The adverb clause usually modifies the verb of the main clause, but it may also modify an adjective or adverb in the main clause.

Halley's Comet had just appeared *when* Mark Twain was born, and he died *when*

it returned.

[The subordinator *when* introduces the two adverb clauses. The first adverb clause modifies the verb *had appeared;* the second modifies the verb *died.*]

Comet Encke is not as glorious *as* it once must have been.

[The subordinator *as* introduces the adverb clause, which modifies the adjective *glorious.*]

Unlike an adjective clause, an adverb clause can often move around freely in the sentence without changing the meaning or confusing the structure of the sentence. (See also section **25**.)

Comet Stefan had been lost for thirty-seven years *until Miss Oterma of Finland rediscovered it in 1942.*
Until Miss Oterma of Finland rediscovered it in 1942, Comet Stefan had been lost for thirty-seven years.
Comet Stefan, *until Miss Oterma of Finland rediscovered it in 1942*, had been lost for thirty-seven years.

Deduct 5 for each blank incorrectly filled.

Subordinate Clause Modifiers:
Adjectives and Adverbs

Exercise 1-9

NAME _____ SCORE _____

DIRECTIONS   Write *adj.* in the blank if the italicized subordinate clause is an adjective modifier and *adv.* if it is an adverb modifier. (To test your classification, try moving the italicized clause to different places in its sentence; notice whether the new arrangement affects the meaning or the structure of the sentence. If the movement of the clause affects either the meaning or the structure of the sentence, you know that it is an adjective clause.)

EXAMPLE

The moon crosses the Sun's path, *which is called the "ecliptic,"* at

two points.   _*adj.*_

1. Many primitive societies believed the Moon or Sun were under

   attack by a demon *when they were in eclipse.*   _*adv.*_

2. *When the Moon was on the ecliptic*, the ancient Babylonians

   knew it would be eclipsed.   _*adv.*_

3. They could calculate the day and hour of the eclipse, *although*

   they could not explain its causes.   _*adv.*_

4. They did not know that the Earth's shadow, *which is about*

   5,700 miles in diameter at the distance of the Moon, caused a

   lunar eclipse.   _*adj.*_

5. A solar eclipse, *which was far more terrifying to them*, also

   was not understood.   _*adj.*_

6. Solar and lunar eclipses occur *when the Moon is on the*

   ecliptic.   _*adv.*_

7. *As it encounters the Earth's shadow*, the Moon slowly disap-

   pears.   _*adv.*_

8. The Moon does not totally disappear *because some sunlight*

   bends around Earth's atmosphere and lights the lunar surface.   _*adv.*_

9. The extent to which the Earth's atmosphere affects the sun-

   light determines the color and brightness *that the Moon re-*

   tains during the eclipse.   _*adj.*_

10. During some eclipses the Moon glows a deep red *which indicates there is a large amount of dust in Earth's atmosphere.* _adj._

11. *If storm clouds fill the skies and blot out the light,* the eclipse will be very dark. _adv._

12. Poets, *to whom the drama of eclipses has great appeal,* often use the deep red eclipse as a portent of disaster. _adj._

13. A solar eclipse occurs *when the Moon moves to the other side of the ecliptic.* _adv._

14. Behind the Moon stretches the "umbra" *which is a dark, cone-shaped shadow.* _adj._

15. The tip of the umbra reaches Earth and produces a dark spot *that races across Earth's surface.* _adj._

16. A total solar eclipse is visible only to people *who are within the darkened spot.* _adj._

17. The writer Herodotus described a solar eclipse *whose appearance had historical impact.* _adj._

18. The sun was directly over head *as the Medes and Lydians battled each other on May 28, 585 B.C.* _adv._

19. Suddenly day turned into night, and the battle abruptly stopped *as the two armies gazed in wonder at the eclipse.* _adv._

20. It was a sign from the gods, they decided, so *when the sun reappeared* they declared a truce and lived in peace for fifteen years. _adv._

1e Learn to use main clauses and subordinate clauses in various types of sentences.

Sometimes a writer has two or more related ideas to set forth. Depending on the relationship of the ideas and on the desired emphasis, the writer may choose to express the ideas in separate sentences or to combine them in one of several ways.

Types of Sentences   There are four types of sentences: *simple, compound, complex,* and *compound-complex.* Which of these types a given sentence is depends on the number of main and subordinate clauses it includes.

Simple Sentences   The simple sentence consists of only one main clause and no subordinate clauses. A simple sentence is often short but not necessarily so: one or more of the basic sentence parts—the subject, verb, or complement— may be compound and many single-word and phrase modifiers may be attached to the main clause.

> SIMPLE   The Moon's shadow is the umbra.

> SIMPLE   **Attempting to date historical events,** scientists rely on calculations *about*
>
> *eclipses* **made by Theodore Oppolzer.**
>
> [The main clause, or basic formula, "Scientists rely on calculations," has been expanded by two verbal phrases (in boldface) and one prepositional phrase (in italics).]

> SIMPLE   The **ancient** Chinese exploded firecrackers, sounded gongs, and chanted
>
> songs **to signal eclipses.**
>
> [The verb and complement are compound; a single-word modifier and a verbal phrase (both in boldface) also expand the main clause.]

Compound Sentences   A compound sentence consists of two or more main clauses (but no subordinate clauses) connected by a coordinating conjunction (*and, but, or, nor, for, so, yet*) or by a conjunctive adverb (such as *thus* or *therefore*) or other transitional expressions (such as *as a matter of fact*). (A semicolon may substitute for the coordinating conjunction; see section **14**.) In a compound sentence the connecting word (in boldface below) acts like the fulcrum of a seesaw, balancing grammatically equivalent structures.

> COMPOUND   The Moon travels at 2,100 miles per hour in its orbit, and the shadow
>
> sweeps eastward across the Earth at the same speed.

[The first main clause is balanced by the grammatically equivalent second main clause. The clauses are connected by the coordinate conjunction *and*.]

COMPOUND   Only people standing where the umbra touches the Earth see a total

solar eclipse; however, all people on the hemisphere facing the Moon

can see a lunar eclipse.

[The conjunctive adverb, *however*, balances the first main clause against the grammatically equivalent second main clause.]

Complex Sentences   A complex sentence consists of one main clause and one or more subordinate clauses. The subordinate clause in a complex sentence may function as the subject, a complement, a modifier, or the object of a preposition. As is true of the compound sentence, the complex sentence has more than one subject and verb; however, at least one of the subject-verb pairs is introduced by a subordinator such as *what, whoever, who, when,* or *if* (in boldface below) which makes its clause dependent on the main clause.

COMPLEX   The Greek fleet was embarking from the port of Athens on August 3,

431 B.C., ***when a total solar eclipse took place.***

[The subordinate clause functions as a modifier—as an adverb clause.]

COMPLEX   The Greek commander Pericles explained to his men ***that some large***

object was blocking the Sun's light.

[The subordinate clause functions as the complement (direct object).]

COMPLEX   Pericles' explanation of ***what caused the eclipse*** marks one of the earliest

records of humans understanding the phenomenon.

[The subordinate clause functions as the object of the preposition *of*.]

Compound-Complex Sentences   A compound-complex sentence consists of two or more main clauses and at least one subordinate clause. Thus it has three or more separate sets of subjects, verbs, and sometimes complements.

COMPOUND-COMPLEX By about 400 B.C. the Greeks could explain *what caused a solar eclipse*, but they still viewed lunar eclipses as signs or omens *that foretold disasters.*

[The subordinate clauses (in italics), introduced by the subordinators *what* and *that* (in boldface), function as complement (direct object) and modifier (adjective) respectively.]

Compound Subjects and Verbs
and Compound Sentences

Exercise 1-10

NAME _____ SCORE _____

DIRECTIONS   Underline the simple subject or subjects in each of the following main clauses once and the verb or verbs twice. If the sentence is a compound sentence, insert an inverted caret (**V**) between the two main clauses. (Notice that the main clauses are correctly joined by a comma plus a coordinating conjunction, by a semicolon, or by a semicolon plus a conjunctive adverb or transitional phrase.) In the blank write *sub* if the subject is compound, *verb* if the verb is compound, and *CS* if the sentence is compound.

EXAMPLES

Occasionally an asteroid passes between a distant star and Earth

and causes that star momentarily to blink out. _____*verb*_____

Astronomers describe this brief eclipse of the star as an "occulta-

tion," **V** and they use the occultation to measure the size of the as-

teroid. _____*CS*_____

1. An eclipse of our Sun and an occultation of a distant star cast

   similar shadows on Earth. _____*sub*_____

2. Astronomers usually cannot predict a distant star's shadow

   path, **V** but they can predict the exact path of the Sun's shadow

   across Earth. _____*CS*_____

3. Pallas is the second largest minor planet in our solar system; **V**

   it eclipsed the distant star Vulpeculae in 1983. _____*CS*_____

4. The shadow's path crossed North America; **V** therefore, it lay

   potentially within reach of the largest concentration of ama-

   teur astronomers in the world. _____*CS*_____

5. The International Occultation Timing Association is centered

   in Silver Spring, Maryland, **V** and it coordinated an intense

   study of the occultation. _____*CS*_____

6. During the occultation, Pallas slowly passed in front of the

   star and finally blotted it from view. _____*verb*_____

7. Viewers intensely studied the brief occultation through telescopes and hurriedly photographed it. *verb*

8. They also measured the size of Pallas's shadow on Earth and quickly estimated the asteroid's size. *verb*

9. Study of the occultation provided some information about the eclipsed star, but it provided even more information about Pallas. *CS*

10. Pallas is roughly 520 kilometers long and 516 kilometers wide, and it has no large, easily identifiable surface irregularities. *CS*

Subjects and Verbs in Main and Subordinate
Clauses: Complex Sentences

Exercise 1–11

NAME _____ SCORE _____

DIRECTIONS Each sentence below contains one main clause and one subordinate clause—each clause, of course, with its own subject and verb. Underline the subjects once and the verbs twice. In the blank, write the subordinator that introduces the subordinate clause. (Remember that a relative pronoun subordinator—for instance, *who*, *whom*, *that*, *which*—often serves as the subject or complement of its own clause. Remember also that an entire subordinate clause may serve as the subject or complement of a main clause.)

EXAMPLES

Because the Moon is so near and easy to see, it usually

is the first object viewed by amateur astronomers.   *Because*

Even extremely low-powered telescopes reveal that the

Moon is riddled with craters, mountain ranges, val-

leys, and flat expanses called "maria."   *that*

1. Anyone who studies the Moon soon becomes aware

   of four particularly large formations.   *who*

2. The crater Petavius resembles a giant terraced cir-

   cle which is about 110 miles in diameter with ram-

   parts 11,000 feet high.   *which*

3. Even large telescopes reveal a crater floor that is

   relatively smooth.   *that*

4. Posidonius is a huge walled plain whose bound-

   aries are steep walls.   *whose*

5. The great walled plain was formed when the Moon

   was volcanically active.   *when*

6. Because the plain floor originated as a lava flow, it

   is very smooth.   *Because*

7. Scientists also believe that volcanic activity created

   the gigantic mountain-walled plain of Clavius.   *that*

8. The mountain range that encircles Clavius rises at least two miles above the plain.

that

9. Although the inner plain is a fairly smooth lava flow, the walls are rugged.

although

10. The Moon's darkest area, which astronomers have named "the Basin Grimaldi," becomes visible about a day before a Full Moon.

which

Deduct 5 for each incorrect answer.

Subordinate (Dependent) Clauses: Functions in Sentences

Exercise 1–12

NAME _____ SCORE _____

DIRECTIONS   Classify each italicized subordinate clause in the following sentences as a subject (*S*), a complement (*C*), or a modifier (*M*). As you do the exercise, notice the subordinator that introduces the clause.

EXAMPLE
Many astronomers argued for years *that the moon was under-studied.*   *C*

1. *If the Moon were farther from Earth,* some astronomers would find it more interesting.   *M*

2. Some astronomers only want to study objects *that are at the farthest limits of their telescopes.*   *M*

3. In 1837, several German astronomers did lunar studies *that led to detailed maps of the Moon's surface.*   *M*

4. For many years afterwards, astronomers believed *that further investigation would be unnecessary.*   *C*

5. Johannes Hevelius and his wife, *who worked with a telescope set up on their balcony,* produced the first good map of the Moon.   *M*

6. *As Hevelius identified the Moon's features,* he named them after towns and countries on Earth.   *M*

7. Hevelius decided not to name them after friends, *because he could not be sure to include everyone.*   *M*

8. *Whoever was left out* would feel deprived of immortality.   *S*

9. After they studied the large dark areas of the Moon, Johannes and Elizabeth named them Mare, *which is Latin for "the sea."*   *M*

10. In 1651, Riccioli and his assistant Grimaldi decided *that they would draw a new map.*   *C*

11. Riccioli named the craters after great men *even though some had never looked through a telescope.*   _M_

12. *When Riccioli named the two largest craters after himself and Grimaldi,* he insured their lasting fame.   _M_

13. Nearly all the craters on this side of the Moon *that Riccioli left unnamed* have since been named after famous astronomers.   _M_

14. The image of the Moon *that you see through a telescope* has been inverted.   _M_

15. *That the Man in the Moon is upside down* may at first confuse you.   _S_

16. You can orient yourself *if you first identify the features.*   _M_

17. Then you will see *that Mare Imbrium and Mare Serenitatis form the eyes* and *that Mare Nubium is the mouth.*   _C_

18. *What appears to be a furrowed brow* is actually the narrow Mare Frigoris.   _S_

19. *Although these flat, dark expanses are called maria, or seas,* they are improperly named.   _M_

20. Scientific evidence suggests *that the Moon contains no water.*   _C_

2

In general, write complete sentences.

Once you become aware of the parts of the sentence (section **1**), you will sense the difference between a complete sentence and an incomplete one, a fragment. Although fragments are usually not a clear way to communicate with your reader, they may be effective, and even necessary, in a few instances, particularly in answering questions, stating exclamations, and recording dialogue.

> QUESTION AND FRAGMENT ANSWER   Are craters on the Moon considered evidence of volcanic activity? *Yes, especially those that resemble volcano craters on Earth.*

> SENTENCE AND FRAGMENT EXCLAMATION   A person standing in one of the large craters would be in the midst of a vast plain surrounded by distant mountains. *How inspiring!*

> DIALOGUE   "Moon craters are explosion pits caused by violent impacts," the astronomer argued. "The Moon has no atmosphere to affect the impacts. Every thousand years or so a large object in excess of forty thousand tons will collide with the Moon. It will leave a huge impact pit several miles in diameter. *Dramatic evidence of the constant bombardment of the Moon.*"

Fragments are used in dialogue simply to record people's speech patterns. The fragment used in answering a question or in stating an exclamation allows an idea to be communicated without repeating most of the preceding sentence.

Effective sentence fragments, like those used in answering questions, stating exclamations, and recording dialogue, are written intentionally. The very shortness of most fragments calls attention to them; thus they are used for emphasis. Ineffective fragments, however, are rarely written intentionally. Rather they are written because the writer could not sense the difference between a sentence part and a complete sentence.

2a Learn to sense the difference between a phrase, especially a verbal phrase, and a sentence.

Any sentence becomes a fragment when the verb is replaced by a verbal.

> SENTENCE   A crater one hundred or more miles in diameter *is* a walled plain.

> VERBAL PHRASES   A crater one hundred or more miles in diameter *being* a walled plain.
>
> A crater one hundred or more miles in diameter *having been* a walled plain.

Sometimes a prepositional phrase is incorrectly punctuated as a sentence, usually because the phrase is either very long or is introduced by words like *for example* or *such as.*

SENTENCE	Some Moon features may have been formed by impact with very large meteorites.
PREPOSITIONAL PHRASES	For example, Mare Crisiam and Mare Imbrium. In Mare Imbrium, a plain 700 miles in diameter, with vast mountain ranges at its circumference.

An appositive is a word or word group following a noun or pronoun that defines or restates the noun or pronoun. An appositive cannot stand alone as a sentence.

SENTENCE	The article's description of the strange creatures strolling the shores of blue lunar seas was clearly a hoax.
APPOSITIVE	A profitable deception reprinted as a pamphlet and earning nearly $200,000.

Another common fragment is caused by the separation of the two parts of a compound predicate.

SENTENCE	By 1900 few astronomers still believed that the Moon held intelligent life.
PREDICATE	But still would argue that it contained vegetation.

2b Learn to sense the difference between a subordinate clause and a sentence.

Any sentence can be made a fragment by inserting a subordinator before or after the subject. (See the list of subordinators in the Appendix.)

SENTENCE	In 1835 the *New York Sun* carried a long article that described the bat-men, bird-men, and bison inhabiting the Moon.
SUBORDINATE CLAUSES	In 1835 *after* the *New York Sun* carried a long article that described the bat-men, bird-men, and bison inhabiting the Moon. In 1835 the *New York Sun* *which* carried a long article that described the bat-men, bird-men, and bison inhabiting the Moon.

2c Learn the best way to correct a fragment.

An obvious way to correct a fragment is to supply the missing part—to make the fragment into a sentence. But most fragments are best corrected by reconnecting them to the sentences they belong with. Examine the following paragraph in which the word groups that are likely to be incorrectly written as fragments are printed in italics.

During an eclipse of the Moon, the shadow of the Earth momentarily blocks the Sun's heat *and rapidly cools down the Moon*. The temperature drops more than 300° in an hour. The Moon's surface does not cool uniformly *because solid rock and dust lose heat at different rates.*

Deduct 2 for each error in underlining and 2 for each blank incorrectly filled.

Sentences and Fragments: Verbs and Verbals   Exercise 2–1

NAME _____ SCORE _____

DIRECTIONS   In the following word groups underline each subject with one straight line, each verb with two straight lines, and each verbal with a wavy line. If a word group contains no true subject and/or verb for a main clause, indicate an incomplete sentence by writing *frag.* in the blank for either subject or verb or for both. Notice that a sentence may have both a verb and one or more verbals.

	SUBJECT	VERB
EXAMPLE The Moon having a cover of dust and rubble called "regolith."		*frag.*
1. Meteorites constantly bombarding the Moon.		*frag.*
2. The Moon having no atmosphere, therefore lacking protection from meteorites.		*frag.*
3. The smallest cosmic dust particles collide with its surface.		
4. Creating craters of every size.	*frag.*	*frag.*
5. Each collision shattering rock and scattering dust.		*frag.*
6. Scientists name this disturbing of the lunar soil "gardening."		
7. By studying the soil and rock brought back by Apollo astronauts.	*frag.*	*frag.*
8. Scientists have learned much about the Moon's composition.		
9. The Moon contains no sedimentary rocks resulting from deposits in water.		
10. Instead all lunar rocks are igneous, having been formed by the cooling of molten lava.		
11. The maria, low dark areas, once were considered to be seas.		

12. The light colored <u>areas</u> of the Moon called
    highlands.   _____   *frag.*

13. <u>They</u> <u>are known</u> to be much older than the
    maria.   _____   _____

14. Moon <u>rocks</u>, easily distinguished from Earth
    rocks by chemical analysis or by examining
    them under a microscope.   _____   *frag.*

15. Lunar <u>rocks</u> containing no water.   _____   *frag.*

16. Earth <u>rocks</u> nearly always <u>contain</u> a percent
    or two of water.   _____   _____

17. Lunar <u>rocks</u>, being beautifully preserved,
    never having reacted with water to form clay
    or rust.   _____   *frag.*

18. The <u>crystals</u> in Moon rock <u>look</u> fresher than
    those from a water-bearing lava, just erupted
    from a terrestrial volcano.   _____   _____

19. Moon <u>rocks</u> also forming amidst almost no
    free oxygen.   _____   *frag.*

20. Some Moon <u>rocks</u> <u>contain</u> perfectly preserved
    iron crystals.   _____   _____

Deduct 2 for each error in underlining and 2 for each blank incorrectly filled.

Subordinate Clauses and Sentences   Exercise 2-2

NAME _____ SCORE _____

DIRECTIONS   In the following word groups underline each subject with one straight line, each verb with two straight lines, and each subordinator with a wavy line. (Remember that a subordinator like *who, which,* or *that* may also be the subject of its own clause.) If the word group has only a subordinate clause or clauses, write *frag.* in the blank to indicate an incomplete sentence. If the word group has no subordinate clause or has a subordinate clause plus a main, or independent, clause, write *C* in the blank to indicate a complete sentence.

EXAMPLES

Because Moon rocks have never been exposed to water or oxygen.   *frag.*

Contact with Earth's atmosphere would rust them badly, which

would render them scientifically useless.   *C*

1. When samples from lunar missions are stored on Earth in con-
   tainers that have a pure nitrogen atmosphere.   *frag.*

2. Filters remove all terrestrial dust that could contaminate the
   samples.   *C*

3. When scientists request lunar samples for testing.   *frag.*

4. They receive only the amount that is necessary for their tests.   *C*

5. When sample material has been exposed to Earth's atmosphere, it cannot be returned to the storage chambers.   *C*

6. Although the same chemical elements exist in Earth rocks and
   the proportions are different.   *frag.*

7. Lunar rocks contain more of the common elements calcium,
   aluminum, and titanium than do Earth rocks.   *C*

8. Rarer elements like hafnium and zirconium which melt at
   higher temperatures.   *frag.*

9. Because sodium and potassium melt at lower temperatures,
   the heat from lava would boil them away.   *C*

10. Therefore, the Moon was left enriched with higher temper-
    ature elements and lacking in lower temperature ones.   *C*

11. Because the Moon's interior was formed by volcanic activity which then created the jumble of mountains, plains, and plateaus on the surface. — *frag.*

12. There is some evidence that the Moon's core may still be hot and even partly molten. — *C*

13. Like the Earth it may also contain a small iron core. — *C*

14. Although long-term experiments on the Moon's surface would answer many more questions. — *frag.*

15. Particularly if astronauts could drill for samples deep in the Moon's crust. — *frag.*

Deduct 3 1/2 for each error in identifying fragments and 3 1/2 for each incorrect revision.

Sentences and Fragments   Exercise 2-3

NAME _____ SCORE _____

DIRECTIONS   In the following paragraphs are ten fragments of various types—prepositional and verbal phrases, subordinate clauses, appositives, and parts of compound predicates. First, circle the numbers that stand in front of fragments, then revise the fragments by attaching them to the sentences they belong with. (See **12b** and **12d** if you need help with punctuation.)

①Prior to the return of lunar rock samples, ²We had no way to determine the Moon's age, ③And thus develop a clearer understanding of its evolution. ⁴Testing on meteorites indicated that the solar system formed about 4.6 billion years ago. ⁵Similar testing on Earth and Moon rocks suggested similar ages for the Earth and Moon, ⑥Making them as old as the solar system. ⁷The oldest known rocks on Earth are, however, only 3.8 billion years old, ⑧Leading to the speculation that continued volcanic activity on our planet destroyed the oldest rocks.

⁹The Moon rocks fill in some of this time gap between the Earth's oldest preserved rocks and the formation of the solar system. ¹⁰Lava from the dark maria are the Moon's youngest rocks, ⑪But are as old as the youngest rocks found on Earth. ¹²Rocks from lunar highlands are even older, ⑬Most highland samples being 4.0 to 4.3 billion years old. ⑭As scientists studied samples returned by Apollo 17 astronauts, ⑮They realized that the rocks were 4.6 billion years old. ¹⁶These rocks are fragments formed when the Moon was solidifying, ⑰Crystalline records of the Moon's actual formation. ⑱While the still-molten Moon gradually cooled and solidified into different kinds of rocks, ¹⁹The Moon was bombarded

by huge rocks, some the size of small states like Rhode Island or Delaware. [20]This bombarding created huge craters,[21] which are the most dramatic features of the lunar landscape.

Deduct 4 for each error in identifying fragments and 3 for each incorrect revision.

Fragments: Effective and Ineffective   Exercise 2–4

NAME _____ SCORE _____

DIRECTIONS   The following paragraphs include six effective fragments (see page 53) and thirteen ineffective fragments, incomplete sentences that the writer did not plan. Circle the number that stands in front of each fragment. Then revise the ineffective fragments either by rewriting them as complete sentences or by connecting them to the sentences they belong with. (See **12b** and **12d** if you need help with punctuation.) Place an X by the number of each effective fragment.

X
①A mountain over 10,000 feet high, created not by forces within the planet but by the force of objects crashing down from above.

X
②A riverlike channel half a mile wide and 80 miles long that once flowed with molten rock instead of water.

X
③A layer of fine soil 20 yards deep, produced by meteorites relentlessly crushing the planet's surface.

⁴These surface features of the Moon are the relics of an evolutionary process radically different from Earth's. ⑤Long before Earth had any of its present features, ⁶the Moon had developed its current physical appearance. ⁷In fact, the surface of the Moon we see today was essentially complete over 3 billion years ago. ⑧However, despite our great scientific knowledge of the Moon, ⁹many questions about it remain unanswered. ⑩Because Apollo and Soviet Luna missions only sampled nine sites on the Moon, ¹¹much of what we know is still theory. ¹²We know very little about its far side and nothing about its poles. X⑬So much to learn!

¹⁴Apollo spacecraft used a laser device to measure accurately the heights of features over much of the lunar surface, ⑮and discovered from these careful

measurements, (16) That the Moon is not a perfect sphere. ¹⁷It is slightly egg-shaped, (18) The small end of the egg pointing toward the Earth.

¹⁹There are other striking differences between the front and back hemispheres of the Moon, (20) The front (Earth-facing) side being covered with large dark maria, (21) And the far side nearly all light-colored, rugged terrain. ²²Underneath the maria on the front side the crust is about 60 km thick, (23) Contrasting with the crust on the far side which is over 100 km thick.

²⁴Is the Moon's interior molten? ²⁵How old are the youngest lunar rocks? (26) Unable to answer either question / ²⁷We obviously have far to go to complete our understanding of the Moon's formation. ²⁸Is the Moon a dead planet? (29) Apparently not. ³⁰For over 300 years astronomers have noted reddish glows, clouds, and mists on the Moon's surface. ³¹Why are these events important? (32) Because they suggest continued volcanic activity.

(33) As a consequence of our studying the Moon in recent years, (34) We have come to think of it as a planet with a history and character all its own. ³⁵We may even think of it now as a kind of museum, (36) A world that preserves the history and development of our solar system. ³⁷In the future we will return to the Moon for study and perhaps for other reasons, (38) Perhaps as a first step on a long journey to deep space or perhaps to create permanent bases for science, exploration, and industry.

3

Learn the standard ways to link two closely related main clauses.

In section **1** you studied the two main ways to expand a sentence—subordination and coordination. Subordination often requires the use of a comma or commas for the subordinated addition to the main clause. (See also **12b** and **12d**.)

Coordination, too, requires a comma when two main clauses are connected by a coordinating conjunction—*and, but, or, nor, for, so,* and *yet*.

> Science fiction literature has speculated for years about life on Mars, *but* visits by spacecraft to the planet have dispelled the idea.

If the coordinating conjunction is removed, the two main clauses may still be connected; however, the standard mark of punctuation between the two clauses then becomes the semicolon.

> Science fiction literature has speculated for years about life on Mars; visits by spacecraft to the planet have dispelled the idea.

Even if another type of connective—a conjunctive adverb like *then, therefore,* or *however*—is inserted between the main clauses, a semicolon is still the standard mark of punctuation to be used after the first main clause.

> Science fiction literature has speculated for years about life on Mars; *however,* visits by spacecraft to the planet have dispelled the idea.

If a comma is used between two main clauses not connected by a coordinating conjunction, the sentence contains a *comma splice.* In other words, the comma has been made to perform a function that standard usage has not given it.

> COMMA SPLICE   Science fiction literature has speculated for years about life on Mars, visits by spacecraft to the planet have dispelled the idea.
>
> COMMA SPLICE   Science fiction literature has speculated for years about life on Mars, however, visits by spacecraft to the planet have dispelled the idea.

Some students feel they can avoid comma splices by omitting all commas from their writing. And they are right. But in so doing they violate standard practices of punctuation even further. Instead of writing comma-splice sentences, they write *fused* (or run-together) sentences. And fused sentences are even more ineffective than comma-splice sentences because they are more difficult to understand at first reading.

> FUSED SENTENCE   The first astronomer to argue for an advanced Martian civilization was Percival Lowell he believed he could detect signs of construction on the Martian surface.

3a The standard punctuation of two main clauses not connected by a coordinating conjunction is the semicolon.

> Lowell interpreted certain dark marks on Mars as canals; he decided that Martians had erected an elaborate irrigation system.   [The semicolon acts like the fulcrum of a seesaw, with the idea in one main clause balanced by the idea in the other.]

There are two other ways to avoid a comma-splice or fused sentence.

> TWO SENTENCES   Lowell interpreted certain dark marks on Mars as canals. He decided that Martians had erected an elaborate irrigation system. [Placing the two ideas in separate sentences emphasizes them equally.]

> SUBORDINATION   After Lowell interpreted certain dark marks on Mars as canals, he decided that Martians had erected an elaborate irrigation system.   [Subordinating one of the ideas establishes a cause and effect relationship.]

3b The standard punctuation of two main clauses connected by a conjunctive adverb or a transitional phrase is the semicolon.

> Early reconnaissance of Mars revealed a landscape like the Moon's; *however,* later photographs by Mariner spacecraft revealed a far more complex planet.

> Mariner 4 initiated the exploration of Mars; *in fact,* scientists have explored only the Moon and Earth more intensely.

Notice that a conjunctive adverb or a transitional phrase may also be placed in the middle of a main clause and that the standard marks of punctuation are then commas.

> The very qualities that make Mars intriguing, *however,* also complicate exploration.

> Later photographs revealed, *in fact,* that Mars continues to be a volcanically active and changing planet.

You may need to consult or even memorize the list of commonly used conjunctive adverbs and transitional phrases in the Appendix.

3c The standard mark of punctuation for a divided quotation made up of two main clauses is the semicolon or an end mark (a period, question mark, or exclamation point).

> "Mariner spacecraft performed far longer than was expected," said the scientist; "they were designed to work three months, yet Mariner 1 lasted four years."

> "Mariner spacecraft performed far longer than was expected," said the scientist. "They were designed to work for three months, yet Mariner 1 lasted four years."

Comma Splices and Fused Sentences   Exercise 3–1

NAME _____   SCORE _____

DIRECTIONS   In each of the following sentences insert an inverted caret (**V**) between main clauses. Then indicate in the first blank at the right whether the sentence is correctly punctuated according to standard practice (*C*), contains a comma splice (*CS*), or is fused (*F*). Correct each error by the method you consider best, showing in the second blank whether you have used subordination (*sub.*), a period (*.*), a semicolon (*;*), or a comma plus a coordinating conjunction (*conj.*).

EXAMPLE

An American Viking spacecraft landed on Mars in

1976, it tested the soil to determine whether or

not life was present.   _____CS_____   _____sub._____

1. An early test indicated that the Martian soil
   V *but*
   could take in and use carbon, repeating the

   test gave the opposite result.   _____CS_____   _____conj_____

2. In another test, a "soup" was prepared that
   V
   could support micro-organisms; Martian soil

   was injected into the soup.   _____F_____   _____;_____

3. Scientists hoped that any micro-organisms in
   V *so*
   the soil would eat the soup then they would

   give off carbon dioxide or carbon monoxide

   which the scientists could detect.   _____F_____   _____._____
                                  V *because*
4. Again the results were ambiguous, the soup

   emitted some carbon dioxide but then ceased.   _____CS_____   _____sub._____

5. Scientists decided that a chemical reaction in

   the soil had caused the emission and that no

   micro-organisms were present.   _____C_____   _____

6. Subsequent experiments also gave ambiguous
   V *and*
   results, most scientists agreed that they saw

   no reason to believe that Mars held life.   _____CS_____   _____conj._____

7. Some scientists still would like to test water
   from Martian polar caps,ᵛ ʙᵉᶜᵃᵘˢᵉ water gives them a
   better chance of finding life.   _CS_ _sub._

8. Life as we know it on Earth could, in theory,
   survive in a relatively narrow band of our solar system.ᵛᴶ the band extends from inside the
   orbit of Venus to just outside the orbit of
   Mars.   _F_ _._

9. This small area is known as the "ecosphere,"ᵛ
   ᵃⁿᵈ it has a range of temperatures that could be
   tolerated by living organisms.   _CS_ _conj._

10. One possible exception is Saturn's satellite Ti-
    tan which could possibly support life in its
    methane atmosphere despite the $-70°C$ sur-
    face temperature.   _C_ _____

Deduct 4 3/4 for each blank incorrectly filled and 4 3/4 for each incorrect revision.

Comma Splices and Fused Sentences   Exercise 3–2

NAME _____ SCORE _____

DIRECTIONS   In each of the following sentences insert an inverted caret (**V**) between main clauses. Then indicate in the blank whether the sentence contains a comma splice (*CS*) or is fused (*F*). Rewrite each comma splice or fused sentence using two of the four possible methods: subordination, an end mark (two sentences), a semicolon, or a comma plus a coordinating conjunction. (You may want to discuss the effect each of the methods has on the ideas in the two clauses: to emphasize one or both ideas, to balance one idea with another, to establish a relationship between the ideas.)

EXAMPLE

Astronomers need good "seeing," viewing that is free of city lights,

clouds, and air turbulence $\overset{\vee}{}$ observatories usually are built atop

mountains to achieve good seeing.   _____*F*_____

Astronomers need ... turbulence. Observatories ...
seeing. Because astronomers need ... turbulence,
observatories ... seeing.

1. In 1892 Percival Lowell, a native of Boston, resolved to found

    an observatory to study Mars $\overset{\vee}{}$ he built the observatory on

    Mars Hill in Flagstaff, Arizona, to achieve good "seeing."   _____*CS*_____

    In 1892 after Percival Lowell ... "seeing."
    In 1892 Percival Lowell ... Mars. He built ...
    "seeing."

2. Peering through the Mars Hill telescope, Lowell meticulously

    sketched the surface of Mars $\overset{\vee}{}$ indeed, he sketched a pano-

    rama of bright and dark expanses, polar caps, and a maze

    of canals.   _____*CS*_____

    Peering through ... Mars; indeed, he ... canals.
    Peering through ... Mars. Indeed, he ... canals.

3. Lowell's drawings of the canals ignited public interest in

    Mars $\overset{\vee}{}$ however, other astronomers were unable to see the

    canals.   _____*CS*_____

    Lowell's drawings ... in Mars; however, other ...
    the canals.
    Lowell's drawings ... in Mars. However, other ...
    the canals.

4. In recent years the United States has landed spacecraft on the Martian surface and photographed the planet with orbiting satellites ⱽ none of these scientific missions, however, can explain what inspired Lowell's canal sketches.   _F_

In recent years ... satellites ; none ... canal sketches.
In recent years ... satellites. None ... canal sketches.

5. Carl Sagan compared Lowell's drawings with photographs taken by Mariner spacecraft ⱽ the drawings, he discovered, do not correspond to anything in the photographs.   _F_

Carl Sagan compared ... spacecraft. The drawings ... photographs.
Carl Sagan compared ... spacecraft ; the drawings ... photographs.

6. "The canals of Mars seem to be some malfunction, under difficult seeing conditions, of the human hand/eye/brain combination," Sagan argues ⱽ "I have the nagging suspicion, however, that some essential feature of the Martian canal problem still remains undiscovered."   _CS_

"The canals of Mars ... argues. "I have ... remains undiscovered."
"The canals of Mars ... argues; "I have ... remains undiscovered."

7. Sagan has in mind Lowell's undisputed skill as an astronomer and his equally undisputed honesty ⱽ in fact, Sagan cannot believe that Lowell could sketch the same canal patterns repeatedly without having seen something on the Martian surface.   _CS_

Sagan has ... honesty ; in fact, ... Martian surface.
Sagan has ... honesty. In fact, ... Martian surface.

Deduct 3 1/2 for each blank incorrectly filled and 3 1/2 for each incorrect revision.

Comma Splices, Fused Sentences, and Fragments: A Review

Exercise 3–3

NAME _____ SCORE _____

DIRECTIONS   Classify each of the following word groups as a fragment (*frag.*), a comma splice (*CS*), a fused sentence (*F*), or a correct sentence (*C*). Revise each faulty word group.

EXAMPLE
Four Viking spacecraft ~~arriving~~ *arrived* at Mars in 1976 to study it from the

surface and from orbit.　　　　　　　　　　　　　　　　　　　*frag.*

1. Much of the Viking activity was aimed at studying the presence of water on Mars. *a*lthough scientists have detected water
   ice in comets and in frozen outer planets, Mars is the only
   other planet over which water has flowed.　　　　　　　*F*

2. Scientists believe that Mars once had an atmosphere; however,
   intense activity by the developing Sun burned away the atmosphere.　　　　　　　　　　　　　　　　　　　　　　　*CS*

3. ~~So that~~ *T*he water on Mars now must be the result of volcanic
   activity.　　　　　　　　　　　　　　　　　　　　　　*frag.*

4. "The surface of Mars is obviously of volcanic origin," NASA
   spokesmen explain. "*a*s volcanism formed the planet, it also
   released water vapor which immediately froze."　　　　*CS*

5. "Surface temperatures are sufficiently cold to keep the water
   frozen," they added.　　　　　　　　　　　　　　　　*C*

6. Much of the remaining Martian water is stored in the north
   polar ice cap. *p*hotographs from Viking 2 revealed that Martian winds have eroded the ice caps into a complicated spiral
   shape.　　　　　　　　　　　　　　　　　　　　　　　*F*

7. Great dunes *are* composed of sand-sized clumps of silt and ice and
   shaped by Martian winds.　　　　　　　　　　　　　　*frag.*

8. Similar dunes appear all over the planet, ~~they~~ *and* are testimonials to the importance of the wind in sculpting the Martian terrain. _CS_

9. Scientists call such wind-made forms Eolian features, look up Eolian (or Aeolian) in your dictionary. _CS_

10. On occasion Martian winds create dust storms that completely cover the planet, during these storms surface structures are obscured and astronomers can only wait to discover what changes the storms have brought to the Martian landscape. _F_

4

Master the uses and forms of adjectives and adverbs.

Both adjectives and adverbs function as modifiers; that is, they make the meaning of the words they refer to more exact. In the examples below, notice that the meaning becomes clearer and more detailed as modifiers are added (adjectives are in boldface, adverbs in italics).

> The spacecraft photographed the ice on Mars.
>
> The **Viking** spacecraft photographed the **polar** ice on Mars.
>
> The *surprisingly* **successful Viking** spacecraft *repeatedly* photographed the **eroded polar** ice on Mars.

The adjectives—*successful, Viking, eroded, polar*—modify the noun subject *spacecraft* and the noun complement *ice*. Typically, adjectives modify nouns and sometimes pronouns. The adverbs—*surprisingly* and *repeatedly*—modify the adjective *successful* and the verb *photographed*. Typically, adverbs modify verbs and modifiers (both adjectives and adverbs).

A modern dictionary will show you the current usage of adjective and adverb modifiers. But here are a few guidelines.

4a Use adverbs to modify verbs, adjectives, and other adverbs.

> Colonization of Mars has *always* been an intriguing idea.   [*Always* modifies the verb *has been*.]
>
> Colonization of Mars has *often* provided an *extremely* intriguing plot for science fiction stories.   [*Often* modifies the verb *has provided*; *extremely* modifies the adjective *intriguing*.]
>
> Colonization of Mars *surprisingly often* is the topic of conversation among scientists.   [*Often* modifies the verb *is*; *surprisingly* modifies the adverb *often*.]

4b Distinguish between adjectives used as complements and adverbs used to modify verbs.

Adjectives, like nouns, are used as complements after linking verbs such as *be, appear, become, feel, look, seem, smell,* and *taste*. Such adjective complements refer to the subjects of their clauses.

> Although Martian weather often is *bad*, scientists seem *fascinated* with the prospect
>
> of adapting to it.
>
> [*Bad* refers to the subject of the subordinate clause, *weather*; *fascinated* refers to the subject of the main clause, *scientists*.]

They say that they are *optimistic*, especially after the successes of the Viking landers.

> [*Optimistic* refers to the subject of the subordinate clause, *they*.]

Undaunted were the scientists.

> [For emphasis, the complement, *undaunted*, comes before but still refers to the subject, *scientists*.]

A sensory verb like *feel*, *taste*, or *look* is followed by an adverb instead of an adjective when the modifier refers to the verb.

> The astronaut looked *gloomily* out the window at the Martian sandstorm. [Compare "The astronaut looked gloomy," in which *gloomy*, an adjective complement, modifies the subject, *astronaut*.]

A linking verb followed by an adjective complement may also be modified by one or more adverbs, coming either before or after.

> The astronaut *suddenly* looked gloomy *yesterday*. [Both adverbs modify *looked*.]

4c Use the appropriate forms of adjectives and adverbs for the comparative and the superlative.

Many adjectives and adverbs change form to indicate degree. The comparative degree (a comparison of two things) is usually formed by adding *-er* to the modifier or by putting *more* or *less* before the modifier. The superlative degree (a comparison of three or more things) is formed by adding *-est* to the modifier or by putting the word *most* or *least* before the modifier. Some desk dictionaries show the *-er* and *-est* endings for those adjectives and adverbs that form their comparative and superlative degrees in this way (for example, old, old*er*, old*est*). Most dictionaries show the changes for highly irregular modifiers (for example, good, *better*, *best*). As a rule of thumb, most one-syllable adjectives and most two-syllable adjectives ending in a vowel sound (*tidy, narrow*) form the comparative with *-er* and the superlative with *-est*. Most adjectives of two or more syllables and most adverbs form the comparative by adding the word *more* (*less*) and the superlative by adding the word *most* (*least*).

> NONSTANDARD The Viking lander performed more better than previous landers. [The *-er* shows the comparative degree; *more* is superfluous.]
>
> STANDARD The Viking lander performed better than previous landers.
>
> NONSTANDARD It was the better prepared of all the American and Russian landers. [*Better* is used to compare only two things.]
>
> STANDARD It was the best prepared of all the American and Russian landers.

Note: Not all adjectives and adverbs have a form for the comparative and superlative degrees. Most adjectives made from nouns—like *governmental*, for example—have no other forms. (One does not say that something is "more governmental" than something else or that something is the "most governmental" of all.) Other modifiers, like *perfect* and *unique*, are in themselves an expression of the superlative degree.

4d Avoid the awkward substitution of a noun form for an adjective.

We correctly use many nouns as modifiers of other nouns—*soap* opera, *book* club, *moon* rocket—because there are no suitable adjective forms available. But when adjective forms are available, you should avoid awkward noun substitutes.

AWKWARD   Education television presented a special on the Viking missions.

BETTER   *Educational* television presented a special on the Viking missions.

4e Avoid the double negative.

The term *double negative* refers to the use of two negatives to express a single negation.

NONSTANDARD   He did not have no memory of the Martians.   [double negative: *not* and *no*]

STANDARD   He did not have a memory of the Martians.   [single negative: *not*]

OR

He had no memory of the Martians.   [single negative: *no*]

Another redundant construction occurs when a negative such as *not, nothing,* or *without* is combined with *hardly, barely,* or *scarcely.*

NONSTANDARD   He couldn't hardly stop talking about the Martians.

STANDARD   He could hardly stop talking about the Martians.

NONSTANDARD   The Martian was elected without scarcely any opposition.

STANDARD   The Martian was elected with scarcely any opposition.

Deduct 5 1/2 for each blank incorrectly filled.

Adjectives and Adverbs

Exercise 4-1

NAME _____ SCORE _____

DIRECTIONS   In each of the following sentences cross out the incorrect modifier within the parentheses and write in the blank the choice that represents standard usage. In the sentence, underline the word or words being modified by the modifier you chose. (Consult your dictionary if you are in doubt about the proper form of the comparative or superlative degree of an adjective or adverb.)

EXAMPLE
We (sure, surely) will colonize space before many more

years have passed.   *surely*

1. Some of NASA's (more persuasive, most persuasive)
   scientists have been arguing for the colonization of
   the Moon.   *most persuasive*

2. Congress listened (careful, carefully) to the argu-
   ments and gave NASA permission to plan a Moon
   colony.   *carefully*

3. The (more recent, most recent) plans call for NASA
   first to build a space station.   *most recent*

4. The next step in colonization is almost (certain,
   certainly) to be a manned lunar station.   *certain*

5. Scientists (most, almost) always point to a lunar
   colony as necessary for other space exploration.   *almost*

6. The practical benefits seem (obvious, obviously) to
   those scientists.   *obvious*

7. Energy savings are one of the (more important,
   most important) benefits.   *most important*

8. It will be easy to launch space exploration from the
   Moon's (relative, relatively) weak gravity.   *relatively*

9. Many necessary materials also can be mined or
   manufactured (more easily, most easily) on the
   Moon than on the Earth.   *more easily*

10. They can be produced and injected into space with (relative, ~~relatively~~) ease.

relative

11. Space workers can (~~easy,~~ easily) use the materials to construct space industries, satellites, settlements, vehicles, and depots.

easily

12. (Hopeful, ~~Hopefully~~) NASA scientists now are talking about having the lunar base in place by 2020.

Hopeful

13. Plans now include underground buildings to provide (necessary, ~~necessarily~~) protection from cosmic rays, solar flares, and potential military threats.

necessary

Below, make the choices that avoid double negatives.

14. Building the space platform had proceeded (with, ~~without~~) scarcely a problem.

with

15. Then the Senate committee began to investigate and could discover hardly (~~nothing,~~ anything) that it liked.

anything

16. The chairman (could, ~~could not~~) hardly control the meetings because the members became so upset.

could

17. Most of them were upset because their states did not receive (~~no,~~ any) government contracts to help with the building.

any

18. I did not know (~~no one,~~ anyone) in the government could act so childishly.

anyone

Adjectives and Adverbs   Exercise 4-2

NAME _____ SCORE _____

DIRECTIONS   While preserving the meaning, rewrite each of the following sentences, changing the italicized adjective to an adverb and the italicized noun to a verb or an adjective, as in the example below. (You will have to make a few other changes in the sentence in addition to changing the italicized words.)

EXAMPLE
Neil Armstrong felt a *total happiness* when he first stepped onto the Moon.

Neil Armstrong felt totally happy when he first stepped onto the Moon.

1. The Lunar Rover took a *slow tour* of the Moon.

   The Lunar Rover slowly toured the Moon.

2. The President extended a *warm welcome* to the returning astronauts.

   The President warmly welcomed the returning astronauts.

3. The astronauts' dignity and composure made a *strong impression* on everyone.

   The astronauts' dignity and composure strongly impressed everyone.

4. The astronauts' reactions to their lunar visits often were a *great delight* to the American public.

   The astronauts' reactions to their lunar visits often greatly delighted the American public.

5. During one lunar walk two astronauts demonstrated an *unexpected enthusiasm* for golf.

   During one lunar walk two astronauts were unexpectedly enthusiastic about golf.

5

Master the case forms of pronouns to show their functions in sentences.

The form that a noun or pronoun has in a sentence indicates its function, or *case: subjective, objective,* or *possessive.* Nouns usually change their form for only one case—the possessive. (In section **15** you will study the ways the apostrophe indicates that change.) Certain pronouns, however, change their form for each case, and you must be aware of the various forms if you want to use these pronouns correctly.

SUBJECTIVE	OBJECTIVE	POSSESSIVE
I	me	mine
we	us	our OR ours
he, she	him, her	his, her, OR hers
they	them	their OR theirs
who OR whoever	whom OR whomever	whose

5a A pronoun has the same case form in a compound or an appositive construction as it would have if it were used alone.

When you are using a single pronoun, you may have no difficulty choosing the right case.

> *I* saw the space shuttle with *her.*

But when other pronouns or nouns are added, you may become confused about case and write, "Him and me saw the space shuttle with Mel and she." If you have a tendency to make such errors in case, think of the function each pronoun would have if it were used in a separate sentence.

> *He* saw the space shuttle.   [NOT *Him* saw the space shuttle.]
> *I* saw the space shuttle.   [NOT *Me* saw the space shuttle.]
> I saw the space shuttle with *her.*   [NOT I saw the space shuttle with *she.*]

Then you will be more likely to write the correct case forms:

> *He* and *I* saw the space shuttle with Mel and *her.*

5b The case of a pronoun depends on its use in its own clause.

When a sentence has only one clause, the function of the pronoun may seem clear to you.

> *Who* is funding the space shuttle?   [*Who* is the subject of the verb *is funding.*]

But when another clause is added, you must be careful to determine the pronoun's use in its own clause.

I know *who* is funding the space shuttle.   [Although *who* introduces a clause that acts as the direct object of the verb *know*, in its own clause *who* is the subject of the verb *is funding.*]

An implied rather than a stated clause often follows the subordinating conjunctions *than* or *as.*

She did as well in the training as *I*.   [The implied meaning is "as I did."]
John knows you better than *me*.   [The implied meaning is "than John knows me."]

5c In formal writing use *whom* for all objects. (See also **5b**.)

The scientist *whom* they named to head the mission has resigned.   [object of the verb *named*]
The scientist to *whom* they assigned the mission has resigned.   [object of the preposition *to*]
Whom did they choose to replace him?   [object of the verb *choose*]

5d In general, use the possessive case before a verbal used as a noun.

A gerund is a verbal that ends in *-ing* and is used as a noun (see **1d(1)**). The possessive case is used before a gerund, which acts as a noun, but not before a participle, which also sometimes has an *-ing* ending but acts as an adjective.

Bob's parents got tired of *his* complaining that his new telescope would not work. [*Complaining* is a gerund and functions as the object of the preposition *of*.]
That afternoon they found *him* looking through the big end of the telescope. [*Looking* is a participle, an adjective modifying *him*.]

5e Use the objective case for direct and indirect objects, for objects of prepositions, and for both subjects and objects of infinitives (*to* plus the verb).

The salesman gave *me* instructions for using the telescope.
Between *you* and *me*, I was too excited to remember *them*.
As a result it was easy for *him* to use the telescope but impossible for *me*.   ["To do it" is implied after *for me.*]

5f Use the subjective case for subjects and for subject complements.

She and *I* watched the Moon-landing on television.
The owner of the television is *he*.   [You may find it more comfortable to avoid using the pronoun as a complement. If so, write "He is the owner of the television."]

5g Add *-self* to a pronoun (*himself, herself, itself, ourselves, themselves*) when a reflexive or an intensive pronoun is needed.

A reflexive pronoun follows the verb and refers to the subject; an intensive pronoun emphasizes the noun or pronoun it refers to.

I blamed *myself* for not seeing the launch.   [*Myself* refers back to *I.*]

I myself will take the blame for not seeing the launch.   [*Myself* intensifies *I.*]

The pronoun ending in *-self* is not used as a subject or an object unless it refers to the same person as the subject.

The other astronomers asked *me* to represent *them*.   [NOT *myself* and *themselves*]

He blamed *himself* for not being awake to watch the launch.   [*Himself*, the object, refers to the same person as *He*, the subject.]

Deduct 6 2/3 for each blank incorrectly filled.

Case of Pronouns

Exercise 5-1

NAME _____ SCORE _____

DIRECTIONS   In the following sentences cross out the incorrect case form or forms in parentheses and write the correct form in the blank.

EXAMPLE
Galileo's assistant handed (he, him) a stone and a

feather.   *him*

1. Most of (we, us) recognize the names of the famous

   physicists.   *us*

2. (Who, Whom) does not know of Galileo, Newton,

   and Einstein?   *who*

3. In the seventeenth century Galileo's ideas placed

   him in conflict with Church authorities, (who,

   whom) finally forced him to recant.   *who*

4. Today you and (I, me) recognize some of the ideas

   as common sense, but others seem to contradict

   common sense.   *I*

5. Galileo first placed (hisself, himself) in danger by

   arguing the Copernican theory that the Earth or-

   bits the Sun.   *himself*

6. Church officials reacted by forcing (he, him) to say

   that this was only a hypothesis.   *him*

7. Galileo hoped that, because (he, him) and Pope

   Urban were friends, he would avoid further perse-

   cution.   *he*

8. At the same time, he invited controversy both with

   his ideas and with (him, his) choosing to publish

   not in Latin but in vernacular Italian.   *his*

9. Galileo's next publication explained the laws that govern bodies in motion, and he set himself in conflict with all (who, ~~whom~~) followed Aristotle. _____who_____

10. Aristotle believed that objects fall at speeds proportional to their weights. (Who, ~~Whom~~) could argue that if a feather and a stone are dropped at the same time from the same height they will reach the ground at the same time? _____who_____

11. Galileo argued that Aristotle had not fully imagined the problem; (his, ~~him~~) not imagining that the air would exert different influences on the stone and feather led to false conclusions. _____his_____

12. Galileo argued that, in a vacuum, a stone and a feather dropped from the same height at the same time would reach the ground at the same time. The vacuum would permit (~~they~~, them) to fall with no resistance. _____them_____

13. To all of (~~we~~, us) the idea of a vacuum is acceptable, but in the seventeenth century a vacuum was considered unnatural. _____us_____

14. Church authorities believed (~~theirselves~~, themselves, ~~them~~) justified in branding Galileo a heretic and threatening him with torture. _____themselves_____

15. Neither you nor (I, ~~me~~) could fail to understand why Galileo chose to recant and to avoid torture. _____I_____

Deduct 6 2/3 for each blank incorrectly filled.

Case of Pronouns

Exercise 5-2

NAME _____ SCORE _____

DIRECTIONS   In the following sentences cross out the incorrect case form or forms in parentheses and write the correct form in the blank.

EXAMPLE

In the sixteenth century, few of (us, ~~we~~) would have gone against the authority of the Church and the ancient philosophers.

_us_

1. Galileo is a familiar historical type, one (~~who,~~ whom) we honor because he defied tradition.

whom

2. Isaac Newton is another one (who, ~~whom~~) changed history because he defied it.

who

3. Newton's personality contrasted completely with Galileo's and did not set (~~he,~~ him) in public conflict with authority.

him

4. Newton was quiet, moody, and introspective and would seem to (~~you and I,~~ you and me) particularly unfit to defy tradition.

you and me

5. In addition to being somewhat reclusive, Newton was a devout Christian (who, ~~whom~~) could be judged a fanatic.

who

6. Newton's parents soon judged (him, ~~he~~) to be unsuited for farm work.

him

7. They sent him to Cambridge University to study under a faculty (who, ~~whom~~) had been depleted by the civil war.

who

8. Isaac Barrow, an amateur mathematician, tutored Newton until (~~him,~~ he) judged the young man prepared to replace him.

_he_

9. Barrow realized that Newton could teach (him, ~~he~~) more than he could teach Newton.

him

10. Newton began work at Cambridge in virtual isolation; even the reclusive Newton soon needed more intellectual stimulation than (he, ~~him~~) was getting.

_he_

11. The astronomer Edmund Halley, (~~whom~~, who) later became famous for correctly predicting the cyclic orbit of the comet, became a close confidant.

who

12. At Halley's urging Newton published his work in a volume commonly known to (~~we~~, us) today as _Principia_.

_us_

13. Suddenly, all the scientific leaders of Newton's day realized that they had among (~~themselves~~, them) a genius.

them

14. Newton moved to London and was appointed master of the Royal Mint, a post intended to make (~~he~~, him) financially secure.

him

15. Newton applied (himself, ~~him~~) well to the task: he initiated the practice of fluting the edges of coins to prevent the precious metal from being shaved off, and he personally attended the hanging of counterfeiters.

himself

6

Make a verb agree in number with its subject; make a pronoun agree in number with its antecedent.

Subjects and verbs must have the same number: a singular subject requires a singular verb, and a plural subject requires a plural verb. (Remember that an -*s* ending shows plural number for the subject but singular number for the verb.)

SINGULAR   The *member* of the Stargazer's Club *uses* a refractor telescope.

PLURAL   Five *members* of the Stargazer's Club *use* refractor telescopes.

Similarly, a pronoun must agree in number with its antecedent, the noun or pronoun it refers to.

SINGULAR   The *boy* brought *his* camera because *he* wanted to photograph through *his* telescope.

PLURAL   All the *members* brought *their* cameras because *they* wanted to photograph through *their* telescopes.

6a The verb agrees in number with its subject.

(1) The verb must be matched with its subject, not with the object of a preposition or with some other word that comes between the subject and verb.

The *combination* of cameras with telescopes *has become* common.   [*Combination*, not *telescopes*, is the subject.]

A *camera*, together with the necessary attachments, significantly *increases* the money invested in stargazing.   [Most writers agree that nouns following expressions like "together with," "in addition to," and "along with" do not affect the number of the subject. Notice that the whole phrase is set off by commas.]

Subjects and verbs that end in -*sk* or -*st* must be carefully matched. Because of our tendency to leave out certain difficult sounds when speaking, many of us also fail in our writing to add a needed -*s* to a verb or to a subject ending in -*sk* or -*st*.

Artists are often hired to interpret photographs taken by astronomers.
Because the photographs lack detail, the *artist* often paints from his imagination.

(2) Subjects joined by *and* usually take a plural verb.

The club president and his brother *have been observing* Saturn most of the night.

Exception: If the two subjects refer to the same person or thing, or if *each* or *every* comes before the subject, the verb is singular.

The club president and organizer of tonight's star watch *hopes* to be the first to sight the comet.

Every club member and every professional astronomer *dreams* of owning the perfect telescope.

(3) Singular subjects joined by *or, nor, either . . . or,* and *neither . . . nor* usually take a singular verb.

Either a 3-inch refractor or a 6-inch reflector *is* a good starting-size telescope.

Exception: If one subject is singular and one plural, the verb is matched with the nearer subject, or the sentence is revised to avoid the agreement difficulty.

Neither the member nor his guests *were prepared* for the sudden rainstorm.

OR

The member *was* not *prepared* for the sudden rainstorm, and neither *were* his guests.

(4) When the subject follows the verb (as in sentences beginning with *there is* or *there are*), special care is needed to match up subject and verb.

There *is* a wide *range* of prices among the refractor telescopes.

There *are* expensive and inexpensive refractor *telescopes.*

Included among the expensive types *are* refractor *telescopes* with lenses larger than 3 inches.

(5) A relative pronoun (*who, whom, which, that*) used as the subject of a clause is singular or plural depending on its antecedent.

There are motorized telescope mounts that automatically *turn* and *elevate* the telescope. [*Mounts,* the antecedent, is plural; therefore *that* is considered plural.]

Every amateur astronomer who *plans* to photograph the stars needs a motorized telescope mount. [*Astronomer,* the antecedent, is singular; therefore *who* is considered singular.]

(6) Pronoun subjects like *each, one, anybody, everybody, either,* and *neither* usually take singular verbs.

Each of us *plans* to trade his or her small refractor for a larger one.

Everybody with a small refractor *is planning* to trade it for a larger one.

Pronoun subjects like *all, any, half, most, none,* and *some* may take either a singular or plural verb—the context determines the verb form.

All of the refractors *use* lenses to focus light.

All of the incoming light *is* refracted or bent by the lens.

(7) In general, use a singular verb with collective nouns regarded as a unit and with nouns that are plural in form but singular in meaning.

The number of inches in diameter of the main lens or mirror *determines* a telescope's capability.   [*The number* is usually regarded as a unit.]

A *number* of types of telescopes *contain* lenses and mirrors.   [A *number* usually refers to individuals or items.]

(8) The verb agrees with the subject, not the subject complement, but it is usually best to avoid disagreement of verb and subject complement by revising the sentence to eliminate the linking verb.

AWKWARD   My usual *snack* at stargazing parties *is* a *Mars Bar* and *Moon Pie*. [The verb *is* correctly agrees with the subject *snack*, but the disagreement of verb and subject complement seems awkward to many writers.]

REVISED   At stargazing parties I usually snack on a *Mars Bar* and *Moon Pie*. [Replacing the linking verb with an active verb eliminates the problem of disagreement of verb and subject complement.]

(9) Even though they have the -s ending, nouns like *news*, *civics*, and *measles* take singular verbs. The dictionary is the best guide for determining which nouns with plural endings take singular verbs.

Economics usually *determines* how good a telescope you will own.   [The dictionary describes *economics* as singular.]

(10) Single titles, even if plural in form, are considered singular in number, as are words referred to as words.

"The Three Sisters" *was* the title the Mayas gave to one constellation. *Catadioptrics is* often misspelled. Do you know what it means?

6b A pronoun agrees in number with its antecedent (see also 27b).

(1) Use a singular pronoun to refer to such antecedents as *each, everyone, nobody, one, a person, a woman, a man*.

Each of the women takes *her* turn viewing.

Today writers make every effort to avoid sexism in the use of personal pronouns. Whereas writers once wrote, "Each of us should do his best," they now try to avoid using the masculine pronoun to refer to both men and women. To avoid sexism, some writers give both masculine and feminine pronoun references.

Each of us took *his* or *her* turn.
Each of us took *his/her* turn.

Other writers prefer to use *one's* in place of *his* or *her*.

One should take *one's* turn.

Perhaps the easiest way to avoid sexism is to use plural pronouns and anteced-ents—unless a feminine or a masculine pronoun is clearly called for, as *her* would be in reference to Sally Ride.

> All of them took *their* turns.
> All of us took *our* turns.

(2) Use a plural pronoun to refer to two or more antecedents joined by *and;* use a singular pronoun to refer to two or more antecedents joined by *or* or *nor.*

> Maria *and* Elaine have taken *their* turns using the new telescope.
> Neither Maria *nor* Elaine wants *her* turn to be over.

If it is necessary to have one singular and one plural antecedent, make the pronoun agree with the closer antecedent.

> Neither Maria nor her *friends* know when *their* turns will end.

Again, as with the verb (see **6a(6)**), it is sometimes best to rephrase to avoid the pronoun agreement difficulty.

> Maria does not know when *her* turn will end, and neither do her friends.

(3) Use either a singular or a plural pronoun to refer to a collective noun like *team, staff,* or *group,* depending on whether the noun is considered a unit or a group of individuals.

> The observatory *staff* is planning *its* next public viewing.   [Here *staff* acts as a unit. Notice that both the pronoun and the verb must agree with the subject.]
> The *staff* are disagreeing about what *their* responsibilities will be during the public viewing.   [The individuals on the staff are being referred to; thus both the pronoun and the verb are plural.]

When the collective noun is considered plural, as *staff* is in the preceding example, many writers prefer to use *staff members* rather than a noun that looks singular in number.

> The staff *members* are disagreeing about what *their* responsibilities will be during the public viewing.

(4) The pronoun that refers to such antecedents as *all, most, half, none,* and *some* is usually plural, but in a few contexts it can be singular.

> *All* of them took *their* turns.
> *Most* of the viewers saw more than *they* ever had before.
> *Most* of their preparation proved *itself* worthwhile.

Deduct 5 for each blank incorrectly filled.
Agreement of Subject and Verb

Exercise 6–1

NAME _____ SCORE _____

DIRECTIONS   In each of the following sentences underline the subject of the verb in parentheses with one line; then match it mentally with the correct verb. Cross out the verb that does not agree with the subject, and write the verb that does agree in the blank.

EXAMPLE

Exploration of the outer planet (~~present~~, presents) scien-

    tists with a variety of problems.   *presents*

1. The most significant problem (is, ~~are~~) time.   *is*

2. For all its apparent power, a rocket (is, ~~are~~) a puny

    thing on the scale of the solar system.   *is*

3. Direct flights to Neptune by robot explorer (re-

    quire, ~~requires~~) forty years.   *require*

4. By relying on computations discovered by a gradu-

    ate student in aeronautics, a spacecraft now

    (~~make~~, makes) the forty-year journey to Neptune

    in twelve years.   *makes*

5. Gary Flandro's computations (explain, ~~explains~~)

    that Jupiter's gravity alters the velocity and direc-

    tion of spacecraft voyages.   *explain*

6. Flandro (~~compare~~, compares) the effects Jupiter

    exerts on comets to those it could exert on space-

    craft.   *compares*

7. Planning such a flight (~~depend~~, depends) on a rare

    alignment of Jupiter, Saturn, Uranus, and Nep-

    tune.   *depends*

8. Flandro's computations in 1966 demonstrated that

    the four planets (~~was~~, were) properly aligned dur-

    ing Thomas Jefferson's presidency.   *were*

9. He realized that they (~~was,~~ were) going to be properly aligned again in 1977. _were_

10. NASA officials quickly realized that this (was, ~~were~~) a rare opportunity to save time and money. _was_

11. All resources (~~was,~~ were) funneled into planning Voyager missions to the outer planets. _were_

12. A number of problems immediately (beset, ~~besets~~) a mission as ambitious as this one. _beset_

13. The number of problems, particularly funding problems, (~~increase,~~ increases) as launch time nears. _increases_

14. If everyone involved (is, ~~are~~) stubborn and lucky, the spacecraft is eventually launched. _is_

15. Scientists (refer, ~~refers~~) to this Voyager mission as the Grand Tour. _refer_

16. Neither Uranus nor Neptune, the first two goals of the Grand Tour, (is, ~~are~~) easily visible from Earth. _is_

17. Both Uranus and Neptune (~~is,~~ are) comparatively small planets. _are_

18. Each (is, ~~are~~) almost as much larger than Earth as Earth is larger than the Moon. _is_

19. Jupiter, together with Saturn, (is, ~~are~~) comparatively large. _is_

20. Jupiter's mass and diameter (make, ~~makes~~) it a true planetary giant. _make_

Deduct 10 for each error in agreement.

Agreement of Subject and Verb

Exercise 6–2

NAME _____ SCORE _____

DIRECTIONS   In the following sentences the subjects and verbs are in agreement. Re-write the sentences, making all italicized singular subjects and verbs plural and all itali-cized plural subjects and verbs singular. (You will need to drop or add an article—*a*, *an*, *the*—before the subject and sometimes change another word or two to make the sentence sound right.) When your answers have been checked, you may want to read the sentences aloud to accustom your ear to the forms that agree with each other.

EXAMPLE
Recent *study indicates* that Jupiter and Saturn are reduced copies of the Sun.

Recent studies indicate that Jupiter and Saturn are reduced copies of the Sun.

1. The *planets are composed* of 97% hydrogen and helium.

   The planet is composed of 97% hydrogen and helium.

2. *Each* of them *is* a gas giant with a thick atmosphere.

   Both of them are gas giants with thick atmospheres.

3. There *are traces* of other gases, rocks, and metals.

   There is a trace of other gases, rocks and metals.

4. The *cores* of Uranus and Neptune *are* rock and *are covered* by a mantle of methane, ammonia, and water.

   The core of Uranus and Neptune is rock and is covered by a mantle of methane, ammonia, and water.

5. The *atmosphere* of each planet *is* rich in hydrogen and helium.

   The atmospheres of both planets are rich in hydrogen and helium.

6. *Teams* of NASA scientists *are* still *monitoring* Voyager spacecraft.

   A team of NASA scientists is still monitoring Voyager spacecraft.

7. The *encounter* of Voyager 2 with Uranus *occurred* on January 24, 1985.

   The encounters of Voyager 2 with Uranus occurred on January 24, 1985.

8. *Photographs* from Voyager 2 on Christmas Day, 1985, *show* details on Uranus 3,000 kilometers across.

   A photograph from Voyager 2 on Christmas Day, 1985, shows details on Uranus 3,000 kilometers across.

9. At its closest approach Voyager's *photographs detect* features 20 kilometers across.

   At its closest approach a Voyager photograph detects features 20 kilometers across.

10. The *moons* of both planets *are* also *included* in some photographs.

   The moon of each planet is also included in some photographs.

7

Use the appropriate forms of verbs.

You will remember from section **1** that the verb is the most essential part of the basic formula for a sentence. Sentences may be written without subjects—though few are, of course. And sentences are frequently written without complements. But without a verb, there is no sentence. To use this essential part of the sentence correctly, you must know not only how to make the present tense of the verb agree with its subject in number (see section **6**) but also how to choose the right tense of the verb to express the time you intend: present, past, future, present perfect, past perfect, or future perfect.

Verbs have three main tenses—present, past, and future—and three secondary tenses—present perfect, past perfect, and future perfect. A verb's ending (called its *inflection*) and/or the helping verb or verbs used with it determine the verb's tense.

PRESENT	fly
PAST	flew
FUTURE	will fly
PRESENT PERFECT	has or have flown
PAST PERFECT	had flown
FUTURE PERFECT	will have flown

Actually, there are several ways to form a given tense in English. For the past tense, for example, you could write any of these forms:

He *flew* experimental airplanes.

He *was flying* experimental airplanes.   [continuing past time]

He *did fly* experimental airplanes.   [Emphatic. Notice that this form of the past tense uses *did* plus the present form of the main verb, *fly*.]

He *used to fly* experimental airplanes.   [*Used to* (NOT *use to*) suggests an action that no longer occurs.]

Native speakers of English use most forms of a verb correctly without even thinking. But there are a few forms and a few verbs that give many of us difficulty; this section concentrates on these forms and these verbs.

7a Avoid misusing the principal parts of verbs and confusing similar verbs. (See the Appendix for a list of the principal parts of some of the most common troublesome verbs.)

Most verbs are *regular* verbs; that is, they form their tenses in a predictable way. The *-ed* ending is used for the past tense and all the perfect tenses, including the past participle form of a verbal. The *-ing* ending is used to form the progressive and the present participle.

PAST   He *entered* the astronaut training program.

PRESENT PERFECT   He *has entered* the astronaut training program.

PAST PERFECT   He *had entered* the astronaut training program before he earned his pilot's license.

FUTURE PERFECT   Twelve minutes into the maneuvers the shuttle *will have entered* the Moon's gravitational field.

PAST PARTICIPLE   *Having entered* the atmosphere, the pilot watched as computers began to control the shuttle.

PROGRESSIVE   He *is entering* the atmosphere. [also *was entering, has been entering, had been entering, will have been entering*]

PRESENT PARTICIPLE   *Entering* the atmosphere, he turns the controls over to computers.

Most dictionaries do not list the principal parts of a regular verb like *enter: enter* (Present), *entered* (Past and Past Participle), and *entering* (Present Participle).

But if a verb is irregular—that is, if it forms its past tense in some way other than by adding an *-ed*—the dictionary will usually list three or four principal parts.

race, raced, racing [Notice that only a *-d* is added to form the past and past participle; therefore the principal parts may be listed in the dictionary.]

drive, drove, driven, driving [This verb has four listings in the dictionary because it changes form for the past and the past participle as well as the present participle.]

If a verb undergoes no change except for the *-ing* ending of the present participle, the dictionary still lists three principal parts because the verb is not a regular verb.

burst, burst, bursting

Be careful to distinguish between verbs with similar spellings like *sit/set, lie/lay,* and *rise/raise.* Remember that *sit, lie,* and *rise* cannot take objects but *set, lay,* and *raise* can.

        object

Before Luke *sat down* to rest, he *raised* the hood of his land skimmer and *laid out*

  object

his tools to repair the engine.

The tools *were set* on a workbench that *sat* nearby.

Notice in the second example above that the word you expect to be the object of *set*—that is, *tools*—is made the subject of the sentence. Thus the subject of the sentence is not acting but is being acted upon. In such a case, the verb is said to be *passive*.

The verbs *set, lay,* and *raise* can be made passive, but the verbs *sit, lie,* and *rise* cannot be because they cannot take objects.

> The tools were *set* down.   [NOT *sat* down]
> The tools were *laid* down.   [NOT *lain* down]
> The hood was *raised*.   [NOT was *risen*]

Of these six difficult verbs, the most troublesome combination is *lie/lay* because the past tense form of *lie* is *lay*.

> He *lays* out the tools and then *lies* down to rest.
> After he had *laid* out the tools, he *lay* down to rest.

Be careful to add the *-d* or *-ed* ending to the past and perfect tenses of verbs like *use* and to verbs that end in *-k* or *-t*.

> He has use*d* only ten minutes of his space walk.
> He ask*ed* the ground crew in Houston for more information.

Be careful to spell correctly the principal parts of verbs like *occur, pay,* and *die* that double or change letters.

> occur, occu*rr*ed, occu*rr*ing
> pay, pa*id*, paying
> die, died, d*y*ing.

7b Make the tense forms of verbs and/or verbals relate logically between subordinate clauses and the main clause and in compound constructions.

Verbs in Main and Subordinate Clauses   When both the main-clause verb and the subordinate-clause verb refer to action occurring now or to action that could occur at any time, use the present tense for both verbs.

> When scientists *study* the universe for signs of other life, they usually *are listening* for radio messages. [*Are listening*, the progressive form, denotes action that takes place in the past, present, and (probably) future.]

When both the main and the subordinate verbs refer to action that occurred at a definite time in the past, use the past tense for both verbs.

> While Carl Sagan *was leading* the Mariner project, he *hoped* to discover other life forms. [*Was leading*, the past progressive form, suggests an action that took place in the past but on a continuing basis.]

When both the main and the subordinate verbs refer to action that continued for some time but was completed before now, use the present perfect tense for both verbs.

Sagan *has* not *stopped* expecting to discover other life forms just because the Mariner lander *has found* no signs of life on Mars.

Notice that the present tense can be used with the present perfect tense without causing a shift.

Some scientists *have stopped* believing in extraterrestrial life because the Mariner experiments *can*not *detect* life on Mars.

Some scientists *do* not *believe* in extraterrestrial life because they *have found* no sounds of it in this solar system.

Main Verbs and Verbals   When the main verb's action occurs at the same time as the verbal's, use the present-tense form of the verbal.

Sagan *continues* to believe in extraterrestrial life.

Sagan *continued* to believe in extraterrestrial life.

Continuing to believe in extraterrestrial life, Sagan strongly *suggests* radio astronomy as the best way to contact other civilizations.

Continuing to believe in extraterrestrial life, Sagan strongly *suggested* radio astronomy as the best way to contact other civilizations.

On the few occasions when the action of the verbal occurs before the action of the main verb, use the present-perfect tense form of the verbal.

Sagan *would like to have resolved* the issue of the existence of other life forms while he headed the Mariner project.   [Compare "Sagan *wishes he had resolved* the issue."]

Having failed to resolve the issue of the existence of other life forms, Sagan focused his talents on radio astronomy, which he hoped would provide new evidence of other life forms.   [The failure to resolve occurred before Sagan turned to radio astronomy.]

Compound Constructions   Be sure that verb tenses in compound predicates are consistent.

Sagan steadfastly *argues* for the presence of other life forms in the universe and *concentrates* his research on finding them.

7c In writing, use the subjunctive mood in the few expressions in which it is still appropriate.

Although the subjunctive mood has been largely displaced by the usual form of the present tense (the *indicative* mood), the subjunctive is still used in a few instances: (1) to express a condition contrary to fact, (2) to state a wish, (3) in *that* clauses of demand, recommendation, or request.

If she *were asked*, Mrs. Williams would return to Mars.

She wishes that she *were* free to return.

The possibility that she will be asked to return requires that she *be prepared* to leave at a moment's notice.

Deduct 4 for each item incorrectly treated.

Verb Forms

NAME _____ SCORE _____

DIRECTIONS   Use your dictionary to look up the principal parts of the verbs listed below. If the verb is a regular verb—that is, adds an -ed for the past and the past participle and an -ing for the present participle—write *regular* in the blank. But if the verb is not predictable in its tense forms, write *irregular* in the blank and fill in the two or three other parts that your dictionary lists after the present tense form.

EXAMPLES

try   *tried trying*   *irregular*

talk   *regular*

1. see   *saw seen seeing*   *irregular*

2. last   *regular*

3. grow   *grew grown growing*   *irregular*

4. write   *wrote written writing*   *irregular*

5. drown   *regular*

6. send   *sent sending*   *irregular*

7. fly   *flew flown flying*   *irregular*

8. attack   *regular*

9. break   *broke broken breaking*   *irregular*

10. choose   *chose chosen choosing*   *irregular*

11. lead   *led leading*   *irregular*

12. kiss   *regular*

13. prepare   *prepared preparing*   *irregular*

14. occur   *occurred occurring*   *irregular*

15. take   *took taken taking*   *irregular*

16. fill   *regular*

17. pass _____ *regular*

18. add _____ *regular*

19. think *thought thinking* ___ *irregular*

20. carry *carried carrying* ___ *irregular*

21. start _____ *regular*

22. surpass _____ *regular*

23. hit *hit hitting* ___ *irregular*

24. sail _____ *regular*

25. fail _____ *regular*

Deduct 5 for each blank incorrectly filled.

Troublesome Verbs

Exercise 7–2

NAME _____ SCORE _____

DIRECTIONS   In the following sentences cross out the incorrect form or forms of the verb in parentheses and write the correct form in the blank.

EXAMPLE

On the evening of June 18, 1178, several monks in England might have (~~saw~~, seen) the formation of a crater on the Moon.

seen

1. Accounts of the sighting that were (~~wrote~~, written) by Gervase of Canterbury describe a dramatic event.

written

2. According to Gervase, the Moon was in a slim crescent when the event (~~takes~~, took) place.

took

3. Suddenly, Gervase reports, "a flaming torch (sprang, sprung) up."

sprang or sprung

4. An explosion (~~strew~~, ~~strewn~~, strewed) "fire, hot coals, and sparks" across the face of the Moon.

strewed

5. After the explosion the Moon's surface appeared to writhe like a snake, and these distortions (~~persist~~, persisted) for several minutes.

persisted

6. "When the Moon (~~returns~~, returned) to normal, the whole crescent took on a blackish appearance," Gervase concluded.

returned

7. Is it possible that the monks actually (~~witness~~, witnessed) a meteor impact on the Moon?

witnessed

8. Dr. Jack Hartung, of the State University of New York at Stony Brook, (~~establishes~~, established, has established) new credibility for the meteor theory when he identified the crater Giordano Bruno as the likely impact site.

established

9. Scientists (~~know,~~ have known) of Bruno only in recent years.

   have known

10. Bruno (is, ~~was~~) hidden on the far side of the Moon, visible to humans only from Lunar orbiters.

   is

11. Photographs reveal a vast system of rays that (~~radiates,~~ radiate) from a central impact point.

   radiate

12. "What are the rays?" researchers (~~wonder,~~ wondered).

   wondered

13. They are the paths of material that (burst, ~~bursted,~~ ~~busted~~) from the surface when the meteor landed.

   burst

14. Other scientists (~~choose,~~ chose) to investigate the probable size of the impact explosion.

   chose

15. They (~~decide,~~ decided) that the explosion on the Moon's far side would easily have been large enough to generate the phenomena described by Gervase.

   decided

16. Scientists also (knew, ~~have known~~) that the Moon wobbles slightly from side to side, a movement called *libation.*

   knew

17. They (~~realize,~~ realized) that such a gigantic impact would affect the Moon's motion enough to impart a libation that would still be discernible.

   realized

18. Astronauts (~~leave,~~ left) equipment on the Moon to measure the wobble.

   left

19. The equipment (~~proves,~~ proved) that the Moon still wobbles exactly as it should if it was staggered by a meteor impact about 800 years ago.

   proved

20. Crater Bruno must have (~~begin,~~ ~~began,~~ begun) its existence just as Gervase described it in 1178.

   begun

Deduct 6 2/3 for each blank incorrectly filled.

Verb Forms   Exercise 7–3

NAME _____ SCORE _____

DIRECTIONS   In the following sentences cross out the incorrect form or forms of the verb in parentheses and write the correct form in the blank.

EXAMPLE
I would like (~~to be~~, to have been) a witness to the super-

nova of 1054 that gave rise to the Crab nebula.   *to have been*

1. Western astronomers (realized, ~~realize~~) in the last century that Chinese and Japanese records contained accounts of a bright new star seen in 1054.   *realized*

2. In 1921 American astronomer John Duncan (~~finds~~, found) that the Crab nebula's expansion rate indicates that it must have been formed about 900 years earlier.   *found*

3. In 1928 Edwin Hubble realized that the ancient Chinese references to a "guest star" and the origin of the Crab nebula (~~was~~, were) the same event.   *were*

4. Oriental records (~~indicates~~, indicate) that the guest star became so bright that it was visible in daytime and could be observed for an entire year.   *indicate*

5. Recently astronomers have discovered cave drawings by native Americans in the Southwest that (~~has~~, have) helped to date the supernova more exactly.   *have*

6. Having used the cave drawings to confirm one sighting of the supernova on July 5, 1054, scientists (~~begin~~, began) researching for other records.   *began*

7. Recently scholars have discovered an autobiography in which the author, an Arab physician, (identifies, ~~identified~~) the presence of the new star and blames it for an epidemic.

   identifies

8. The physician, Ibn Butlan, explains that his people found it impossible (to escape, ~~to have escaped~~) the influence of the star.

   to escape

9. As it (~~grows~~, grew) in brightness, he explains, the epidemic flourished.

   grew

10. He must often have wished that he (~~was~~, were) in another place and time.

    were

11. All about him great masses of people (~~die~~, died), and he was left feeling completely helpless before the cosmic power.

    died

12. Butlan goes on to say that in the autumn of 1054 over 14,000 people were buried in a churchyard in Constantinople—after all the cemeteries (~~are~~, were) filled.

    were

13. Of course, the superstitions of Butlan's age (~~require~~, required) that a physician have as much knowledge of signs and portents as of science.

    required

14. Astrology was a powerful instrument for Butlan's practice of medicine, and he (~~uses~~, used) it to make his diagnoses.

    used

15. However, the research of modern scholars enables us now (to understand, ~~to have understood~~) the true effects of the explosion of the supernova on our planet.

    to understand

MANUSCRIPT FORM

8

Follow acceptable form in writing your paper.

Your instructor may indicate the exact form needed for preparing your papers. Usually an instructor's guidelines include the points discussed in this section.

8a Use proper materials.

If you handwrite your papers, use wide-lined, $8\frac{1}{2} \times 11$-inch theme paper (not torn from a spiral notebook). Write in blue or black on one side of the paper only.

If you type your papers, use regular white $8\frac{1}{2} \times 11$-inch paper (not onionskin, or erasable bond). Use a black ribbon, double-space between lines, and type on one side of the paper only.

If you use a word processor to prepare your papers, make sure the typeface and the paper you plan to use will be acceptable to your instructor. Ask your instructor to examine a sample from your printer to see if it is acceptable quality.

8b Arrange the writing on the page in an orderly way.

Margins and Indention   Theme paper usually has the margins marked for you. But with unlined paper, leave about one inch of margin at all sides. Indent the first line of each paragraph about one inch if you handwrite and five spaces if you type, but leave no long gap at the end of any line except the last one in a paragraph.

Paging   Use Arabic numbers (2, 3, and so on) in the upper right-hand corner to mark all pages.

Title   On the first page, center your title about $1\frac{1}{2}$ inches from the top or on the first ruled line. Do not use either quotation marks or underlining with your title. Capitalize the first word of the title and all other words except articles, prepositions, coordinating conjunctions, and the "to" in infinitives; then begin the first paragraph of your paper on the third line. Leave one blank line between your title and the first paragraph. (Your instructor may ask you to make a title page. If so, you may or may not rewrite the title on the first page of the paper.)

Identification   Instructors vary in what information they require and where they want this information placed. The identification will probably include your name, your course title and number, the instructor's name, and the date.

Punctuation   Never begin a line of your paper with a comma, a colon, a semi-colon, or an end mark of punctuation; never end a line with the first of a pair of brackets, parentheses, or quotations.

Poetry   If you quote four or more lines of poetry, indent the lines about one inch from the left margin and arrange them as in the original. Long prose quotations (more than four lines) should also be indented. (See also **16a**.)

8c Write clearly and neatly.

Write so that your instructor can read your paper easily. Most instructors will accept a composition that has a few words crossed out with substitutions written neatly above, but if your changes are so plentiful that your paper looks messy or is difficult to read, you should recopy the page.

8d Divide words at the ends of lines according to standard practice.

The best way to determine where to divide a word that comes at the end of a line is to check a dictionary for the syllable markings (usually indicated by dots). In general, though, remember these guidelines: never divide a single-syllable word; do not carry over to the next line a syllable like "ed" or one letter of a word; divide a hyphenated word only at the hyphen. Keep in mind that an uneven right margin is expected and that too many divisions at the ends of lines make a paper difficult to read.

8e Proofread your papers carefully.

Always leave a few minutes at the end of an in-class writing assignment for proofreading. Few people write good papers without revising their first drafts. When you need to make a change, draw a straight horizontal line through the part to be deleted, insert a caret (**Λ**) at the point where the addition is to be made, and write the new material above the line. When writing out-of-class papers, try to set your first draft aside for several hours or even for a day so that you can proofread it with a fresh mind.

9/10

Use capitals and italics in accordance with current practices.

A recently published dictionary is the best guide to current standards for capitals, italics, abbreviations, and numbers. There are a few general rules to follow for these problems in mechanics (sections **9**, **10**, and **11**), but whenever you are in doubt about how to handle a particular word, you should consult an up-to-date dictionary.

9a Capitalize words referring to specific persons, personifications, places, things, times, organizations, peoples and their languages, religions and their adherents, holy books, holy days, and words denoting the Supreme Being. Capitalize words derived from proper names and words used as essential parts of proper names.

PERSONS	Shakespeare, Buddha, Mr. White
PERSONIFICATIONS	John Doe, Uncle Sam, Mother Nature
PLACES	Puerto Rico; LaGrange, Georgia; Western Avenue; the West (referred to as an area)
THINGS	the Statue of Liberty, the Bible, History 111, the First World War
TIMES	Wednesday, July 4; Thanksgiving; the Age of Enlightenment
ORGANIZATIONS	the Peace Corps, the Rotary Club, Phi Beta Kappa
RACES AND LANGUAGES	Oriental, English, Latin
RELIGIONS AND THEIR ADHERENTS	Islam, Christianity, Judaism, Moslem, Christian, Jew
HOLY BOOKS AND HOLY DAYS	Koran, the Bible, Torah, Ramadan, Advent, Passover
WORDS DENOTING THE SUPREME BEING	Allah, God, Jehovah
WORDS DERIVED FROM PROPER NAMES	Swedish, New Yorker, Anglican
ESSENTIAL PARTS OF PROPER NAMES	the Bill of Rights, the Battle of the Bulge, the New River

9b In general, capitalize a person's title if it immediately precedes the person's name but not a title that follows the name.

> In the last election, Representative Thad Lucas faced Martin Houser, former governor, in the race for senator.

Note that usage varies with regard to capitalization of titles of high rank when not followed by a proper name (Senator OR senator). Titles of family members are capitalized only when they are written in combination with a name (Uncle Ben) or when they are used in place of a name (I asked Father for a loan).

9c Capitalize the first and last words of a title or subtitle and all other key words within it.

> A physicist friend of mine suggested that I read two articles: "What's a Calculator For?" and "Learning to Work with Your Calculator."

Caution: Articles—*a, an, the*—and prepositions, coordinating conjunctions, and the *to* in infinitives are not capitalized unless they are the first or last words.

9d Capitalize the pronoun *I* and the interjection *O*.

9e Capitalize the first word of each sentence, including a quoted sentence.

> Astronomers think that the Mars moon Phobos may be a captured asteroid.
>
> OR
>
> "Astronomers think that the Mars moon Phobos may be a captured asteroid," Mr. White explained.
> "Oh, really!" exclaimed a student.

9f Avoid capitals for words that name classes rather than specific persons, places, or things.

> The doctors held a conference at a convention center in the downtown section of our town.

Also avoid the common tendency to capitalize seasons, directions, and general courses of study.

> This spring I am going to study astronomy at an eastern university.

10 To show italics, underline the titles of books, films, plays, works of art, magazines, newspapers, and long poems; the names of ships and airplanes; foreign words; and words, letters, and figures spoken of as such.

> The word *experience* becomes important when you are actually confronted with a great work of art, whether the work is a piece of sculpture like Modigliani's *Flight*, a novel like James Michener's *Space*, or even a great piece of engineering like the space shuttle *Columbia*.

Caution: Do not underline the title of your own essay or overuse italics for emphasis.

Deduct 6 2/3 for each incorrect revision.

Capitals and Italics   Exercise 9/10–1

NAME _____ SCORE _____

DIRECTIONS   Words in one of each of the following groups should be capitalized and/
or italicized (underlined). Identify the group that needs capitalization and/or italics by
writing either *a* or *b* in the blank at the right. Then make the necessary revision for the
appropriate group of words.

EXAMPLE
(a) a class at our college

(b) *G*eology 203 at *m*arymount *C*ollege   _*b*_

1. (a) responded, "*Y*ou will see me again."

   (b) responded that you will see me again.   _*a*_

2. (a) a course in history

   (b) a course in *S*panish   _*b*_

3. (a) visited another country during the holiday

   (b) visited *C*anada during the *C*hristmas holiday   _*b*_

4. (a) reading *T*he *L*ast of the *M*ohicans by *J*ames *F*enimore *C*ooper

   (b) reading a novel about pioneer times   _*a*_

5. (a) boarded the *Q*ueen *M*ary for its last crossing of the *A*tlantic

   (b) boarded an ocean liner for its last transoceanic voyage   _*a*_

6. (a) a story in a weekly magazine about the death of a popular

   rock singer

   (b) "*S*inging *I*s *B*etter *T*han *A*ny *D*ope," a story in *N*ewsweek

   about the death of *J*anis *J*oplin   _*b*_

7. (a) *R*epresentative *G*ornto visiting *A*rizona

   (b) the representative from our state   _*a*_

8. (a) admired the painting by the artist

   (b) admired *guernica* by picasso   _b_

9. (a) the pronunciation of the word party as "pah-ty" in the

      south

   (b) the pronunciation of words in a southern state   _a_

10. (a) a famous war in history

    (b) the war of 1812   _b_

11. (a) went to see a well-known play during our annual trip to

      a neighboring city

    (b) went to see *hello dolly!* during our annual trip to new york   _b_

12. (a) the president of our country will be inaugurated on tues-

      day, january 20.

    (b) the president of a popular club at our college   _a_

13. (a) keats' courting of death in *la belle dame sans merci*

    (b) the many poems that personify human qualities   _a_

14. (a) economics 200 to be offered in the spring

    (b) a course in economics to be offered in the spring   _a_

15. (a) the grandmother who joined a charitable organization

    (b) my swedish grandmother who joined the salvation army   _b_

11

Learn when to use abbreviations, acronyms, and numbers.

In specialized kinds of writing—such as tables, indexes, and footnotes—abbreviations, acronyms, and figures are appropriate, but in ordinary writing abbreviations are used sparingly, figures are used only for numbers that would require three or more words to write out, and acronyms should be spelled out the first time they are used.

11a Before proper names, use the abbreviations *Mr., Mrs., Ms., Dr.,* and *St.* (for *Saint*) as appropriate. Use such designations as *Jr., Sr., II,* and *Ph.D.* after a proper name.

> *Ms.* Gates invited *Dr.* Fleming to tell the story of *St.* Jude.

11b Spell out names of states, countries, continents, months, days of the week, and units of measurement.

> When Mary was born on *July* 8 at the hospital in La Ceiba, *Honduras*, she weighed seven *pounds*, three *ounces*, but seven days later, at home in New Orleans, *Louisiana*, she weighed nine *pounds*.

11c Spell out *Street, Road, Park, River, Company,* and similar words when used as part of proper names.

> From Riverview *Drive* in Riverview *Park* you can see the Stones *River* and the new Tennessee Valley Authority building.

11d Spell out the words *volume, chapter,* and *page* and the names of courses of study.

> The notes on *chemistry* are taken from *chapter* 9, *page* 46.   [*Ch.* 9, *p. 46* would be acceptable in a footnote.]

11e Spell out the meaning of any acronym that may not be familiar to your reader when you use it for the first time.

> The Jet Propulsion Laboratory (*JPL*) funded the first mission. Consider the publicity that *JPL* received for a relatively small expense.
>
> OR
>
> The *JPL* (Jet Propulsion Laboratory) funded the first mission.

11f Spell out numbers that require only one or two words, but use figures for other numbers.

> After *twenty-two* years of gourmet cooking, he had gone from a size *thirty-two* to a size *forty*.
> Our home covers *1,600* square feet.

Note the ways figures are used in the following instances:

(1) the hour of the day: 4:00 P.M. (p.m.) OR four o'clock in the afternoon
(2) dates: *May 6, 1977*
(3) addresses: *55* North Broadway
(4) identification numbers: Channel *4*, Interstate *40*
(5) pages or divisions of a book: page *40*, chapter *6*
(6) decimals and percentages: *.57* inches, *10* percent
(7) a series of numbers: a room *25* feet long, *18* feet wide, and *10* feet high; The vote was *50* to *6* in favor, with *7* abstentions.
(8) large round numbers: two million light-years
(9) at the beginning of a sentence: One hundred fifty people filed applications.

11g Recognize the meanings of several common Latin expressions, which are usually spelled out in English in formal writing.

> i.e. [that is], e.g. [for example], viz. [namely]
> cf. [compare], etc. [and so forth], vs. OR v. [versus]

Caution: Never write *and etc.*, and use the word *etc.* itself sparingly. In general, naming another item is more effective.

> This course covers rhetoric, punctuation, grammar, mechanics, and spelling. [Naming another item, *spelling*, is more effective than writing *etc.*]

Deduct 6 2/3 for each incorrect item.

Abbreviations and Numbers   Exercise 11–1

NAME _____ SCORE _____

DIRECTIONS   Rewrite each of the following items using an abbreviation or a figure if the abbreviation or the figure would be appropriate in ordinary writing. If not, simply rewrite the item as it stands.

EXAMPLES
three o'clock in the afternoon

3:00 P.M. or p.m.

on Tuesday afternoon

on Tuesday afternoon

1. on page fifteen of chapter three

   on page 15 of chapter 3

2. fourteen thousand dollars

   $14,000

3. Jim Nunnery, the doctor on our street

   Jim Nunnery, the doctor on our street

4. the Raiders vs. the Cowboys

   the Raiders vs. or versus the Cowboys

5. Eighty percent of those registered voted.

   Eighty percent of those registered voted

6. debate about the Equal Rights Amendment

   debate about the ERA

7. life in California in nineteen seventy-seven

   life in California in 1977

8. the economics class in Peck Hall

   the economics class in Peck Hall

9. one hundred pounds

   100 pounds

10. on the twenty-first of January

on January 21

11. Riverview Park off Thompson Lane

Riverview Park off Thompson Lane

12. Susan Collier, our senator

Susan Collier, our senator or Senator

13. Shane Colvin, a certified public accountant

Shane Colvin, a CPA

14. between the United States and Canada

between the United States and Canada

15. a lot that is one hundred feet long and ninety-five feet wide with seventy-five feet of road frontage

a lot that is 100 feet long and 95 feet wide with 75 feet of road frontage

THE COMMA   ,/12

12

Let your sentence sense guide you in the use of the comma.

In speaking, you make the meaning of a sentence clearer or easier to follow by pauses and by changes in voice pitch. When you read the following sentence aloud, notice that you pause twice (and that your voice also drops in pitch) to make the sentence easier for a listener to follow:

> A black hole, perhaps the most fascinating current topic of conversation about the cosmos, originates with the collapse of a star.

In writing, of course, you use punctuation marks, not voice pitch, to make your sentences easier to follow. And you decide where to put the punctuation marks on the basis of your sentence sense (section **1**).

Remember that the word order in an ordinary sentence follows this pattern:

> SUBJECT–VERB–COMPLEMENT.
> Black holes are fascinating.

Often when you write a sentence that varies in some way from this pattern, you will use a comma or commas. If you add something before the subject, you often follow the introductory addition with a comma.

> Addition, S–V–C
> However, black holes are fascinating.

Note: A dash may sometimes be used in the same way as a comma (section **17**).

If you interrupt the sentence pattern, you often use two commas:

> S, addition, V–C.
> Black holes, however, are fascinating.
> S–V, addition, C.
> Black holes are, however, fascinating.

If you add a word or group of words to the end of the sentence pattern, you often use a comma:

> S–V–C, addition.
> Black holes are fascinating, however.

Of all the marks of punctuation, the most frequently used is the comma. Commas have four main uses:

> **a**   to follow a main clause that is linked to another main clause by a coordinate conjunction (*and, but, or, nor, for, so,* or *yet*);

b to follow certain introductory elements;
c to separate items in a series, including coordinate (equal in rank) adjectives;
d to set off nonrestrictive, parenthetical, and miscellaneous elements.

12a A comma follows a main clause that is linked to another main clause by a coordinating conjunction: *and, but, or, nor, for, so,* or *yet.*

Main clauses can stand alone as simple sentences. When they do, they may even be introduced by a conjunction (see **30b(3)**).

> The French astronomer Pierre Simon de Laplace first hypothesized the existence of black holes. But Laplace could not discover proof of their existence.

When the two main clauses are linked by a coordinating conjunction, a compound sentence results.

> PATTERN   **MAIN CLAUSE,** coordinating conjunction **MAIN CLAUSE.**

> The French astronomer Pierre Simon de Laplace first hypothesized the existence of black holes, but Laplace could not discover proof of their existence.

The semicolon may also be used when the two main clauses that are linked by a coordinating conjunction contain other commas.

> In 1796 the French astronomer Pierre Simon de Laplace first hypothesized the existence of black holes, masses so dense that their gravitational pull would allow nothing to escape; but Laplace could not discover proof of their existence. [Remember that the addition of another main clause, rather than the presence of the coordinating conjunction, is the reason for the punctuation mark.]

Notice in the following examples that a comma is used before a coordinating conjunction only when the conjunction links two main clauses.

TWO VERB PHRASES	A black hole's gravity will not allow even light to escape and therefore makes the hole invisible.
TWO SUBORDINATE CLAUSES	Because black holes are by definition invisible and because Laplace could study the skies only with optical instruments, he could not hope to "see" a black hole.
TWO MAIN CLAUSES	Proving the existence of black holes is difficult, but scientists can search for them by looking for their effects on objects that can be seen.

Deduct 6 2/3 for each blank incorrectly filled.

Commas between Main Clauses

Exercise 12–1

NAME _____ SCORE _____

DIRECTIONS   In the following sentences, insert an inverted caret (**V**) wherever two main elements are joined. Then insert either a comma or a semicolon after the first main clause. Write the mark that you have added in the blank at the right as well. If a sentence does not have two main clauses, write *C* in the blank to show that the sentence is correct and needs no punctuation mark.

EXAMPLES

Eventually all stars consume their fuel and die,but the rate and the

method of extinction vary.   _____?_____

The size and mass of stars determine how they evolve beyond the

red giant stage.   _____C_____

1. Large stars occasionally disappear in gigantic explosions,but

   small stars usually shrivel up and fade away.   _____?_____

2. Because our sun is a relatively small star, we know that one

   day it will simply fade away.   _____C_____

3. At the end of the red stage, small stars cannot generate enough

   heat to sustain nuclear reactions,and they just fade away.   _____?_____

4. A small red-giant star collapses,yet it cannot generate the 600-

   million-degree heat necessary to ignite the carbon at its center.   _____?_____

5. The collapsed red giant remains forever in a highly com-

   pressed state;by the force of its own weight it has been com-

   pressed into a space only a millionth as large.   _____;_____

6. Its center does not burn,but its surface appears white-hot.   _____?_____

7. These shrunken white-hot stars are called white dwarfs;they

   slowly radiate their heat and become cold, blackened corpses.   _____;_____

8. A large massive star has a different fate;because it can gener-

   ate heat, it can burn its carbon core.   _____;_____

9. Burning the carbon core creates new elements which are

   burned in turn.   _____C_____

10. After the star creates an iron core, the fire goes out for the last
time.   _C_

11. The continued collapse of the star cannot rekindle the fire,nor
can any increase in heat ignite the nuclear reactions.   _,_

12. As the star continues to collapse, all the material rushes
toward the center of the star.   _C_

13. Finally, like a compressed spring the star rebounds,or, in this
case, it explodes.   _,_

14. One effect of the explosion is to hurl into space atoms of all the
elements—everything from iron to silver, gold, and platinum.   _C_

15. All the elements that the star manufactured over its lifetime
of ten million years or more are hurled into space;thus is born
a supernova.   _;_

12b   A comma usually follows adverb clauses that precede main clauses. A comma often follows introductory phrases (especially adverb phrases) and transitional expressions. A comma follows an introductory interjection or an introductory *yes* or *no*.

The introductory element, which offers a variation from subject-first word order (see also section **30b**), is usually followed by a comma.

> PATTERN   Introductory element**,** **MAIN CLAUSE.**

> *Because our sun is constantly present and apparently unchanging,* we usually think of all stars as immutable.

(1) When an adverb clause precedes the main clause, it is usually followed by a comma.

> *Although our sun is vast and constantly present,* it does not remain unchanged.

There is usually no comma before the adverb clause when it follows the main clause:

> Our Sun, like all other stars, changes *as it consumes itself and gives off light.*

But if the adverb clause at the end begins with *although,* a comma is normally used.

> Throughout the first 90 percent of a star's lifetime its appearance changes very little**,** *although it consumes most of its hydrogen during that time.*

Some writers omit the comma after the introductory adverb clause when the clause is very short or when it has the same subject as the main clause, but there is nothing wrong with including the comma.

> *When a star consumes most of its hydrogen* it visibly changes.
>
> OR
>
> *When a star consumes most of its hydrogen,* it visibly changes.

(2) A comma usually follows an introductory verbal phrase and may follow an introductory prepositional phrase.

> *Gradually swelling and turning red in its outer layers,* the star becomes a huge red ball.   [introductory verbal phrase]
> *In addition to these changes in size and color,* the star undergoes other, less visible changes.   [introductory prepositional phrase]

The comma is often omitted after prepositional phrases if no misreading could result.

> *In 1979* Robert Jastrow popularized the term "red giant" to describe what a star looks like during this stage of its life.
> *While expanding,* the red giant continues to consume its remaining hydrogen.   [A comma prevents misreading.]

(3) A comma follows an introductory transitional expression, an interjection, and some-times a single-word modifier.

To be exact, the red giant consumes the hydrogen by transforming it into helium and releasing vast amounts of energy.

Yes, man has duplicated the process of changing hydrogen into helium.

Uncontrolled, the transformation occurs for brief moments during the explosion of a hydrogen bomb.

Certainly man would benefit enormously by learning to control the transformation and resulting energy release. [Writers may or may not use a comma after an introductory word like *yet, thus,* and *certainly,* depending on how closely they feel the word is related to the rest of the sentence. If they see the word as func-tioning primarily for transition, they use a comma; if they see it primarily as an adverb, closely related to the verb, they do not use a comma.]

Commas after Introductory Elements

Exercise 12–2

NAME _____ SCORE _____

DIRECTIONS   After each introductory element, either write a zero (0) to indicate that no comma is needed or add a comma. Also write the zero or the comma in the blank.

EXAMPLES

Blazing brilliantly, a supernova is even visible to the naked eye dur-

ing the day.   ___,___

In 1604 an exploding supernova caused a sensation in Europe.   ___O___

1. In A.D. 1054 Chinese astronomers recorded a supernova explo-

sion.   ___O___

2. Today there is a great cloud of gas known as the Crab Nebula

at the position of the supernova.   ___O___

3. Although the explosion occurred nine hundred years ago, the

Crab Nebula continues to expand at seven hundred miles per

second.   ___,___

4. After exploding, the supernova left behind a core.   ___,___

5. In fact, the core has proved to be far more interesting than the

vast and expanding layers of gas.   ___,___

6. While studying the origins of radio waves in the galaxy, an

astronomy student at Cambridge University identified the

core of a supernova.   ___,___

7. Since then, many similar cores have been discovered.   ___,___

8. Called pulsars, these cores emitted radio signals with such reg-

ularity that scientists at first suspected they were sent by intel-

ligent beings.   ___,___

9. Eventually, scientists realized that pulsars were the condensed

remnants of supernova.   ___,___

10. Lying at the center of the Crab Nebula is a typical pulsar.   ___O___

11. For example, its total radius is no more than ten miles, and it

spins on its axis while broadcasting radio waves.   ___,___

12. Listening with radio telescopes,scientists detect brief regular bursts of radioactivity.

————,————

13. Interestingly enough,scientists do not believe that a pulsar is necessarily the last stage in the evolution of a star.

————,————

14. If the core compresses to a radius of two miles,the theory of relativity predicts the occurrence of an extraordinary phenomenon.

————,————

15. According to the theory,with a radius of two miles the collapsed core will have enormous density and, therefore, enormous gravity.

————,————

16. At that point,the tug of gravity will be so great that even light will not be able to escape.

————,————

17. From that point on the star will be invisible.

———O———

18. Finally,it is a black hole in space.

————,————

19. Inside,the black hole continues to contract.

————,————

20. As it contracts,it grows ever denser.

————,————

**12c Commas are used between items in a series and between coordinate adjec-
tives. A series is a succession of three or more parallel elements.**

(1) Use commas between three or more items in a series.

PATTERN   1, 2, and 3 . . .
OR   1, 2, 3 . . .

                                                                        1
If our Sun became a red giant it would be large enough to destroy Mercury,
        2   **3**
Venus, and Earth.

                                                                        1
We need not worry about being destroyed by our own red giant because the Sun
                                            2
will not reach this stage for another six billion years, the change will be gradual
                    3
when it does occur, and by that time man should be able to move to another part

of the galaxy.

After our Sun becomes a red giant, it will undergo another dramatic change. Three
                                        1   **2**
factors will cause the change: a depletion of the hydrogen fuel, an increase in
                    3
helium, and drastically rising temperatures.

   The comma before the *and* may be omitted only if there is no difficulty reading the series or if the two items should be regarded as one unit.
                                                        1 2   **3**
Red giants are indicated on your star map by the numbers 3, 5, and 7.   [Without

   the last comma the series remains clear: Red giants are indicated on your star

   map by the numbers 3, 5 and 7.]
                                                        1   **2**
For easy identification the stars are marked with numbers, letters, and blue and
        3
white circles.   [*Blue and white* refers as a unit to *circles;* thus there is no comma

before the last *and.*]

   All the commas are normally omitted when a coordinating conjunction is used
between each item in the series.
                    1   **2**   **3**
Some people ignore or misread or even refuse to believe the directions on the star

   maps.

Semicolons may be used between the items in the series if the items themselves contain commas or if the items are main clauses. (See also **12a**.)

          1

As a red giant collapses, it also renews itself: first**,** it forms a core of pure helium**,**

          2

which resulted from fusion of the hydrogen fuel**;** second**,** it becomes hot enough

to fuse helium**,** a process requiring temperatures in excess of 200 million degrees**;**

    3

and third**,** it releases enormous amounts of energy as the helium is transformed

into carbon.

Caution: Remember that no comma is used when only two items are linked by a conjunction.

> *The helium-burning stage* and *the collapse of the red giant* last for about 100 million years.

(2) Use commas between coordinate adjectives that are not linked by a coordinating conjunction.

If the adjectives are coordinate, you can reverse their order or insert *and* or *or* between them without loss of sense.

      a   **b**   **a**

The *violent,* intensely *hot* explosions transform helium into a *stable,* extremely

    b

dense core of carbon.

             a   **b**   **a**

The intensely *hot* and *violent* explosions transform helium into an extremely *dense*

    b

and *stable* core of carbon.

Caution: Adjectives that are not coordinate take no commas between them.

> On the night that we look for red giants the observatory's *large waiting* room is always filled before viewing begins. [You would not say "large *and* waiting room."]

> COORDINATE ADJECTIVES   *small, dying* star [You can say "*dying, small* star" or "*small* and *dying* star."]

> ADJECTIVES THAT ARE NOT COORDINATE   *large waiting* room and *largest refractor* telescope [You would not say "*large* and *waiting* room" or "*refractor largest* telescope."]

Commas between Items in a Series
and between Coordinate Adjectives

Exercise 12–3

NAME _____ SCORE _____

DIRECTIONS   In each sentence, identify each series that needs commas by writing *1*, *2*, *3*, and so on above the items and in the blank on the right; identify coordinate adjectives by writing *a*, *b*, and *c* above the adjectives and in the blank. Insert commas or semicolons where they belong in the sentence and also in the blank to show the punctuation of the pattern. Write *C* in the blank if a sentence has no items in a series or no coordinate adjectives that need punctuation.

EXAMPLES

The black hole continues to shrink and pile its matter into an incred-

ibly tiny, dense lump.   *a, b*

Intuition, common sense, and experience tell us that it can't continue

to shrink forever; yet modern physics says that no force is power-

ful enough to stop the contraction.   *1, 2, 3*

1. If modern physics is correct, the particles of the dead star's

   mass can come infinitely close together.   *C*

2. Modern physics may be wrong, however, and scientists may

   discover a new, contradictory law that will change the way we

   think about the universe.   *a, b*

3. Another prediction based on Einstein's theory is that no object

   can travel faster than light, but a black hole has such powerful,

   unrelenting gravity that even light cannot escape.   *a, b*

4. If light cannot escape, nothing can, so black holes capture

   everything they encounter: gases, light, fragments of rock, and

   even whole asteroids or passing comets.   *1, 2, 3, 4, 5*

5. Some scientists have imagined using black holes as a quick,
   a
   b
   convenient means of space travel.   *a, b*

6. They imagine that the other end of a black hole (called a
   1
   white hole) opens into another time,that a traveler could dis-
   2
   appear into a black hole,and that the traveler could then
   3
   emerge through the white hole into another time.   *1,2,3*

7. Stephen Hawking, whom many people consider the best,most
   a b
   innovative physicist since Einstein, suggests that our universe
   could be thought of as having been created from matter that
   issued from a white hole.   *a, b*

8. Hawking has advanced another theory about mini-black
   holes: the universe began with a huge explosion, called the
   1
   "big bang"; the explosion led to countless collisions among the
   2
   newly formed matter;and some of the collisions resulted in the
   3
   formation of moderate- to microscopic-sized black holes.   *1;2;3*

9. The collision of a mini-black hole with a larger body would
   a   b
   be a dramatic,devastating event.   *a, b*

10. The June 30, 1908, event in Siberia, which has been attrib-
    uted to a meteor or comet, also could have been caused by the
    Earth colliding with a mini-black hole.   *C*

12d Commas are used to set off (1) nonrestrictive clauses and phrases, (2) parenthetical elements such as transitional expressions, and (3) items in dates and addresses.

A parenthetical or nonrestrictive addition that comes before the basic sentence pattern is followed by a comma.

> *One of the most informative books on black holes,* Red Giants and White Dwarfs*, traces the evolution of stars.*

If the parenthetical or nonrestrictive addition comes after the basic sentence, a comma precedes it.

> Red Giants and White Dwarfs *explains why scientists believe that black holes exist, in spite of their inability to see black holes.*

The most common position for the parenthetical or nonrestrictive addition is in the middle of the sentence, where one comma precedes it and another comma follows it.

> In one of his essays, *"The Quest for Black Holes,"* David Darling argues that a black hole may lie at the center of the Milky Way.
>
> He claims that the existence of a massive black hole at the center of any galaxy, *including the Milky Way,* would indicate that the galaxy had evolved from an earlier, more violent one.

(1) Nonrestrictive clauses and phrases are set off by commas. Restrictive clauses and phrases are not set off. (See also **13a**.)

A restrictive clause or phrase limits the meaning of the word it refers to.

> The magazine *that "The Quest for Black Holes" is taken from* is called *Astronomy.* [The *that* clause limits the meaning of the word *magazine.* Note that the relative pronoun *that* always introduces a restrictive clause.]
>
> Anyone *reading this magazine* is impressed with the informative articles. [The verbal phrase *reading this magazine* limits the meaning of the word *anyone.*]

A nonrestrictive clause or phrase does not limit the meaning of the word it refers to; rather, it adds information about a word that is already clearly limited in meaning. The nonrestrictive clause or phrase is set off with commas.

> "The Quest for Black Holes," *taken from the magazine Astronomy,* provides a comprehensive report on the international efforts aimed at proving the existence of black holes. [The verbal phrase *taken from the magazine Astronomy* adds further information about the subject *"The Quest for Black Holes."*]
>
> David Darling, *who is a computer consultant and freelance science writer,* presents very technical information in a way that even an uninformed reader will understand. [The *who* clause adds information about *David Darling.*]

Of course, not all adjective clauses and phrases are as obviously restrictive or nonrestrictive as the ones used in the above examples. Many times you can determine whether a clause or phrase is restrictive or nonrestrictive only by referring to the preceding sentence or sentences.

> Before x-ray astronomy began in the 1960s, astronomers could detect x-rays only as a general but random presence in the galaxy. But after simple x-ray detectors were sent aloft in rockets, the detection of x-rays became much more precise. X-rays, *which had seemed a kind of galactic clutter,* suddenly were discovered to come from a large number of compact, specific sources in the galaxy.   [Without the first two sentences, the *which* clause would be restrictive, or necessary to limit the meaning of x-rays.]

Sometimes, depending on the writer's intended meaning, a clause or phrase may be either restrictive or nonrestrictive. Notice the difference in meaning between the two sentences below, which differ only in punctuation.

> When black holes were first imagined, scientists realized that discovering them would be difficult for astronomers *who used equipment made to discover visible objects.*   [Without the comma before *who*, the sentence suggests that finding black holes would be difficult for astronomers who use optical equipment; other astronomers, however, might be able to find them.]
>
> When black holes were first imagined, scientists realized that discovering them would be difficult for astronomers, *who used equipment made to discover visible objects.*   [With the comma before *who*, the sentence suggests that finding black holes will be difficult for all astronomers because all rely on optical equipment.]

(2) Parenthetical elements, nonrestrictive appositives, absolute and contrasted elements, and words in direct address are set off by commas.

Parenthetical elements include a variety of constructions that introduce supplementary information to a sentence or that make up transitions between sentences.

> We read several essays, *such as "You Can Go Home Again" and "Great Balls of Fire,"* about comets.   [In this sentence *such as* introduces a nonrestrictive phrase. In the sentence "An essay *such as 'You Can Go Home Again'* explains the formation of comet orbits," *such as* introduces a restrictive phrase. Note also that when a comma is used with *such as*, the comma comes before *such*, with no comma after *as*.]
>
> "If you become an astronomer," *Stephen Wallace says,* "your patience will be tried when you have to explain that you don't do horoscopes and that astrology is nonsense."   [An expression such as *Stephen Wallace says (claims, replies,* and so on) is considered parenthetical. See **16a(2)** for further information on the placement of commas in dialogue.]
>
> Freida Brown, *as well as other astrologers,* takes offense to Wallace's characterizing astrology as "romance."   [Expressions like *as well as, in addition to,* and *along with* usually introduce parenthetical matter.]
>
> *In fact,* Brown accuses Wallace of ignoring the historical roots of astronomy in astrology.   [A transitional expression such as *in fact* is always considered parenthetical.]

According to Brown, astrology, *although it usually is dismissed by scientists,* is a science.   [A subordinate clause may introduce parenthetical matter.]

Appositives are usually set off by commas, though on a few occasions they are restrictive.

The essay "*The Tragedy of the American Space Program*" presents a controversial view of the space program.   [The title of the essay is a restrictive appositive needed to identify which essay is being referred to; thus it is not set off with commas.]
"The Tragedy of the American Space Program," *a controversial essay,* argues that America has retreated from an early commitment to exploration of the universe.   [The appositive is nonrestrictive; thus it is set off with commas.]

Absolute phrases are verbal phrases that are preceded by their subjects. They affect the meaning of the entire sentence in which they appear (not just a single word, phrase, or clause). Absolute phrases are always set off by commas.

According to Don Lago, one justification alone should have convinced the country to continue space exploration, *man's need to know effectively countering any argument to cancel the program.*   [The verbal *countering* has its own subject, *need.*]

Contrasted elements are always set off by commas.

Lago believes that the desire for knowledge, *not for wealth or power,* should inspire space exploration.

Words in direct address do just what you would expect them to do: they address someone or something directly. They are always set off by commas.

"Do not fall prey, *America,* to a false practicality," Lago seems to be saying in "The Tragedy of the American Space Program."

(3) Geographical names and items in dates and addresses (except for zip codes) are set off by commas.

Send your application by May 17, 1987, to Box 5393, Raleigh, North Carolina 27606.

Dates are sometimes written and punctuated differently in official documents and reports.

On Friday, 19 June 1987, the finalists checked into the hotel.

When only the month and the year are given, no comma is necessary.

May 1987.

12e A comma is occasionally used to prevent misreading even when it is not called for by any of the principles already discussed.

CONFUSING   Those of you who wish to write for further details.

CLEAR   Those of you who wish to, write for further details.

Commas to Set Off Nonrestrictive Clauses
and Phrases and Parenthetical Elements   Exercise 12–4

NAME _____ SCORE _____

DIRECTIONS   In the following sentences, set off each nonrestrictive or parenthetical addition with a comma or commas. Then in the blank write (1) a dash followed by a comma (—,) if the nonrestrictive or parenthetical addition begins the sentence, (2) a comma followed by a dash (,—) if the nonrestrictive or parenthetical addition ends the sentence, (3) a dash enclosed within commas (,—,) if the nonrestrictive or parenthetical addition comes within the sentence, or (4) *C* if there is no nonrestrictive or parenthetical addition to set off.

EXAMPLE

Any scientist, however dedicated, cannot view the possibility of a col-

lision between a mini-black hole and the Earth with satisfaction.   ,—,

1. The 1908 incident in Siberia, if it involved a mini-black hole,

   could have been much worse than it was.   ,—,

2. One can imagine such a strike wiping out Washington, D.C.,

   or Moscow, for instance, if it happened to be unfortunately

   aimed.   ,—,

3. The collision, resembling the strike of a hydrogen bomb, might

   accidentally cause a nuclear war.   ,—,

4. Thinking it had been attacked, one of the superpowers might

   retaliate against earthly enemies before learning the truth.   —,

5. Of course, even as we discuss mini-black holes, we must remind

   ourselves that they may not exist.   ,—,

6. Isaac Asimov, the author of many books on the cosmos, enjoys

   speculating about what man might be able to do with mini-

   black holes if they were to exist.   ,—,

7. A black hole is, after all, a gateway to enormous energies.   ,—,

8. Any object spiraling into it will radiate a great deal of energy,

   a process that could provide enormous sources of energy.   ,—

9. Most of the energy in any object resides in its mass.   *C*

10. The energy that results from burning coal or oil, for instance, uses only a tiny fraction of 1 percent of the mass of the fuel. —,═,—

11. Even nuclear reactions, the most powerful forces known to man, liberate only a couple of percent of the mass. —,═,—

12. An object spiraling into a black hole or, under certain conditions, skimming it without actually entering it may convert up to 30 percent of its mass into energy. —,═,—

13. And, of course, not every substance can be burned or split or fused in a nuclear reaction. —,═,—

14. Anything, Asimov explains, that falls into a black hole will yield energy. —,═,—

15. The black hole is a universal furnace, a source of unlimited energy. —,═══

16. "How," you may ask, "could humans make use of this universal furnace?" —,═,—

17. "We must capture a mini-black hole," Asimov explains, "by tugging it into the gravitational field of Earth." —,═,—

18. After setting the mini-black hole into an Earth orbit, we could begin feeding it fuel. ═══,—

19. The fuel, probably frozen hydrogen pellets, would be propelled by the black hole but not into it. —,═,—

20. The mini-black hole, working at a safe but visible distance from earth, would initiate nuclear reactions and produce energy to be stored and sent down to Earth. —,═,—

Deduct 7 for each blank incorrectly filled.

All Uses of the Comma

Exercise 12–5

NAME _____ SCORE _____

DIRECTIONS   Decide whether each comma used in the following sentences (a) separates main clauses, (b) sets off an introductory addition, (c) separates items in a series or coordinate adjectives, or (d) sets off a parenthetical or nonrestrictive addition. Write *a*, *b*, *c*, or *d* above each comma and in the blank to the right of the sentence.

EXAMPLE

Let us consider, *d* for a moment, *d* how to describe what would happen

to any object that fell into a black hole.   *d d*

1. According to Einstein's theories, *b* increasing intensity of gravity

   slows the passage of time.   *b*

2. The dominant characteristic of a black hole is its extremely

   intense gravity, *a* so an encounter with a black hole should test

   Einstein's theories.   *a*

3. Scientists believe that an object dropped into a black hole

   would slow down, *c* stop, *c* and then disappear.   *c c*

4. The object, *d* as it fell into the black hole, *d* gradually would

   come under the influence of the powerful gravitational forces.   *d d*

5. It would reach a point called the Schwarzschild radius, *d* where

   gravity is so strong that only an object traveling at the speed

   of light can escape.   *d*

6. As it reached the Schwarzschild radius, *b* the object would ap-

   pear to slow down and finally stop.   *b*

7. And, *d* as it slowed and stopped, *d* it also would grow dimmer

   and then disappear.   *d d*

8. If we imagine an astronaut falling into a black hole and some-

   how retaining consciousness and an awareness of his sur-

   roundings, *b* he would feel no change in the time rate; that

   change is something only a person outside the hole would per-

   ceive.   *b*

9. The astronaut would pass through the Schwarzschild radius
   without knowing it was any kind of barrier,ᵃ and he would
   keep falling toward the black hole's center.   _a_

10. Isaac Asimov suggests a fascinating view of the fall,ᵈ from the
    astronaut's perspective.   _d_

11. The astronaut would see an ever-expanding distance before
    him; although he might fall forever,ᵇ he would never reach the
    center.   _b_

12. This view of a black hole suggests a bottomless,ᶜ fathomless
    hole.   _c_

13. We should recall,ᵈ however,ᵈ that the intense gravity would dis-
    member and atomize the astronaut.   _d d_

14. We can be certain that the physical consequences of falling
    into a black hole would be irreversible and destructive,ᵈ what-
    ever the effects it would have on time.   _d_

Deduct 7 for each blank incorrectly filled.

All Uses of the Comma

Exercise 12-6

NAME _____ SCORE _____

DIRECTIONS   In the following sentences insert all necessary commas. Then write *a*, *b*, *c*, or *d* above each comma and in the blank to the right of each sentence to indicate that the comma (a) separates main clauses, (b) sets off an introductory addition, (c) separates items in a series or coordinate adjectives, or (d) sets off a parenthetical or nonrestrictive addition.

EXAMPLE
$\quad$ *d*
Isaac Asimov, who has written a great deal about black holes, used

them to discuss the beginning and the end of the universe. $\qquad$ *d d*

1. Suppose the universe began as an immeasurably thin expanse
   $\quad$ *c $\quad$ c*
   of gravel, dust, and gas. $\qquad$ *c c*

2. Slowly, over an incredible number of eons, it condensed until
   it formed the cosmic egg. $\qquad$ *d d*

3. The cosmic egg then exploded, and over an equally incredible
   number of eons it will restore matter toward the recreation of
   the cosmic egg. $\qquad$ *a*

4. "We happen to be living," Asimov says, "during the period
   shortly after (15 billion years after) the explosion." $\qquad$ *d d*

5. If the cosmic egg could form once, why could it not form repeatedly? $\qquad$ *b*

6. Why may not the dispersed matter from that first explosion
   $\quad$ *c $\quad$ c*
   collect itself again, contract once more, and form a second cosmic egg? $\qquad$ *c c*

7. The effect of such repeated cosmic egg explosions would be
   $\quad$ *d*
   to create an oscillating universe, expanding and contracting in
   great waves of energy. $\qquad$ *d*

8. Scientists generally agree, however, that the universe is expanding uniformly. $\qquad$ *d d*

9. Some scientists argue that there is not enough mass in the universe to stop the expansion *a* so the universe has no limits to its size.   *a*

10. Other scientists have identified clusters of galaxies that should have been pulled apart by such a constant *c* general expansion of the universe.   *c*

11. These galaxies have more gravitational force than their mass justifies *d* a condition which scientists refer to as the problem of the missing mass.   *d*

12. Asimov asks *d* "Can that missing mass consist of black holes?"   *d*

13. He suggests that there may be many black holes in the universe *c* that they may contain the missing mass *c* and that they may be preventing the galaxies from expanding to destruction.   *c* *c*

14. If black holes exist in numbers sufficient to hold these galaxies together *b* they may help disprove the idea of an expanding universe caused by one big explosion.   *b*

Deduct 10 for each sentence incorrectly punctuated.

All Uses of the Comma   Exercise 12-7

NAME _____ SCORE _____

DIRECTIONS   Write a sentence to illustrate each of the items listed.

EXAMPLE
an absolute element

Each generation has a new phenomenon in the cosmos that most fascinates it, the black hole being the most recent.

1. a complete date

On August 22, 1937, Fritz Zwicky discovered a supernova.

2. a nonrestrictive clause

The supernova, which later proved to be the brightest yet seen, was discovered on one of 1,625 photographs taken by Zwicky.

3. a contrasted element

Discovery of the supernova was a result of careful planning, not luck.

4. a restrictive phrase

Observers at Mt. Palomar still continue the research on supernovae that Zwicky initiated.

5. a transitional expression

Today's research, of course, is more sophisticated.

6. items in a series

Other supernovae searches are carried out in Italy, Switzerland, and Hungary.

7. a parenthetical element introduced by *such as*

Some research efforts, such as Zwicky's, may go unrecognized and unappreciated by the general public.

8. two main clauses linked by a coordinating conjunction

The search for supernovae at Mt. Palomar from 1958 to 1973 yielded the greatest number of discoveries, and Zwicky believed that the 270 found cost an average of $550 each.

9. an introductory verbal phrase

Having been convinced that supernovae searches were inexpensive, other observatories joined the hunt.

10. a complete address, including zip code

For information about current research on supernovae, write to the Smithsonian Astrophysical Observatory, Cambridge, Massachusetts 02138.

13

Superfluous or misplaced commas make sentences difficult to read.

The comma is the most frequently used punctuation mark. It is also the most frequently *mis*used punctuation mark. While trying to master the correct use of the comma, many people tend to overuse it and to misplace it in sentence patterns, especially if they rely too much on the pause test for placement. Some short-winded writers, who pause after every third or fourth word, fill their sentences with commas that make the writing difficult to follow. In the example below, the circled commas should not be included.

CONFUSING People ⊙ who have never been involved in astronomy ⊙ are unaware of ⊙ the great savings in time and labor ⊙ that computers provide astronomers.

Actually, this sentence requires no internal punctuation at all, for the clauses and phrases that have been added to the basic sentence pattern are all restrictive; they are necessary to define or to limit the meaning of the words they modify.

CORRECT People who have never been involved in astronomy are unaware of the great savings in time and labor that computers provide astronomers.

Section **13** is included as a caution against overuse and misplacement of commas. **The circled commas throughout the examples in this section should be omitted.**

13a Do not use a comma to separate the subject from its verb or the verb from its complement.

Remember that commas are used to set off nonrestrictive or parenthetical additions. Do not use them to separate the parts of the basic (Subject-Verb-Complement) sentence.

Studying how stars change ⊙ is the primary interest of many astronomers.
[The subject, *studying*, should not be separated by a comma from its verb *is*.]
Most astronomers agree ⊙ that they can learn a great deal from the death of a star. [The verb, *agree*, should not be separated by a comma from its complement, the *that* clause.]

13b Do not use a comma after a coordinating conjunction; do not use a comma before a coordinating conjunction when only a word, phrase, or subordinate clause (rather than a main clause) follows the conjunction. (See also **12a**.)

A star's life is long and peaceful, but ⊙ its death can be brief and dramatic.
[The comma comes **before, not after,** the coordinating conjunction.]
Most astronomers will spend their careers hoping to see a star's final explosion ⊙ but will never witness the event. [compound predicate—no comma before *but*]

13c Do not use commas to set off words or short phrases (especially introductory ones) that are not parenthetical or that are very slightly so.

Before World War II (,) astronomers began using radio telescopes.
Research (,) for astronomers (,) means studying the information that the sky holds.

13d Do not use commas to set off restrictive clauses, phrases, or appositives. (See also **12d**.)

The death of a star can be so dramatic (,) that for a few days the star outshines all its millions of neighbors put together.   [No comma is needed because the *that* clause is necessary to define or limit *dramatic*.]
The book (,) *Einstein's Universe* (,) helps lay readers understand the theory of relativity.   [No commas are needed because the title *Einstein's Universe* is a restrictive appositive needed to define or limit *book*.]
Physicists (,) trying to explain black holes (,) must understand Einstein's ideas about the relationship between gravity and time.   [No commas are needed because the verbal phrase is a restrictive addition needed to define or limit *physicists*.]

13e Do not use a comma before the first or after the last item in a series.

Journals such as (,) *Scientific American, Nature,* and *Astronomy* (,) publish the most recent news of astronomy.

13f In general, do not use a comma before an adverb clause at the end of a sentence. (See also **12b**.)

Most serious astronomers head straight for their computers (,) when they finish collecting images and other data with their telescopes.   [If the *when* clause came at the beginning of the sentence as an introductory addition, it would be followed by a comma.]

13g Do not use a comma between adjectives that are not coordinate. (See also **12c**.)

Serious (,) young astronomers make many (,) important sacrifices in order to spend time studying the sky.

Superfluous Commas

Exercise 13-1

NAME _____ SCORE _____

DIRECTIONS   Each of the following sentences is correctly punctuated. Explain why a comma is not added to each sentence at the place or places indicated in the question by listing the rule of caution (see **13a–13g**) that applies.

EXAMPLE
Searching for comets is no longer the most fascinating task for as-

tronomers.

Why is *comets* not followed by a comma?   _a_

1. A scientist like Albert Einstein effectively changes the way

   people look at the cosmos.

   Why is *like Albert Einstein* not set off with commas?   _d_

2. Einstein's years of greatest productivity began when he was

   twenty-five years old.

   Why is there no comma before *when*?   _f_

3. By the age of thirty-eight he had completed theories that re-

   built the universe and was on his way to becoming famous.

   Why is there no comma before *and*?   _b_

4. Einstein lived nearly another thirty-eight years, but in that

   time he worked without success on a project to unify electric-

   ity and gravity.

   Why is there no comma after *but*?   _b_

5. The landmarks of Einstein's work are *Special Relativity* (1905)

   and *General Relativity* (1915).

   Why is *of Einstein's work* not set off by commas?   _d_

6. All subsequent research has shown that we actually live in a

   universe much like that which Einstein described.

   Why is there no comma after *shown*?   _a_

7. Many people believe that Einstein proved that all things are

   "relative."

   Why is there no comma after *believe*?   _a_

8. Actually, he discovered what was absolute despite the confusion, illusions, and contradictions produced by relative motions or gravity.

   Why is there no comma after *contradictions*?   *e*

9. The term "relativity" should remind us that observers are participants in the system they are studying.

   Why is *relativity* not set off by commas?   *d*

10. In social behavior all of us are aware of distinctions between "self " and "other."

    Why is there no comma after *behavior*?   *c*

11. Observers on Earth have one view of the Sun, but observers in another galaxy have another view of the Sun.

    Why is there no comma after *but*?   *b*

12. Astronauts flying above the Earth feel themselves at rest with the Earth hurtling past them.

    Why is *flying above the Earth* not set off by commas?   *d*

13. The astronauts reason that the Earth has tremendous energy of motion.

    Why is there no comma after *reason*?   *a*

14. The astronauts' colleagues who are standing on Earth are insensible to this energy of motion.

    Why is *who are standing on Earth* not set off by commas?   *d*

15. Therefore it must be simultaneously correct to say that the Earth has great energy of motion and no energy of motion.

    Why is there no comma before *and*?   *b*

14

Use the semicolon between parts of equal grammatical rank: (a) between two main clauses not joined by a coordinating conjunction and (b) between coordinate elements that already contain commas.

A semicolon indicates that one part of a coordinate construction is finished. The semicolon acts like the fulcrum of a seesaw, balancing parts of equal grammatical rank.

> One group of scientists is convinced that the search for extraterrestrial intelligent life (ETI) is a worthwhile undertaking; another group argues that such a quest is a waste of time, money, and intellectual resources. [two main clauses with no coordinating conjunction]
>
> The equipment that will search for ETI is the most sophisticated yet devised for this purpose: a chest-high VAX mainframe computer; linkage of the computer to a 26-meter (85-foot) radiotelescope, part of NASA's Deep Space Tracking Network; and a complex assembly of specially created computer software. [items in a series, some of which already contain commas]

14a Use the semicolon to separate two main clauses not joined by a coordinating conjunction or two main clauses that contain commas and are also joined by a coordinating conjunction.

PATTERN   MAIN CLAUSE; MAIN CLAUSE.

> In the middle of the nineteenth century Karl Friedrich Gauss, the brilliant German mathematician, suggested that the human race should try to communicate with other intelligent races; he wanted to plant a gigantic forest in the shape of a right triangle. [two main clauses with no coordinating conjunction]
>
> Astronomers on other planets who saw this symbol would recognize it as a sign of our understanding of the Pythagorean theorem, a sign of our intelligence, and a sign of our desire to communicate; so they would respond to our greeting. [The first clause already contains commas, so a semicolon must be used before the coordinating conjunction *so*.]

Caution: In a divided quotation, be especially careful to use a semicolon between the two main clauses of a sentence when they are not connected by a coordinating conjunction.

> "We must study nearby stars," Frank Drake said in 1960; "only there are we likely to find evidence of intelligent life."

Remember that a conjunctive adverb, like *however*, or a transitional expression, like *for example* (see section **1**), is not the same as a coordinating conjunction—*and, but, or, nor, for, so,* or *yet.* Thus when a conjunctive adverb or a transitional expression is used to link two main clauses, a semicolon must come before it.

> Drake trained a radio telescope on two nearby stars, Tau Ceti and Epsilon Eridoani; *however,* he never detected the kind of pulsed or coded radio signal that another intelligent race might use to send a message.

14b   Use the semicolon to separate a series of equal elements which themselves contain commas.

> The detection of just one ETI signal would help answer many fundamental questions: what are we doing here; where are we going; are there other living beings in space; and, if so, what are they like?
>
> Carl Sagan and other notable scientists believe that advanced civilizations exist elsewhere in great numbers—according to some estimates, 100,000 or more; that searching for these civilizations is vital and relatively inexpensive; and that the new NASA program is likely to succeed.

14c Use the semicolon between parts of equal rank only, not between a clause and a phrase or a subordinate clause and a main clause.

> The NASA search for ETI will be a success, because it will either find other intelligent civilizations in our galaxy or it will provide convincing evidence that they do not exist.   [The subordinate clauses, introduced by *because,* are not equal in rank to the main clause; thus a semicolon would be inappropriate.]

Deduct 3 1/3 for each incorrect use of the semicolon and for each blank incorrectly filled.

Semicolons   Exercise 14–1

NAME _____ SCORE _____

DIRECTIONS   In the following sentences insert an inverted caret (**V**) between main clauses and add semicolons as needed. In the blank, copy the semicolon and the word or transitional expression immediately following, along with the comma if there is one. Write *C* in the blank if the sentence is correctly punctuated. (Not all sentences have two main clauses).

EXAMPLE
Passengers traveling at a constant speed in a straight line have no
sensation of motion;indeed, they feel exactly as they would if they
were at rest.   *;indeed,*

1. When people listen to a passing train, they hear the pitch of
the train whistle change;as the train approaches, the whistle
makes the sound "hee" and as it departs, the sound "haw."   *; as*

2. These phenomena are examples of relativity, but observers
were aware of them long before Einstein.   *C*

3. In 1842 Christian Doppler explained the changes in pitch of
the train whistle;he pointed out that the pitch or frequency
changes indicated the speed of the train.   *;he*

4. A listener hears a train's whistle because of pressure waves
emitted by the whistle;the sound waves move toward the listener at a steady speed.   *; the sound*

5. As the train moves toward the listener, the speed of sound
through the air does not change;however, each successive
wave has less distance to travel to reach the listener's ear.   *;however,*

6. As the waves become crowded together, they arrive at the listener's ear at a faster rate—a higher frequency—per second
than if the train were at rest.   *C*

7. When the train is pulling away, successive waves have farther
to travel;they are spaced out and arrive with lower frequency
or lower pitch.   *;they*

8. This effect occurs elsewhere; it helps, for example, to explain changes in light.

   ; it helps,

9. Light and sound are both measured in frequencies; a change in frequency changes the pitch of sound and the color of light.

   ; a change

10. White light can be broken into a spectrum of colors: red, orange, yellow, green, blue, indigo, and violet; the acronym ROY G. BIV helps students remember the spectrum.

    ; the acronym

11. The frequency of blue light is about twice that of red light; the higher frequency corresponds to higher energy and temperature.

    ; the higher

12. When a glowing object experiences a lowering of frequency, energy, and temperature, its color will change gradually to red; in contrast, a change to blue means an increase in the three characteristics.

    ; in contrast,

13. If a star were traveling away from an observer at the speed of light, its light would be "redshifted" completely, and it would become visible.

    C

14. A star traveling toward an observer would completely "blueshift"; its waves of light would pile atop each other and achieve infinite energy and temperature.

    ; its waves

15. Naturally, some stars move toward us as others move away; as a result, red shifts and blue shifts are about equal in number.

    ; as a result

Commas and Semicolons   Exercise 14–2

NAME _____ SCORE _____

DIRECTIONS   In the following sentences insert either a semicolon or a comma as needed within the sentences and also in the blank.

    EXAMPLE

Studies of the stars within our galaxy have indicated that roughly

    equal numbers of stars travel toward and away from Earth; how-

    ever, studies of other galaxies have yielded different results.   _____;_____

1. By 1917, studies of the spectra of nearby galaxies showed all

   but the closest to have a redshift; this indicates that the galax-

   ies are receding from us.   _____;_____

2. As more and more galaxies were studied, it turned out that all

   the galaxies except the two that are closest to us have a red-

   shift.   _____,_____

3. Because the size of this redshift increased steadily the farther

   the galaxies were from the Earth, scientists realized that they

   might have discovered a clue to the origin of the universe.   _____,_____

4. After Edwin Hubble studied this redshift, he advanced in 1929

   what is called Hubble's Law.   _____,_____

5. "The rate at which a galaxy is receding from us," Hubble ex-

   plained, "is directly related to its distance from us."   _____,_____

6. If Galaxy A is receding from us at ten times the velocity of

   Galaxy B, then Galaxy A is ten times as far from us as Gal-

   axy B.   _____,_____

7. Later studies revealed that other galaxies not only are moving

   away from us but are gaining in speed, the farther away the

   galaxy, the greater its velocity and the greater its increase in

   velocity.   _____,_____

8. At first glance, it seems as if the whole universe is speeding

   away from us, and, somehow, we seem to be the key to the

   behavior of an expanding universe.   _____,_____

9. In 1917, the Dutch astronomer William de Sitter used the equations of general relativity to theorize an expanding universe, a portrait of galaxies speeding away from each other at constant rates.   ____ ; ____

10. No matter which galaxy we live in, it seems that all other galaxies are speeding away from us.   ____ ; ____

11. As the universe ages, it expands; but when it was young, what did it resemble?   ____ ; ____

12. In 1927, the Belgium astronomer Georges Lemaître suggested that billions of years ago all the matter in the universe stood in one place and formed a structure he called the "primeval atom," which others have called the "cosmic egg."   ____ ; ____

13. Lemaitre did not guess how long the cosmic egg existed or how it was formed, nor did he speculate on the cosmic egg's explosion.   ____ ; ____

14. At some point, however, it exploded in what the Russian physicist George Gamow called the "big bang," and the force of that explosion was so great that the galaxies still speed away from the universe's center.   ____ ; ____

15. The forces of the Big Bang and of the continued expansion of the universe are enormous, yet gravity exerts a remarkable influence.   ____ ; ____

16. Gravitational force must have slowed the expansion process; therefore, it must continue to influence the rate.   ____ ; ____

17. Scientists cannot accurately measure the density of the matter in the universe; therefore, they do not know just how much influence gravity has on expansion.   ____ ; ____

15

Use the apostrophe (a) to indicate the possessive case—except for personal pronouns, (b) to mark omissions in contracted words and numerals, and (c) to form certain plurals.

The apostrophe, in most of its uses, indicates that something has been omitted.

> don't   [do *not*]
> they're   [they *are*]
> children's books   [books *of* or *for* children]
> the artist's paintings   [paintings *of* or *by* the artist]

15a Use the apostrophe to indicate the possessive case.

In general, a noun or a pronoun does not come immediately before another noun or pronoun: we do not write "children books" or "artist painting." When we do need to use a noun or pronoun before another noun or pronoun, we make the first one possessive by using an apostrophe. In a sense, we say that the first noun or pronoun owns the second one.

> parent's duty   [duty of one parent]
> parents' duty   [duty of two or more parents]
> everyone's duty   [duty of everyone]
> crater's edge   [edge of the crater]
> craters' edges   [edges of the craters]

(1) Add the apostrophe and an s ('s) to a noun or indefinite pronoun to indicate the singular possessive case. (See the list of indefinite pronouns in the Appendix.)

> The astronaut's picture hung on the president's wall.
> One's questions often go unanswered.

Option: To form the possessive case of a singular noun that ends in *s*, add either the apostrophe and *s* or only the apostrophe.

> Mars' terrain   OR   Mars's terrain
> Columbus' ship   OR   Columbus's ship

(2) Add the apostrophe (') to all plural nouns that end in s to indicate the plural possessive case. Add the apostrophe and an s ('s) to all plural nouns not ending in s to indicate the plural possessive case.

Always form the plural of the noun first. Then, if the plural noun ends in *s*, add only the apostrophe to show the possessive case.

> photographer [singular]   photographers [plural]
> dignitary [singular]   dignitaries [plural]
> The photographers' pictures hung in several dignitaries' offices.

If the plural noun does not end in *s*, add the apostrophe and an *s* to show the possessive case.

> man   [singular]   men   [plural]
> woman   [singular]   women   [plural]
> Men's and women's roles on space shuttle missions are interchangeable.

(3) Add the apostrophe and an s to the last word of compounds or word groups.

> my father-in-law's car
> someone else's turn
> the secretary of state's position

(4) Add the apostrophe and an s to each name to indicate individual ownership, but to only the final name to indicate joint ownership.

> John's and Andrew's schools were studying the solar system.   [John and Andrew attend different schools.]
> John and Andrew's school was playing in the tournament.   [John and Andrew attend the same school.]

15b Use the apostrophe to indicate omissions in contracted words and numerals.

Be careful to place the apostrophe exactly where the omission occurs.

> The class of '92 [1992] *can't* decide what to include in the time capsule *that's* [that is] to be blasted out of the solar system.

15c Use the apostrophe and an s to form the plural of lower-case letters. If needed to prevent confusion, the apostrophe and an s can be used to form the plural of figures, symbols, abbreviations, and words referred to as words, but frequently only an s is added.

> final *k*'s
> the 1970's   OR   the 1970s
> V.F.W.'s   OR   V.F.W.s
> *and's*   OR   *ands*

15d The apostrophe is not needed for possessive pronouns—*his, hers, its, ours, yours, theirs,* and *whose*—or for plural nouns not in the possessive case.

> *Whose* messages are these—*yours* or *theirs*?
> *Her* department regularly held *its* reception at the *Joneses.*   [*Joneses* is plural but not possessive.]

Deduct 4 1/4 for each blank incorrectly filled.

Apostrophes

NAME _____ SCORE _____

DIRECTIONS   Add all apostrophes needed in the following sentences. In the blank enter each word, number, or letter to which you have added an apostrophe. Be careful not to add needless apostrophes. If a sentence is correct, write *C* in the blank.

EXAMPLE
There's no apostrophe after the *s* in the word group "physics majors."

there's

1. One of England's most famous monuments is Stonehenge.

England's

2. The ancient collection of giant stones draws thousands of tourists each year to Salisbury Plain.

C

3. Stonehenge has been shrouded in mystery during most of its history with each successive generation offering its exploration of the giant stones' significance.

stones'

4. In 1965 Gerald Hawkins' study of Stonehenge dramatically altered our perception of why it was built.

Hawkins'

5. Hawkins' expertise as an astronomer helped him discover Neolithic man's understanding of astronomy.

Hawkins' man's

6. Hawkins realized that from inside the concentric rings of giant stones a viewer's line of sight is defined by the arches formed by several stones.

viewer's

7. The most famous of these lines of sight directs a visitor's attention to a single stone, the Heelstone, which stands about 100 feet outside the rings.

visitor's

8. The Heelstone's placement, Hawkins realized, means that it's an indicator of the rise of the midsummer sun.

Heelstone's it's

9. Hawkins then realized that other stones indicate sunrise and sunset at other periods during the year as well as the position of the full moon at important times.

         C

10. Early priest-astronomers were using Stonehenge as a tool with which to compute important astronomical events.

         C

11. Its likely that one of the stones' functions was to predict eclipses.

         It's stones'

12. At the latitude of Stonehenge the Moons cycle repeats itself every 56 days.

         Moon's

13. Since Hawkins' pioneering work in the 1960s, hundreds of other ancient monuments have been analyzed for their astronomical significance.

         C or 1960's

14. The North American Plains Indians medicine wheels are large arrangements of stones.

         Indians'

15. Like Stonehenge, they represent an early peoples attempts to mark the movements of objects in the sky.

         people's

16. Almost everyone thinks of Neolithic Indians as unlearned and primitive.

         C

17. The medicine wheels significance is to contradict this perception.

         wheels'

18. The underestimation of the Indians abilities came partly from the modern-day judgment that such sophistication must be based on literacy.

         Indians'

19. Its also caused by the modern absence of personal experience with the skies cycles.

         It's skies'

Deduct 5 for each error.

Apostrophes

NAME _____ SCORE _____

DIRECTIONS   Rewrite the following word groups as a noun or a pronoun preceded by another noun or pronoun in the possessive case.

EXAMPLES
a responsibility of everybody

everybody's responsibility

the responsibilities of the United Nations

the United Nations' responsibilities

1. the records of NOW

   NOW's records

2. a poem by Galway Kinnell

   Galway Kinnell's poem

3. the opinions of the investigators

   the investigators' opinions

4. the representative of the United States

   the United States' (or States's) representative

5. the skeletons of the dinosaurs

   the dinosaurs' skeletons

6. an invitation sent by Mr. and Mrs. James

   Mr. and Mrs. James' (or James's) invitation

7. the antenna of the satellite

   the satellite's antenna

8. an address by the governor of Texas

   the governor of Texas' (or Texas's) address

9. the interests of the babies

   the babies' interests

10. a telescope shared by Sarah and Karen

    Sarah and Karen's telescope

11. the example of the women

    the women's example

12. a reunion at the Burtons
the Burtons' reunion

13. opinions held by one
one's opinions

14. the angle of the eclipse
the eclipse's angle

15. the temple of Zeus
Zeus' (or Zeus's) temple

16. the riddle of the Sphinx
the Sphinx's riddle

17. the visits of Anna and Stacy to New York
Anna and Stacy's visits to New York

18. the lawnmower of the son-in-law
the son-in-law's lawnmower

19. the hood of the Rolls Royce
the Rolls Royce's hood

20. the word processor of Jennifer
Jennifer's word processor

16

Learn to use quotation marks to set off all direct quotations, titles of short works, and words used in a special sense, and to place other marks of punctuation in proper relation to quotation marks.

When you use quotation marks, you let your reader know that you are quoting directly (that is, you are stating in the exact words) what someone has written, said, or thought.

> "Will you return this book to the library for me?" the note asked.
> "I'll be glad to," I told my friend when I saw her. But I thought to myself, "I think I'll check it out in my name and read it this weekend."

16a Use quotation marks for direct quotations and in all dialogue. Set off long quotations by indention.

(1) Use double quotation marks (" ") before and after all direct (but not indirect) quotations; use a single quotation mark (') before and after a quotation within a quotation.

INDIRECT QUOTATION	He asked me if I wanted to visit Golden Gate Park.
INDIRECT QUOTATION	I told him that we could drive there this afternoon. [*That* frequently introduces an indirect quotation.]
DIRECT QUOTATION	He asked me, "Do you want to visit Golden Gate Park?"
DIRECT QUOTATION	The brochure for Golden Gate Park recommends the astronomy exhibit as a modern introduction to the "music of the spheres." [A phrase from the brochure is quoted.]
QUOTATION WITHIN A QUOTATION	Diana asked, "Did you see the exhibit 'Galileo and Gravity,' which is on the second floor?"

(2) In quoting dialogue (conversation), a new paragraph begins each time the speaker changes.

> Five-year-old Michael proudly announced to his brother, "I had a dream last night. I rode up and down on the escalator one thousand times with Mama and Daddy."
> "Did I ride the escalator with you?" asked four-year-old Bobby hopefully.
> "Nope. You weren't in the dream," the older boy responded smugly.
> "Well, tonight I'm going to dream about eating five thousand chocolate ice-cream cones," Bobby blurted out, "and you won't get any because you won't be in the dream!"

Note: Commas set off expressions such as *he said* that introduce, interrupt, or follow direct quotations.

The guide cautioned, **"**Be careful, please, while we are in the construction area.**"**
"Be careful, please,**"** the guide cautioned, **"**while we are in the construction area.**"**
"Be careful, please, while we are in the construction area,**"** the guide cautioned.

If the quoted speech is a question or an exclamation, a question mark or exclamation point—instead of a comma—follows the quoted passage.

"Do not touch!**"** the guide scolded a child. "Each of the tiles is numbered and must be placed on the shuttle in sequence."

Caution: Remember that a divided quotation made up of two main clauses or two complete sentences must be punctuated with a semicolon or an end mark.

"Each tile is shaped to fit the contour of the shuttle's exterior,**"** the guide explained**;** **"**the numbers on the tiles tell workers exactly where the tiles are to be placed.**"**

OR

"Each tile is shaped to fit the contour of the shuttle's exterior,**"** the guide explained**.** **"**The numbers on the tiles tell workers exactly where the tiles are to be placed.**"**

(3) Prose quotations that would require four or more lines of typing and poetry that would require four or more lines are indented from the rest of the text.

Prose   When you quote one paragraph or less, all lines of a long quotation (more than four lines) are indented ten spaces from the left margin and are double-spaced. When you quote two or more paragraphs, indent the first line of each complete paragraph thirteen spaces rather than the usual ten. Use quotation marks only if they appear in the original. (If the quotation is run in with the text, remember that it should begin and end with a double quotation mark.)

In The Mind's I, Douglas R. Hofstadter and Daniel C. Dennett attempt to lead readers to examine who they are in new and different terms. In their introduction they ask questions that suggest how thoroughly they intend to disturb old habits of thinking.

> Our world is filled with things that are neither mysterious and ghostly nor simply constructed out of the building blocks of physics. Do you believe in voices? How about haircuts? Are there such things? What are they? What, in the language of the physicist, is a hole--not an exotic black hole, but just a hole in a piece of cheese for instance? Is it a physical thing? What is a symphony? Where in space and time does ''The Star-Spangled Banner'' exist? (6,7)

Poetry   Fewer than four lines of poetry may be run into the text. If run in, the quoted material should begin and end with a double quotation mark. Use quotation marks only if they appear in the original.

In The Prelude, Wordsworth uses an image that reminds us of the view of Earth from a spacecraft or from the Moon: "Yet still the solitary cliffs / Wheeled by me--even as if the earth had rolled / With visible motion her diurnal round." [Use a slash to mark the end of a line when poetry is run into the text.]

OR

In The Prelude, Wordsworth uses an image that reminds us of the view of Earth from a spacecraft or from the Moon:

> Yet still the solitary cliffs
> Wheeled by me--even as if the earth had rolled
> With visible motion her diurnal round.
> Behind me did they stretch in solemn train,
> Feebler and feebler, and I stood and watched
> Till all was tranquil as a dreamless sleep.

16b Use quotation marks for minor titles—of short works such as television shows, short stories, essays, short poems, one-act plays, songs, articles from periodicals—and for subdivisions of books.

> As part of the documentation for her paper on Keats' poem "Bright Star," Alice used an article from the book *American Scholar* by Allen Tate titled "A Reading of Keats."
> Don Maclean's song "Starry, Starry Night" expresses his response to Van Gogh's painting *Starry Night*.

16c Use quotation marks to enclose words used in a special sense.

> The term "research paper" is broadly applied to anything from a three-source, five-page paper to a one-hundred-source, book-length doctoral dissertation. [*Research paper* may be either italicized or enclosed in quotation marks: see section **10**.]

Avoid the tendency some writers have of using quotation marks freely throughout a paper to call attention to what they consider clever phrasings. Often what they think are clever phrases are really only trite expressions, slang, or colloquialisms that could be better phrased. (See also **20c**.)

> INEFFECTIVE The computer was "up to" more of its "strange" ways: it "knocked off" the crew members one by one.
>
> BETTER The computer demonstrated a terrifying intelligence: it killed the crew methodically and mercilessly.

16d Do not overuse quotation marks.

Quotation marks are not used for titles that head compositions. Quotation marks also are not used to enclose a cliché or to mark a *yes* or *no* in indirect discourse.

Yes, he did accuse her of beating around the bush.

NOT

"Yes," he did accuse her of "beating around the bush."

16e Follow the conventions of American printers in deciding whether various marks of punctuation belong inside or outside the quotation marks.

(1) The period and the comma are usually placed inside the quotation marks.

"Well," he said, "I'm ready for the samples."

Exception: If you are citing a page reference for a quotation, place the comma or the period after the page citation—and thus after the quotation marks.

When Livvie let go of old Solomon's watch, she released herself to life, and "all at once there began outside the full song of a bird" (77).

(2) The semicolon and the colon are placed outside the quotation marks.

He read the instructions on the container labeled "Lunar Soil": "Open only in sterile environment."
Another container was labeled "Lunar Film"; it had to be decontaminated before it could be passed to the press corps.

(3) The dash, the question mark, and the exclamation point are placed inside the quotation marks when they apply to the quoted matter and outside the quotation marks when they apply to the whole sentence.

"What's up?" the laboratory assistant asked.   [The question mark applies to the quoted matter.]
Did you notice the container marked "This side up"?   [The question mark applies to the whole sentence.]
At what point did he say, "Why are you telling me this?"   [a question within a question—one question mark inside the quotation marks]

Deduct 10 for each blank incorrectly filled.

Quotation Marks   Exercise 16–1

NAME _____ SCORE _____

DIRECTIONS   In the sentences below, insert all needed quotation marks. Then enter the quotation marks and the first and last word of each quoted part in the blanks. Be sure to include the other marks of punctuation used with the quotation marks in their proper position—either inside or outside the quotation marks. Do not enclose an indirect quotation. Write *C* in the blank if a sentence is correct without quotation marks.

EXAMPLE

"May the force be with you," a popular saying, originated

in the movie *Star Wars*.   *"May—you,"*

1. In *The Right Stuff* Tom Wolfe explains that Chuck Yeager was born so far back in the Appalachian Mountains that "they had to tote in sunshine in a bucket."   *"they—bucket."*

2. Back in those isolated hills and hollows people said, "I don't hold with it," when they disapproved of something.   *"I – it,"*

3. "H'it weren't nothing I hold with, but I helped him with it anyways" might be another typical sentence.   *"H'it —anyways"*

4. Later in life Yeager's speech was imitated by other pilots, thereby becoming the standard pilot speech which Wolfe calls "poker-hollow West Virginia drawl."   *"poker—drawl."*

5. "Yeager became the individual who ranked foremost in the Olympus [of pilots], the ace of all the aces, as it were, among the true brothers of the right stuff," says Wolfe.   *"Yeager—stuff,"*

6. As he recounts the heroics of Yeager and other remarkable pilots, Wolfe adds authenticity by skill-
fully using pilot jargon: "augered in," to mean flying a plane into the ground; "envelope" to refer to
the limits of a plane's abilities; "the right stuff," to
give the ultimate compliment to a pilot's abilities.

"the right stuff,"

7. Yeager always had the inscription "Glamorous
Glennis" written on the nose of his aircraft—from
the P-51 that he flew in combat to the X-1 in which
he broke the "sound barrier."

C

8. On the night before he was to attempt to break the
sound barrier in the X-1 "Glamorous Glennis,"
Yeager fell off a horse and broke several ribs. "I
sorta . . . dinged my . . . ribs," he told his friend
Jack Ridley.

"I — ribs,"

9. Yet he climbed into the X-1, ignited the four rocket
chambers, and flew off to experience what became
known as the ultimate in flying: "booming and
zooming."

"booming-zooming."

10. Observers on the ground spoke to Yeager by radio,
eagerly awaiting his encounter with the "barrier."
Just as he reached the speed of sound, Yeager reported in his best "poker-hollow West Virginia
drawl," "Had a mild buffet there . . . jus' the usual
instability. . . ."

"Had-instability...."

THE PERIOD
AND OTHER MARKS   ./ ?/ !/ :/ —/ ()/ []/ // . . ./ 17

17

Learn to use the end marks of punctuation—the period, the question mark, and the exclamation point—and the internal marks of punctuation—the colon, the dash, parentheses, brackets, and the slash—in accordance with conventional practices.

The end marks of punctuation give most writers little difficulty except when they are used with direct quotations.

17a The period follows declarative and mildly imperative (command) sentences, indirect questions, and many abbreviations.

DECLARATIVE SENTENCE George Wethergill, director of the Department of Terrestrial Magnetism at the Carnegie Institution of Washington, explains that he most wants to discover how the planets formed**.**

MILDLY IMPERATIVE SENTENCE Read about Wethergill's theories of planet formation**.**

INDIRECT QUESTION He was asked how the planets formed**.**

ABBREVIATION Dr**.** Eugene Levy, who will give a lecture at 4:00 p.m**.**, also has studied planet formation.

17b The question mark follows direct (but not indirect) questions.

DIRECT QUESTION Would you like to know more about Dr. Levy's ideas**?**

QUOTED QUESTION "In Dr. Levy's theory of planet formation what starts the process**?**" I wondered.   [No comma or period follows the question mark used at the end of a quoted passage.]

Sometimes a declarative or imperative sentence can be made into a question by simply changing the period to a question mark.

Dr. Levy proved his theory**?**   [Compare "Did Dr. Levy prove his theory?" in which the verb must change to form a question.]

17c The exclamation point follows emphatic interjections and statements of strong emotion.

Dr. Levy's experiments suggest that the process of planet formation may be universal; therefore, planetary systems may have formed all over the galaxy. Amazing**!**
"Bravo**!**" cried the audience when the rock group Cosmic Disc completed its performance.   [No comma or period follows the exclamation point used at the end of a quoted passage.]

Avoid using an exclamation point just to make your writing sound exciting or important.

> In 1983, the IRAS satellite detected evidence of possible planet formations coming from up to 50 nearby stars. [The content of the sentence, not an exclamation point at the end, communicates the writer's belief in the importance of the facts.]

OTHER MARKS

Of the internal marks of punctuation (those that do not mark the end of a sentence), the semicolon (see section **14**), the colon, and the dash are most closely related to the period because they bring the reader to a full stop—rather than to a pause as the comma does. Notice the difference between the way you read aloud a sentence that has a comma and one that has a colon, a dash, or a semicolon.

> Further evidence was collected by Bradford Smith, a planetary scientist at the University of Arizona. [a slight pause for the comma]
> Smith decided to concentrate on one possible site of planet formation: a star called Beta Pictoris, 50 light-years from Earth. [a full stop for the colon]
> Smith detected a dust cloud shaped like a cosmic disc—a swirling cloud of particles beginning to clump together; he suspects the presence of planet-size objects that he is unable to see. [a full stop for the dash and for the semicolon]

You have already studied the comma (section **12**) and the semicolon (section **14**). As you learn about the other commonly used marks of internal punctuation, you will become aware of the overlapping functions of some punctuation marks—that is, of the occasions when several different marks of punctuation are appropriate.

17d The colon, following a main clause, formally introduces a word, a phrase, a clause, or a list. It is also used to separate figures in scriptural and time references and to introduce some quoted sentences.

Following a main clause or sentence pattern, the colon and the dash often may be used interchangeably. The colon is a more formal mark of punctuation than the dash.

> In 1984 another scientist detected additional evidence of nearby planet formation: an object perhaps 10 times as massive as Jupiter orbiting a star named Von Biesbroeck 8.
> Telescopes used in detecting these sites of possible planet formation are not ordinary instruments: they collect infrared radiation rather than light. [The dash is not generally used when a main clause is being introduced.]
> The infrared telescopes generate interesting maps of the sky: splashes of color, pulsations of intense heat, and vast expanses of empty space. [A dash could also be used to introduce this list.]

> Levy repeats the opinion of most scientists: "What we really need is a space-borne telescope." [The dash is not used to introduce quotations.]

Except for this last example, in which a quotation is introduced following an expression such as *he said* (in this case, *Levy repeats*), there is no reason to interrupt a sentence with a colon. Do not use a colon between a subject and verb or between a verb and its complement or object.

> A space-borne telescope is more stable than an earthbound telescope, will not have its viewing distorted by the atmosphere, and will detect radiation that the atmosphere would filter out. [A colon after *telescope* would interrupt the sentence pattern.]
>
> A space-borne telescope has several advantages over earthbound telescopes: it does not have to see through the atmosphere; it can be completely motionless; and it can detect radiation that usually does not pass through the atmosphere. [The colon introduces a list of main clauses following a sentence pattern.]

The colon is also used between chapter and verse in scriptural passages and between hours and minutes in time references.

> Exodus 5:24
> 6:15 P.M.

17e Like the colon, the dash may introduce a word, a phrase, a clause, or a list that follows a sentence pattern; unlike the colon, it may interrupt a sentence pattern to mark a sudden break in thought, to set off a parenthetical element for emphasis or clarity, or to set off an introductory list.

> When I fly, I am more affected by claustrophobia—that's the fear of being closed in, isn't it?—than by acrophobia. [Dashes, or sometimes parentheses, are used to set off a sudden break in thought.]
>
> Three fears, or phobias—claustrophobia, acrophobia, aviophobia—are behind the anxiety many people feel when they travel by airplane. [Colons are not used here because they would interrupt the sentence pattern. Commas are not used because the list itself contains commas. Parentheses could be used: see **17f**.]
>
> Claustrophobia (fear of confined spaces), acrophobia (fear of heights), and aviophobia (fear of flying)—all three are behind the anxiety many people feel when they travel by airplane. [The colon is not used here because it would interrupt the sentence pattern. Use the dash when an introductory list precedes the sentence pattern.]
>
> Three fears, or phobias, are behind the anxiety many people feel when they travel by airplane—claustrophobia, acrophobia, and aviophobia. [The colon is also appropriate here to set off a list following the sentence pattern.]

17f Parentheses (1) set off supplementary or illustrative matter, (2) sometimes set off parenthetical matter, and (3) enclose figures or letters used for numbering, as in this rule.

The primary use of the parentheses is to set off supplementary or illustrative material that is loosely joined to the sentence.

Claustrophobia (the fear of confined spaces) affects many people when they get on elevators. [The parentheses set off the definition; commas could also be used.]

More women than men admit to having aviophobia (see definition on preceding page). [A lowercase letter begins the information in parentheses and a period follows the parentheses when the material in parentheses forms a part of the sentence.]

Parenthetical matter   Three marks of punctuation are used to set off parenthetical matter. The most commonly used are commas, which cause the reader only a pause and so keep the parenthetical matter closely related to the sentence. The least frequently used are parentheses, which minimize the importance of the parenthetical matter by setting it off distinctly from the sentence. Dashes, the third mark used to enclose parenthetical matter, emphasize the parenthetical matter, since they cause the reader to stop at the beginning and the end of the matter. (Remember that dashes, or sometimes parentheses, are necessary not only for emphasis but for clarity when the parenthetical matter itself includes commas.)

Women are more willing than men, as studies have shown, to admit their fears. [Commas would be used by most writers to set off this parenthetical matter.]

Women are more willing than men (as studies have shown) to admit their fears. [Parentheses minimize the importance of the parenthetical matter.]

Women are more willing than men—as studies have shown—to admit their fears. [Dashes emphasize the parenthetical matter.]

Many factors—such as length of flight, time of flight, and past experiences—apparently do not affect most people's sense of security in the air. [Dashes are needed for clarity to enclose the parenthetical matter that contains commas. Parentheses could also be used, but they would minimize the importance of the list of factors.]

17g Brackets set off editorial comments in quoted matter.

When you need to explain something about a quotation, enclose your explanation within brackets to show that it is not part of the quoted matter.

Katherine Anne Porter uses a common metaphor to describe death: "She [Granny Weatherall] stretched herself with a deep breath and blew out the light." [The writer of the sentence added the name to explain the identity of *she*.]

17h The slash indicates options and shows the end of a line of poetry run in with the text. (See also **16a**.)

In *The Prelude*, Wordsworth uses an image that reminds us of the view of Earth from a spacecraft or from the Moon: "Yet still the solitary cliffs **/** Wheeled by me—even as if the earth had rolled **/** With visible motion her diurnal round." [Note the space before and after each slash in the poetry.]

17i Use ellipsis points (three spaced periods) to mark an omission from a quoted passage and to mark a reflective pause or hesitation.

> In 1951, when he learned of the Big Bang theory of creation, Pope Pius XII declared, "True science . . . discovers God as though God were waiting behind each door opened by science."

> The old man looked away, rocking gently, resting his head against the ladderback chair. "Well, maybe I have . . . maybe I haven't," he said. "I disremember."
> —ROBERT HERRING

If ellipsis points are used to indicate that the end of a quoted sentence is being omitted, and if the part that *is* quoted forms a complete sentence itself, use the sentence period plus ellipsis points.

> Planets lose some heat the way a hot potato cools. . . .   —NATIONAL GEOGRAPHIC

Deduct 10 for each incorrect sentence.

End Marks of Punctuation   Exercise 17–1

NAME _____   SCORE _____

DIRECTIONS   Write a sentence to illustrate each of the following uses of an end mark of punctuation.

EXAMPLE
a quoted direct question

Wilson asked him, "Did you see the Pleiades last night?"

1. a mildly imperative sentence

Please take your telescope to the garage, Andy.

2. a direct question

Do you know where I left my book about the return of Halley's comet?

3. a sentence containing an abbreviation

We noticed Mr. and Mrs. Wilson on St. George Street, just down from the planetarium.

4. an exclamation

What a wonderful time we had at the planetarium!

5. a declarative sentence containing a direct quotation

"Until the comet hit Earth," my teacher explained, "the dinosaurs ruled Earth."

6. an indirect quotation

Scientists said that a comet hit Earth and caused the extinction of dinosaurs.

7. a declarative sentence containing a quoted direct question

Scientists had studied geological records of the extinction and finally wondered, "Could a celestial object have caused this ?"

8. an indirect question

We wondered what caused them to think about a celestial object.

9. a declarative sentence containing a quoted exclamation

The scientist who first considered that solution was quoted as saying, "What a perfect theory this is !"

10. a quotation that includes the ellipsis mark

The <u>Dictionary of Dinosaurs</u> reports that, "But for heavenly intervention ... you would be living in the same world with dinosaurs."

Internal Marks of Punctuation   Exercise 17–2

NAME _____ SCORE _____

DIRECTIONS   In the sentences below insert commas, semicolons, colons, dashes, parentheses, and brackets, as needed. Then enter in the blanks the mark or marks you have added. If more than one punctuation mark is possible, choose the one you think most writers would use, but be prepared to discuss the effect of the other possible choice or choices.

EXAMPLE
One of the most celebrated early astronomers was Kepler, a scientist
with many interests who first discovered that the planets move
about the Sun.   ___,___

1. Kepler discovered the orbits of planets about the sun, but he
    was unable to resolve a larger question: why the planets be-
    haved as they did.   ___, :___

2. Of course, Isaac Newton solved that problem.   ___,___

3. Newton (1642–1727) was born on Christmas Day about six
    months after the death of his father.   ___( )___

4. He was a tiny puny baby who, as one of his neighbors said,
    "could have been put into a quart pot."   ___, ,___

5. Newton's law of gravitation enables us to understand the ef-
    fects of gravitation, but it does not define gravity. ___,___

6. Like electricity and magnetism, [it gravity] is an invisible force. ___[ ]___

7. We know how all three forces operate, and we can make use
    of some of them, but we do not yet know just what they are. ___, or ,___

8. Like Kepler, Newton was a man of many talents.   ___,___

9. Newton, because he was interested in nearly everything scien-
    tific, made other significant discoveries.   ___, ,___

10. Pick up a prism, turn it so you can watch the light divide into
    a spectrum, and think of Isaac Newton.   ___, ,___

11. Newton first explained to us the compound nature of light,the idea that light waves of several colors combine to make white light. _____,_____

12. And because Newton also invented calculus,think of him as you attend your next math class. _____,_____

13. Newton also was interested in optical inventions;for example, he designed the first practical reflecting telescope. __;__,__

14. Like most great scientists,Newton believed that his successes were the consequences of the work of scientists who preceded him. _____,_____

15. He said,"If I seem to see farther than other men,it is because I am standing on the shoulders of giants." __,__,__

SPELLING AND HYPHENATION sp 18

18

Learn to spell and hyphenate in accordance with the usage shown in an up-to-date dictionary.

Everyone notices the sign that invites you to eat at the "Resturant" or the one that offers "Wood for Sell." And, right or wrong, most people tend to brand both the owner and the maker of such a sign as uneducated. There is simply no other error in composition that is so universally recognized and deplored as the misspelled word. Because of the stigma of illiteracy that it carries, misspelling should be the first and most important concern of any poor speller.

If you are a poor speller, one who regularly misspells enough words to have your classwork or professional work graded down, you should begin a definite program for improving your spelling skills. There are many excellent spelling manuals available today that make use of the latest psychological studies to present words in a logical, easy-to-learn order.

You may also find the following procedures helpful.

(1) Learn the rules of spelling presented in this section of the book.

(2) Proofread your papers carefully at least once for misspelled words only.

As you write a rough draft, it is often difficult, and always distracting, to look up a great number of words, but you can put a check or some other identifying sign above those words you have any doubts about so that you can look up their spelling when you proofread.

If you have difficulty spotting misspelled words in your own composition, try to slow down your reading of the rough draft by pointing to each word with a pencil. Or even read your writing from right to left instead of the usual left to right to be sure that you see individual words rather than groups of words. You need, whenever possible, to make more than two drafts of your paper because you will be unlikely to see your errors in a rough draft that has many words and phrases crossed through or that has barely legible handwriting.

(3) Keep a list of the words you tend to misspell.

The words that you misspell on your writing assignments should be recorded in the Individual Spelling List at the end of this *Workbook*. Because most people have a tendency to misspell certain words repeatedly, you should review your own spelling list frequently to break your bad spelling habits.

A comparison of your spelling list with someone else's will usually show—surprisingly enough—only two or three words in common. The mastery of spelling is an individual matter, differing with each person. You get some benefit from mastering lists of frequently misspelled words, but your own Individual Spelling List is the all-important one for you to work with.

(4) Write the words you misspell by syllables; then write the definitions of the words; finally, use the words in sentences.

      E NIG MAT IC   puzzling or baffling [The poem was *enigmatic* until I learned the meanings of five key words that the poet used.]

      AT TRIB UTE   as a noun, an object or quality that belongs to or represents someone or something [The *attributes* of Santa Claus have been expanded over the years.]

On the following pages are rules that will help you to avoid misspelling many commonly used words. Following the explanation of each rule is an exercise to reinforce the rule in your mind.

Deduct 3 1/3 for each blank incorrectly filled.

Misspelling Because of Mispronunciation

Exercise 18-1

NAME _____ SCORE _____

18a To avoid omitting, adding, transposing, or changing a letter in a word, pronounce the word carefully according to the way the dictionary divides it into syllables.

The places where common mistakes are made in pronunciation—and spelling—are indicated in boldface.

OMISSIONS	candidate, everything, government
ADDITIONS	athlete, laundry, drowned
TRANSPOSITIONS	perform, children, tragedy
CHANGE	accurate, prejudice, separate

DIRECTIONS   With the aid of your dictionary, write out each of the following words by syllables, indicate the position of the primary accent, and pronounce the word correctly and distinctly. In your pronunciation avoid any careless omission, addition, transposition, or change.

EXAMPLE
similar   *sim´i·lar*

1. accidentally   *ac·ci·den´tal·ly*

2. supposedly   *sup·pos´ed·ly*

3. prisoner   *pris´o·ner*

4. environment   *en·vi´ron·ment*

5. destruction   *de·struc´tion*

6. escape   *es·cape´*

7. circumstance   *cir´cum·stance*

8. surprise   *sur·prise´*

9. further   *fur´ther*

10. candidate   *can´di·date*

11. recognize   *rec´og·nize*

12. temperament   *tem´per·a·ment*

13. asked   *asked*

14. interpret   *in·ter′pret*

15. perhaps   *per·haps′*

16. prepare   *pre·pare′*

17. partner   *part′ner*

18. describe   *de·scribe′*

19. especially   *es·pe′cial·ly*

20. mischievous   *mis′chie·vous*

21. family   *fam′i·ly*

22. prescription   *pre·scrip′tion*

23. used   *used*

24. hindrance   *hin′drance*

25. interest   *in′ter·est*

26. athletic   *ath·let′ic*

27. hungry   *hun′gry*

28. library   *li′brar·y*

29. represent   *rep·re·sent′*

30. sophomore   *soph′o·more*

Deduct 6 for each blank incorrectly filled.

Confusion of Words Similar in Sound and/or Spelling   Exercise 18-2

NAME _____ SCORE _____

18b Distinguish between words that have a similar sound and/or spelling, such as *lose-loose* and *to-too-two*.

DIRECTIONS   In the following sentences, cross out the spelling or spellings in parentheses that do not fit the meaning, and write the correct spelling in the blank. Consult your dictionary freely.

EXAMPLE

In January 1984 President Reagan announced that he was (holey, holy, wholly) committed to building a permanent manned space station.

wholly

1. Instead of receiving wholehearted support from the scientific community for his idea, Reagan immediately (herd, heard) a chorus of boos.

heard

2. From James Van Allen, the great physicist, came the (prophecy, prophesy) that work done by astronauts in a space station would be "enormously inefficient."

prophecy

3. Tom Gold, another fine scientist, predicted that the astronauts would, in (effect, affect), engage in "just a lot of busy work."

effect

4. *Nature*, the oldest and most prestigious scientific journal in the world, identified the fundamental issue that runs (threw, through) all the objections.

through

5. Scientists (quiet, quite) properly fear that the space station program will consume all NASA funds.

quite

6. NASA will be forced to (choose, chose) between funding many smaller, very valuable projects and funding the space station.

choose

7. The smaller research and development projects will (loose, lose) funding.

lose

8. The same scientists also predict that only poor research will result from the platform. They cite (instances, ~~instants~~) of experiments on the space shuttle that have been ruined by an astronaut's sneeze.

instances

9. Most experiments aboard the platform need to be kept (~~stationery~~, stationary).

stationary

10. For example, any observations requiring a telescope need to be motionless, but (there, ~~they're~~, ~~their~~) is a change in a spacecraft's rotation if an astronaut turns her head.

there

11. In general, scientists say that they need everything aboard the platform (except, ~~accept~~) astronauts.

except

12. If NASA followed the (~~council~~, counsel) of this group of scientists, astronauts would be replaced with computers.

counsel

13. Another group of scientists offers (~~advise~~, advice) of an entirely different kind.

advice

14. They promote the space platform as an expression of the noblest (ideas, ideals) of humanity.

(either answer is appropriate)

15. A (~~principle~~, principal) spokesperson for this group is the astronomer Robert Jastrow.

principal

16. Jastrow argues that the scientific community consistently underestimates the effects of space exploration on the nation's (~~moral~~, morale).

morale

17. Jastrow is (~~conscience~~, conscious) of the original, very emotional genesis of the space program.

conscious

Deduct 6 2/3 for each blank incorrectly filled.

Adding Prefixes

Exercise 18–3

NAME _____ SCORE _____

18c Add the prefix to the root word without doubling or dropping letters. (The root is the base word to which the prefix or the suffix is added.)

un-	+	necessary	=	unnecessary
mis-	+	spell	=	misspell
dis-	+	agree	=	disagree

DIRECTIONS   In the blank at the right enter the correct spelling of each word with the prefix added. Consult your dictionary freely. Some dictionaries hyphenate some of the following words (see also **18f**).

EXAMPLES

mis-	+	quote	_misquote_
pre-	+	eminent	_preeminent_
1. dis-	+	satisfied	_dissatisfied_
2. dis-	+	appear	_disappear_
3. mis-	+	pronounce	_mispronounce_
4. mis-	+	understand	_misunderstand_
5. mis-	+	step	_misstep_
6. un-	+	noticed	_unnoticed_
7. un-	+	usual	_unusual_
8. dis-	+	approve	_disapprove_
9. dis-	+	similar	_dissimilar_
10. mis-	+	spent	_misspent_
11. mis-	+	behave	_misbehave_
12. dis-	+	able	_disable_
13. mis-	+	interpret	_misinterpret_

14. re- + take   *retake*

15. re- + evaluate   *reevaluate*

Deduct 6 2/3 for each blank incorrectly filled.

Adding Suffixes—Final *e*

Exercise 18–4

NAME _____ SCORE _____

18d(1) Drop the final *e* before a suffix beginning with a vowel but not before a suffix beginning with a consonant.

bride	+	-al	=	bridal	fame	+	-ous	=	famous
care	+	-ful	=	careful	entire	+	-ly	=	entirely

Exceptions: *due, duly; awe, awful; hoe, hoeing; singe, singeing.* After *c* or *g* the final *e* is retained before suffixes beginning with *a* or *o: notice, noticeable; courage, courageous.*

DIRECTIONS   With the aid of your dictionary, write the correct spelling of each word with the suffix added. Write (*ex*) after each answer that is an exception to rule **18d(1)**.

EXAMPLES

argue	+	-ing	*arguing*
dye	+	-ing	*dyeing (ex)*
1. become	+	-ing	*becoming*
2. use	+	-age	*usage*
3. hope	+	-ing	*hoping*
4. excite	+	-able	*excitable*
5. drive	+	-ing	*driving*
6. outrage	+	-ous	*outrageous (ex)*
7. like	+	-ly	*likely*
8. write	+	-ing	*writing*
9. advise	+	-able	*advisable*
10. arrange	+	-ment	*arrangement*
11. value	+	-able	*valuable*
12. manage	+	-ment	*management*
13. advantage	+	-ous	*advantageous (ex)*

14. judge   +   -ment   *judgment (ex)*

15. extreme   +   -ly   *extremely*

Adding Suffixes—Doubling the Consonant

Exercise 18–5

NAME _____ SCORE _____

18d(2) **When the suffix begins with a vowel (*ing, ed, ence, ance, able*), double a final single consonant if it is preceded by a single vowel and is in an accented syllable.** (A word of one syllable, of course, is always accented.)

mop, mopped   [compare with *mope, moped*]
mop, mopping   [compare with *mope, moping*]
con·fer, con·fer´red   [final consonant in the accented syllable]
ben´e·fit; ben´e·fited   [final consonant not in the accented syllable]
need, needed   [final consonant not preceded by a single vowel]

DIRECTIONS   In the blank at the right enter the correct spelling of each word with the suffix added. Consult your dictionary freely.

EXAMPLE
control   +   -ed   *controlled*

1. stop   +   -ing   *stopping*

2. occur   +   -ing   *occurring*

3. pour   +   -ing   *pouring*

4. proceed   +   -ed   *proceeded*

5. unforget +   -able   *unforgettable*

6. begin   +   -ing   *beginning*

7. control   +   -able   *controllable*

8. transmit +   -ing   *transmitting*

9. equip   +   -ed   *equipped*

10. meet   +   -ing   *meeting*

11. prefer   +   -ed   *preferred*

12. big   +   -est   *biggest*

13. push   +   -ed   *pushed*

14. fat   +   -er   _fatter_

15. attach   +   -ed   _attached_

Deduct 10 for each blank incorrectly filled.

Adding Suffixes—Final *y*

Exercise 18–6

NAME _____ SCORE _____

18d(3) Except before *ing*, final *y* preceded by a consonant is changed to *i* before a suffix.

defy	+	-ance	=	defiance	happy	+	-ness = happiness
modify	+	-er	=	modifier	modify	+	-ing = modifying

To make a noun plural or a verb singular, final *y* preceded by a consonant is changed to *i* and *es* is added (see also **18d(4)**).

duty	+	-es	=	duties	deny	+	-es = denies
ally	+	-es	=	allies	copy	+	-es = copies

Final *y* preceded by a vowel is usually not changed before a suffix.

annoy	+	-ed	=	annoyed	turkey	+	-s = turkeys

Exceptions: *pay, paid; lay, laid; say, said; day, daily.*

DIRECTIONS   With the aid of your dictionary, enter the correct spelling of each word with the suffix added. Write (*ex*) after each word that is an exception to rule **18d(3)**.

EXAMPLES
boundary + -es   *boundaries*

pay + -d   *paid (ex)*

1. monkey + -s   *monkeys*

2. try + -es   *tries*

3. accompany + -es   *accompanies*

4. chimney + -s   *chimneys*

5. bury + -ed   *buried*

6. lay + -ed   *laid (ex)*

7. fallacy + -es   *fallacies*

8. hungry + -ly   *hungrily*

9. lonely + -ness   *loneliness*

10. donkey + -s   *donkeys*

Deduct 5 for each blank incorrectly filled.

Forming the Plural

Exercise 18-7

NAME _____ SCORE _____

18d(4) Form the plural of most nouns by (1) adding *s* to the singular form of the noun, (2) adding *es* to singular nouns ending in *s, ch, sh,* or *x,* or (3) changing the *y* to *i* and adding *es* if the noun ends in a *y* preceded by a consonant.

boy→boys	fox→foxes	mystery→mysteries
cupful→cupfuls	Harris→Harrises	beauty→beauties
Drehmel→Drehmels	genius→geniuses	reply→replies

A few nouns change their form for the plural: *woman→women; child→children.* And a few nouns ending in *o* take the *es* plural: *potato→potatoes; hero→heroes.* And a few nouns change an *f* to a *v* and add *s* or *es: calf→calves; knife→knives.*

DIRECTIONS   In the blank enter the plural form of each word. Consult your dictionary freely.

EXAMPLES
day   *days*
scratch   *scratches*

1. speech   *speeches*
2. box   *boxes*
3. industry   *industries*
4. veto   *vetoes*
5. wolf   *wolves*
6. Long   *Longs*
7. witch   *witches*
8. scientist   *scientists*
9. address   *addresses*
10. city   *cities*

11. question   *questions*
12. ghetto   *ghettos or ghettoes*
13. article   *articles*
14. leaf   *leaves*
15. watch   *watches*
16. man   *men*
17. professor *professors*
18. business   *businesses*
19. Jones   *Joneses*
20. army   *armies*

Deduct 5 for each blank incorrectly filled.

Confusion of *ei* and *ie*

Exercise 18–8

NAME _____ SCORE _____

18e **When the sound is *ee* (as in *see*), write *ei* after *c* (*receipt, ceiling*), and *ie* after any other letter (*relieve, priest*); when the sound is other than *ee*, usually write *ei* (*eight, their, reign*).**

Exceptions: *either, neither, financier, leisure, seize, species, weird.*

Note: This rule does not apply when *ei* or *ie* is not pronounced as one simple sound (*alien, audience, fiery*) or when *cie* stands for *shə* (*ancient, conscience, efficient*).

DIRECTIONS   With the aid of your dictionary, fill in the blanks in the following words by writing *ei* or *ie*. Write (*ex*) after any word that is an exception to rule **18e**.

EXAMPLES
dec___*ei*___ve

___*ei*___ther (*ex*)

1. rec___*ei*___ve

2. bel___*ie*___s

3. ch___*ie*___f

4. s___*ie*___ge

5. conc___*ei*___ted

6. y___*ie*___ld

7. gr___*ie*___f

8. l___*ei*___sure (*ex*)

9. misch___*ie*___f (*ex*)

10. sl___*ei*___gh

11. th___*ie*___f

12. gr___*ie*___ve

13. spec___*ie*___s (*ex*)

14. w___*ei*___ght

15. c___*ei*___ling

16. rel___*ie*___ve

17. h___*ei*___ght

18. f___*ie*___nd

19. n___*ei*___ther (*ex*)

20. f___*ie*___ld

Deduct 3 1/3 for each incorrect item.

Hyphenated Words

Exercise 18–9

NAME _____ SCORE _____

18f In general, use the hyphen (1) between two or more words serving as a single adjective before a noun, (2) with compound numbers from twenty-one to ninety-nine and with spelled-out fractions, (3) with prefixes or suffixes for clarity, (4) with the prefixes *ex-*, *self-*, *all-*, and *great-* and the suffix *elect*, and (5) between a prefix and a proper name.

(1) a *know-it-all* expression
(2) *sixty-six, one-half*
(3) *re-collect* the supplies (to distinguish from *recollect* an event)
(4) *ex-wife, self-help, all-important, great-grandmother, mayor-elect*
(5) *mid-July, un-American*

DIRECTIONS   Supply hyphens where they are needed in the following list. Not all items require hyphens.

EXAMPLES
a well-spent childhood

a childhood well spent

1. a long-distance call

2. a four-foot barricade

3. a twenty-five-year-old coach

4. ex-President Townes

5. President-elect Drehmel

6. a high-rise apartment

7. a commonly used adjective

8. chocolate-covered cherries

9. students who are career minded

10. the all-seeing eye of the camera

11. a two-thirds vote of the senate

12. Two-thirds of the senate approved.

13. western-style jeans

14. the clumsily executed dance

15. He is forty-five.

16. She is my great-aunt.

17. an all-inclusive study

18. results that are long lasting

19. long-lasting results

20. My small daughter is amazingly self-sufficient.

21. The officer re-searched the suspect.

22. a two-part answer

23. The answer had two parts.

24. The up-and-down motion of the roller coaster made the girl ill.

25. The shop specializes in young people's fashions.

26. I feel all right today.

27. We are all ready to go.

28. a win-at-any-cost attitude

29. in mid-December

30. a walk-in closet

19

Learn the ways that an up-to-date desk dictionary can guide you in the choice of words appropriate to your writing needs.

An up-to-date desk dictionary is a necessary reference tool for today's student and professional person. (A desk dictionary is based on one of the unabridged dictionaries, such as *Webster's Third New International*, usually found on a lectern in the library.) You have already seen how essential a current dictionary is for checking the spelling and hyphenation of words and for finding out when to abbreviate, capitalize, and italicize words. But an up-to-date dictionary serves still other purposes. For example, (1) it shows you how to pronounce a word like *harass;* (2) it lists the forms and possible uses of a verb like *sing;* (3) it explains what a given word means and gives example phrases and sentences which clarify the definition; (4) it gives the synonyms and antonyms of a word like *oppose;* (5) it gives information about a word's origin; and (6) it may provide usage labels for words like *poke, nowheres,* and *irregardless.* A desk dictionary may also supply you with miscellaneous information such as a brief history of the English language, the dates and identities of famous people, geographical facts, and lists of colleges and universities in the United States and Canada. A current desk dictionary, then, is one of the best investments you can make.

19a Learn to use an up-to-date dictionary intelligently.

Study the introductory matter to find out what your dictionary's guides to abbreviations and pronunciation are; to know what plural and tense forms your dictionary lists; to learn what attitude your dictionary takes toward usage labels (dictionaries vary in the kinds of labels they use, and some dictionaries label more words than others do); and to understand the order in which the meanings of words are listed—that is, in order of common usage or of historical development.

19b–19g Use words that have no usage labels unless the occasion demands otherwise.

Most words (and most meanings of words) in dictionaries are unlabeled; that is, they are appropriate on any occasion because they are in general use in the English-speaking world. But some words have labels that indicate they are used (1) by people in one section of the country (*Dialectal, Regional,* sometimes *Colloquial*); (2) by people who are often judged uneducated (*Nonstandard* and *Illiterate;* sometimes words in this category are not listed at all); (3) by people who use popular expressions that often do not remain long in the language (*Slang*); (4) in literature from past times (*Archaic, Obsolete, Obsolescent, Rare*); or (5) by people in a specialized field of study (technical words like *pyrexia*, which a dictionary labels *Pathol.* to indicate that it is a term from pathology).

When the occasion demands the use of a word that is labeled—for example, an address to a medical convention might call for technical language or even jargon—the word may be judged appropriate because the audience will understand it. But in general speaking and writing, you should depend on the multitude of unlabeled words that most audiences or readers can be expected to understand.

LABELED WORDS   *Irregardless* of what my *screwy* friend advised, I was not *fixing to* drive my *pater's* new *set of wheels* in the demolition derby.

UNLABELED WORDS   *Regardless* of what my *crazy* friend advised, I was not *about* (STANDARD)   *to* drive my *father's* new *automobile* in the demolition derby.

There is one class of words—labeled *Informal,* or sometimes *Colloquial*—that is commonly used and understood by most writers and speakers. These words are appropriate in speaking and in informal writing and are usually necessary in recording dialogue because most people speak less formally than they write. But, in general, you should avoid words labeled *Informal* or *Colloquial* in most of your college and professional writing.

INFORMAL   The student *lifted* the passage from a critic he was studying.

STANDARD OR   The student *plagiarized* the passage from a critic he was studying.
FORMAL

Except in dialogue, contractions are usually not appropriate in formal writing.

INFORMAL   *There's* hardly anyone who *doesn't* respond to a good play.

STANDARD OR   *There is* hardly anyone who *does not* respond to a good play.
FORMAL

19h Choose words and combinations of sounds that are appropriate to clear prose writing.

A poetic style is generally not appropriate in college essays or professional reports. Usually such writing seems wordy, vague, and even ridiculous.

FLOWERY   He was a *tower of power* in our community, a blazing *meteor in a prosperous enterprise.*

PLAIN BUT   He was a *powerful* man in our community, a *remarkably successful*
CLEAR   *businessman.*

Deduct 1 1/2 for each blank incorrectly filled.

Using the Dictionary

Exercise 19–1

NAME _____ SCORE _____

The full title, the edition, and the date of publication of my dictionary are as follows: _Random House Dictionary of the English Language, College Edition, 1982._

1. Abbreviations   Where does the dictionary explain the abbreviations it uses?

in the "Guide to the Dictionary"

Write out the meaning of each of the abbreviations following these entries:

extend, v.t. _verb, transitive_

deray, n., Obs. _noun, Obsolete_

nohow, adv., Dial. _adverb, Dialectal_

coracoid, Anat., adj. _Anatomy, adjective_

2. Spelling and Pronunciation   Using your dictionary, write out by syllables each of the words listed below, and place the accent where it belongs. With the aid of the diacritical marks, the phonetic respelling of the word (in parentheses or slashes immediately after the word), and the key at the bottom of the page or in the introductory matter, determine the preferred pronunciation (the first pronunciation given). Then pronounce each word correctly several times.

exquisite _ex'qui·site_

harass _har'ass_

grimace _grim'ace_

pianist _pi·an'ist or pi'an·ist_

Write the plurals of the following words:

deer _deer_

index _indexes or indices_

criterion _criteria_

datum _data_

Rewrite each of the following words that needs a hyphen:

watercolor   _____

selfconscious   *self-conscious*

extracurricular   _____

3. Derivations   The derivation, or origin, of a word (given in brackets) often furnishes a literal meaning that helps you to remember the word. For each of the following words give (a) the source—the language from which it is derived, (b) the original word or words, and (c) the original meaning.

	Source	*Original word(s) and meaning*
nefarious	*Latin*	*ne = not + far = law + ius (ious)*
pseudonym	*Greek*	*pseudonym = false name*
deprecate	*Latin*	*dēprecāt = prayed against or warded off*

4. Meanings   Usually words develop several different meanings. How many meanings are listed in your dictionary for the following words?

discipline, *n.*   *8*   spend, *v.*   *6*   out, *adv.*   *28*

tortuous, *adj.*   *3*   in, *prep.*   *9*   magazine, *n.*   *5*

Does your dictionary list meanings in order of historical development or of common usage?   *common usage*

5. Special Labels   Words (or certain meanings of words) may have such precautionary or explanatory labels as *Archaic, Colloquial,* or *Nautical.* What label or special usage do you find for one meaning of each word below?

lush, *n.*   *Slang*

your'n, *pro.*   *Dialectal*

bust, *v.*   *Informal*

ain't, *v.*   *Nonstandard*

hisself, *pro.*   *Nonstandard*

yare, *adj.*   *Archaic*

USING THE DICTIONARY   Exercise 19–1 (continued)

6. Synonyms   Even among words with essentially the same meaning, one word usually fits a given context more exactly than any other. To show precise shades of meaning, some dictionaries treat in special paragraphs certain groups of closely related words. What synonyms are specially differentiated in your dictionary for the following words?

consider, *v.*   *ponder, deliberate, weigh, study*

sharp, *adj.*   *keen, intelligent, quick*

7. Capitalization   Rewrite the words that can be capitalized.

history   _____

communism   _____

spartan   *Spartan*

pisces   *Pisces*

chauvinist   _____

german   *German*

8. Grammatical Information   Note that many words may serve as two or more parts of speech. List the parts of speech that each of the following words may be: *v., n., adj., adv., prep., conj., interj.*

check   *v., n., adj., interj.*

hold   *v., n.*

off   *adv., prep., adj., n., interj.*

number   *n., v.*

ring   *n., v.*

right   *adj., n., adv., v.*

Note the grammatical information supplied by your dictionary for verbs, adjectives, and pronouns.

List the principal parts of *lie:*   *lay, lain, lying*

List the principal parts of *burst:*   *burst, bursting*

List the principal parts of *cry:*   *cried, crying*

List the comparative and superlative degrees of the adjective *steady:* _____

_____ *steadier, steadiest* _____

List the comparative and superlative degrees of the adjective *big:* _____

_____ *bigger, biggest* _____

Should *which* be used to refer to people? *no* _____

What is the distinction between the relative pronouns *that* and *which?* *That introduces restrictive clauses; which introduces nonrestrictive clauses.*

9. Idiomatic Expressions   List two standard idiomatic expressions for each of the following words.

wait: *wait on or upon, wait up*

track: *keep track of, track down*

die: *die hard, die off*

10. Miscellaneous Information   Answer the following questions by referring to your dictionary. Be prepared to tell in what part of the dictionary the information is located.

In what year was Thomas Edison born? *1847*

Where is Normandy located? *in Northern France along the English Channel*

What was Valhalla? *the hall of Odin and home of the souls of brave heroes*

Does your dictionary have a history of the English language? *Yes*

Does your dictionary have a manual of style? *Yes*

Deduct 7 for each blank incorrectly filled.

Appropriate Usage   Exercise 19-2

NAME _____   SCORE _____

DIRECTIONS   If the italicized word, with the meaning it has in its particular sentence, is labeled in your dictionary in any way, enter the label (such as *Informal* or *Slang*) in the blank. If the word is not labeled, write *Standard* in the blank. Discuss your answers in class to compare the usage labels of various dictionaries.

EXAMPLE
The *Star Wars* movies have introduced some *mighty*
   memorable characters.   _*Informal*_
                           (Webster's New World)

1. Some of the characters that *most* everyone recalls
   are machines or nonhumans.   _*Informal*_
                                (Random House College)

2. The robot C₃PO is *kind of* a blend of an English
   butler—very proper and fastidious—and the
   straight man in a comedy routine.   _*Informal*_
                                       (Random House College)

3. The robot R₂D₂ is a funny, brave little character
   that *sort of* reminds us of Lou Costello.   _*Informal*_
                                                (Random House College)

4. Although Chewbaca *ain't* very articulate, he im-
   presses us with his bravery.   _*Nonstandard*_
                                  (American Heritage)

5. When Chewbaca roars, *don't nobody* feel comfortable.   _*Nonstandard*_

6. Chewbaca, of course, is the constant companion of
   the *wheeler-dealer* Han Solo.   _*Slang*_

7. Other very vivid characters in *Star Wars* movies
   have minor roles; intriguing monsters appear almost *anywheres*. Do you recall the tentacled mon-
   ster that lives in a garbage disposal?   _*Nonstandard*_

8. And think about the dinosaur-like creature to
   whom Jabba the Hutt feeds his enemies and with
   whom Luke has to *reckon*.   _*Idiomatic*_
                               (Random House College)

9. The last *Star Wars* movie introduced the Eewoks, a race of cuddly, funny creatures who *seem to* stand for the virtues of simple, natural life. *Standard*

10. The Eewoks help battle the forces of the Empire, symbolized by giant fighting machines that *anyways* look like crosses between insects and lizards. *Nonstandard*

11. The simple Eewoks defeat the complex machines by tripping them with ropes or *busting* them with rocks and falling trees. *Slang (Webster's New World)* *Standard (American Heritage)*

12. The Eewoks have also been produced as very marketable dolls, *being as* they are extremely cuddly. *Nonstandard*

13. Smaller children respond to them because they are completely innocent *even as* they are completely nonhuman. *Standard*

14. Almost every toy that has *spun off* from the *Star Wars* movies has been successful. *Informal*

Deduct 6 2/3 for each blank incorrectly filled.

Appropriate Usage   Exercise 19–3

NAME _____ SCORE _____

DIRECTIONS   In each sentence, choose the proper word or words from the pairs in parentheses. Cross out the incorrect word or words and write the correct one in the blank. Rely on your dictionary to help you choose the word with the correct meaning or the word that is appropriate in a formal essay.

EXAMPLE
(~~Lots of~~, Many) moviegoers recognize the timeless
    theme of good versus evil in the *Star Wars* movies.   *Many*

1. Many adult moviegoers grew up as fans of old
   westerns which (~~regretfully,~~ regrettably) live on
   only in reruns.   *regrettably*

2. In those movies the distinction between good and
   bad characters (~~would of,~~ would have) been evi-
   dent to anyone.   *would have*

3. The good guy generally wore a white hat, rode a
   beautiful horse, and summoned the (~~calvary,~~ cavalry) when he needed help.   *cavalry*

4. He had a sidekick who was humorous, good-
   natured, and brave and who helped save him at
   the (~~climatic,~~ climactic) moment.   *climactic*

5. The heroine was innocent and beautiful but often
   got herself into predicaments that (~~illicited,~~
   elicited) the hero's actions.   *elicited*

6. All of these characteristics of plot and character are
   common, of course, to *Star Wars*; in fact, George
   Lucas (~~purposefully,~~ purposely) leads us to see the
   similarities.   *purposely*

7. Part of the pleasure of seeing the movies derives from our recognizing the plots and characters at the same time we (marvel, ~~marble~~) at what is new and freshly imagined about the settings and characters.

marvel

8. The roots of *Star Wars* do not allude only to old westerns; Luke, for example, is training to be a Jedi knight, and he reminds us at least (~~partially~~, partly) of other legendary knights.

partly

9. His relationship with his mentor Ben (resembles, ~~dissembles~~) the relationship between the young King Arthur and the magician Merlin.

resembles

10. Luke's efforts to become a Jedi (~~comprise~~, constitute) a quest.

constitute

11. The visit with Yoda, who is both (~~childish~~, childlike) and wise, is a major part of the quest for goodness and strength.

childlike

12. And, of course, the dark side of the quest is symbolized by Darth Vader, who has (collaborated, ~~corroborated~~) with the dark, evil forces.

collaborated

13. The (~~affect~~, effect) of the struggle between Luke and Darth Vader is, finally, to remind us of the struggle between good and bad within everyone.

effect

14. Although Luke intends to (avenge, ~~revenge~~) earlier defeats at Vader's hands, he does not intend to give in to the forces of darkness within him.

avenge

15. As first victory, then defeat, seems (~~eminent~~, imminent) for Luke, we are exultant, then dismayed, because we recognize that struggle within ourselves.

imminent

20

Choose words that are exact, idiomatic, and fresh.

Since the basic unit of communication is the word, you cannot write clearly and accurately unless you have built up a vocabulary of words to express the things you think and feel. Of the 500,000 entries in an unabridged dictionary, most college students can use no more than 15,000 in speaking and writing. Building a vocabulary, then, is a lifetime process. Usually the more people read, the more words they add to their recognition vocabularies. After they have seen the same words many times in different contexts, they add these words to their active vocabularies, the words they actually use in speaking and writing.

People who do not regularly read newspapers, magazines, and books often have few words to draw from whenever they speak or write. They may complain, "I know what I mean, but I can't put it into words." They may also say that some works by professional writers are "too hard to understand." The source of their difficulty in both writing and reading is an inadequate vocabulary.

You can begin now to increase your vocabulary by noticing the words you read in your course work and by looking up definitions of all the words you are uncertain of. Sometimes reading a difficult paragraph aloud emphasizes the words you are not familiar with and, as a result, helps you understand why the paragraph is difficult for you.

While you are increasing your recognition vocabulary, you must take great care to make the best possible use of the words in your active vocabulary.

20a Choose words that express your ideas exactly.

To express yourself exactly, you must choose words that have the denotations (the definitions found in dictionaries) and the connotations (the mental or emotional associations that go with the words) that you intend.

PROBLEM WITH DENOTATION	The failure of the satellite was *contributed* to a faulty computer.
CORRECT DENOTATION	The failure of the satellite was *attributed* to a faulty computer.
PROBLEM WITH CONNOTATION	I took my best friend to my *domicile* for dinner.
CORRECT CONNOTATION	I took my best friend to my *home* for dinner.

Remember that a wrong word is very noticeable when it results in a ridiculous sentence (see also **18b**).

WRONG WORD	Faust pledged his *sole* to the devil in exchange for power and knowledge.
CORRECT WORD	Faust pledged his *soul* to the devil in exchange for power and knowledge.

Whenever possible you should choose concrete rather than abstract words. Abstract words refer to ideas, whereas concrete words refer to definite objects. Abstract words are necessary to state generalizations, but it is the specific word, the specific detail, the specific example that engages the reader's attention. (See also section **31**.)

GENERAL	Astronaut Buzz Aldrin described his walks on the Moon as nice.
SPECIFIC	Astronaut Buzz Aldrin described his walks on the Moon as deeply religious experiences that changed his life.

GENERAL	Astronauts must train a lot if they hope to do well.
SPECIFIC	Astronauts train twelve to fourteen hours each day in preparation for the complex demands of a mission.

20b Choose words that are idiomatic.

Idiomatic expressions are phrases that you use every day without thinking about their meaning: "I ran across an old friend" and "Angie played down the importance of money." Native English speakers use expressions like these naturally; but some idioms may seem unnatural, even ridiculous, to foreigners trying to learn our language.

Even native speakers sometimes have difficulty choosing the correct prepositions to make expressions idiomatic. For example, many would write "prior than" rather than the idiomatic "prior to." The dictionary is the best guide for helping you choose the preposition that should follow a word like *prior* to make an idiomatic expression.

UNIDIOMATIC	Some of the parts for the first space shuttle did not *comply to* NASA standards and were replaced.
IDIOMATIC	Some of the parts for the first space shuttle did not *comply with* NASA standards and were replaced.

20c Choose fresh expressions rather than trite ones.

Many idiomatic expressions have been used so often that they have become trite—worn out and meaningless. At one time readers would have thought the expression "tried and true" was an exact and effective choice of words. But readers today have seen and heard the expression so often that they hardly notice it, except perhaps to be bored or amused by it. Clichés of this sort are common in most people's speech and may even occur at times in the work of professional writers, but they should generally be avoided because they no longer communicate ideas exactly. Beware also of political slogans, advertising jargon, and most slang expressions: they are often so overused for a brief period of time that they quickly become meaningless.

TRITE   Last but not least is the dedicated student who rises at the crack of dawn to hit the books.

EXACT   Last is the dedicated student who rises at 6:00 A.M. to study.

Vocabulary Building   Exercise 20–1

NAME _____

DIRECTIONS   To see how becoming aware of words in your reading can lead to a better recognition vocabulary, try this experiment. Read aloud the first paragraph below, underlining the words whose meaning you are uncertain of; then look up the definitions and write them down; finally, reread the sentences in which these words appear. When you have finished with the first paragraph, go on to the second one. Notice how the words that gave you trouble in the first paragraph seem to stand out in the second paragraph, though sometimes as a different part of speech or in a different tense. If you cannot remember the definitions of the words, look again at your notes.

PARAGRAPH 1

My first visit to the planet Tharsus in the Trefoil Galaxy made me feel like the quintessential tourist. I stepped off the shuttle at Standing Rock, the capital city, into a world that was both familiar and totally new. The ambience at first reminded me of Calcutta back on Earth: the city teemed with life and over the masses lay a constant and almost palpable din. The maelstrom created by too many creatures plying their trades in the narrow streets among squat, stuccoed buildings was both frightening and thrilling. Over the whole scene loomed the giant obelisk for which the city is named, a natural stone shaft nearly 20 stories tall that has the presence of some inscrutable god.

PARAGRAPH 2

Notice the changing responses of a crowd of onlookers at a launch of the space shuttle. Like some ancient obelisk the shuttle rests against the launch tower, self-contained and inscrutable in the distance. The crowd seems almost nervous as it watches the few tiny figures scurry around the base of the vast machine, giving the whole scene the ambience of some pagan rite. As the voices at launch headquarters prophesy the ignition of rocket engines, the crowd becomes quiet and strains forward for the first glimpse of the fiery maelstrom. At ignition the shuttle begins to move slowly, almost reluctantly, resting with surprising grace atop a column of flame, smoke, and dust. Suddenly the din of the engines rolls over the crowd, a nearly palpable slap in their faces, shocking them into one of the quintessential experiences of the space age.

Deduct 5 for each blank incorrectly filled.

Correct and Exact Words

Exercise 20–2

NAME _____ SCORE _____

DIRECTIONS   In the following sentences, choose the proper word or words from the pairs in parentheses. Cross out the wrong or inexact word or words and write the correct answer in the blank. Use your dictionary freely.

EXAMPLE
Of all the movies with a space exploration (motif, ~~motive~~), none is more memorable than *The Empire Strikes Back.*

motif

1. *The Empire Strikes Back* (~~accounts~~, recounts) the continuing adventures of Luke Skywalker.

recounts

2. Luke and the rebel forces are hiding from the Imperial Empire forces, and Luke is learning to (contend, ~~attend~~) with his nemesis, Darth Vader.

contend

3. As the movie (~~precedes~~, progresses, ~~regresses~~), the main theme emerges.

progresses

4. It becomes (~~clear as rain~~, ~~plain to anyone~~, clear) that Luke senses that he and Vader are powerfully linked.

clear

5. Luke's relationship with Vader is also linked (to, ~~with~~) his relationship to Princess Leia.

to

6. Not until the movie nears its end do viewers fully (~~apprehend~~, comprehend) these relationships.

comprehend

7. As Luke trains with Yoda to become a Jedi knight, Han and Leia (flee, ~~flea~~) Vader.

flee

8. Yoda has been training Jedi knights in the (principles, ~~principals~~) of knighthood for over 300 years.

principles

9. At first he does not wish to train Luke, who he says is too (impetuous, ~~contemptuous~~).

impetuous

10. He wishes Luke were more (introspective, ~~irrespective~~).

introspective

11. However, Yoda does take Luke as a student and begins to teach him how to (~~transpose,~~ ~~transcribe,~~ transcend) his limitations by relying on the Force.

     transcend

12. In one particularly memorable scene Yoda demonstrates his power to move objects using only his psychic energy: he (transports, ~~disports,~~ ~~imports~~) Luke's spaceship from where it has sunk in the swamps to a dry clearing.

     transports

13. Later he explains that by becoming "one with the Force," Luke can learn to see into the future or to sense what is (~~recurring,~~ occurring) in another place.

     occurring

14. Most of Luke's training, however, centers around Vader. Yoda repeatedly (alludes, ~~eludes~~) to the dark side that will tempt Luke as it did Vader, who finally gave in to it.

     alludes

15. Far from being oblivious (~~about,~~ to, ~~of~~) the dark side, Luke is constantly aware of its presence.

     to

16. But what (distinguishes, ~~discriminates~~) Luke from Vader is his ability to control his emotions.

     distinguishes

17. Luke passes the (~~penultimate,~~ ~~ulterior,~~ ultimate) test of that control during his duel with Vader.

     ultimate

18. Vader (taunts, ~~teases~~) Luke and urges him to give in to his feelings of hate.

     taunts

19. When Luke (~~subsists,~~ resists) him, Vader shocks Luke by revealing that he is Luke's father.

     resists

20. (Ironically, ~~Sarcastically,~~ ~~Satirically~~) the clash between good and evil, and between dark and light, has been embodied in this conflict between father and son.

     Ironically

21

Avoid wordiness but include all words needed to make the meaning or the grammatical construction complete.

Almost every writer's first draft includes many words that are not needed and lacks some words that are. A careful revision based on close proofreading is the only way to transform a rough draft into an effective piece of writing.

ROUGH DRAFT
WITH REVISIONS

~~At this point in time,~~ the largest meteorite actually dis-

played in a museum is in the Hayden Planetarium in

New York City. It was found in 1897 on the northwest

coast of Greenland. The American explorer Robert E.

Peary, ~~found it,~~ and it is about four cubic meters in

volume.

21a Use only those words or phrases that add meaning to your writing.

Most wordiness in composition results from writers' attempts to achieve what they think is a "high style"—to write sentences that sound brilliant. Too often they fill out their sentences with clichés, with roundabout phrasing, and with jargon.

WORDY   Actually it is a fact that the largest known meteorite is still in the ground. It is buried where it fell in southwestern Africa. It is about ten cubic meters in volume.

CONCISE   The largest known meteorite remains buried where it fell in southwestern Africa and is about ten cubic meters in volume.

Use one clear word instead of a long phrase whenever possible. Following is a list of some more common wordy phrases and their one-word counterparts.

Wordy	Concise
to be desirous of	want or desire
to have a preference for	prefer
to be in agreement with	agree
due to the fact that	because
in view of the fact that	because or since
in order to	to

Wordy	*Concise*
at this point in time	now
in this day and age	today
with reference to	about
prior to	before
in the event of	if

Another kind of wordiness, occurring particularly in student compositions, results from the writer's lack of confidence in his/her position. Such wordiness frequently includes expressions like "I think," "it seems to me," "in my opinion," and "would be."

WORDY In my opinion, the best reason for leaving the meteorite in the ground would be to create a kind of monument or memorial to the mysteries of the universe.

CONCISE The meteorite should be left in the ground as a memorial to the mysteries of the universe.

21b Restructure sentences whenever necessary to avoid wordiness.

Often you can combine sentences through subordination to avoid wordiness. (See also section **24**.)

WORDY The expression "quasi-stellar radio sources" was coined by radio astronomers in the 1950s, and it refers to the very bright, star-like objects that they discovered at a great distance from Earth and still moving away.

CONCISE In the 1950s radio astronomers discovered "quasi-stellar radio sources," very bright, star-like objects at a great distance from Earth and still moving away.

WORDY Galileo and William Herschel were famous astronomers, and they were immortalized by great poets. Galileo was mentioned by Milton in *Paradise Lost* and Herschel by Keats in "On First Looking Into Chapman's Homer."

CONCISE Galileo and William Herschel were famous astronomers who were immortalized by great poets: Galileo by Milton in *Paradise Lost* and Herschel by Keats in "On First Looking Into Chapman's Homer." [The *who* clause and the colon reduce the two wordy sentences to one concise sentence.]

Wordiness may also be caused by sentences that begin with *there* or *it*. To eliminate this kind of wordiness, restructure your sentences to use an active verb in place of the form of *be* that inevitably follows *there* or *is*.

WORDY There are two famous observatories that have been built atop Mt. Hopkins in Arizona.

CONCISE Two famous observatories have been built atop Mt. Hopkins in Arizona.

WORDY It is obvious that Mt. Hopkins must provide excellent conditions for viewing.

CONCISE Obviously, Mt. Hopkins provides excellent viewing conditions.

21c Avoid needless repetition of words and ideas.

Repetition of the same word or idea in several consecutive sentences results in monotonous writing. Using pronouns helps as much as anything to avoid this problem.

REPETITIOUS The astronomer Fred Whipple was responsible for developing several observatories. Whipple developed two of the observatories on Mt. Hopkins.

CONCISE The astronomer Fred Whipple was responsible for developing several observatories, two of them on Mt. Hopkins.

Note: Several popular expressions are always repetitious: *each and every, any and all, various and sundry, if and when, combine together, return back.* Other such expressions include *red in color, triangular in shape,* and *city of Cleveland.*

REPETITIOUS Each and every telescope is affected by artificial light.
CONCISE Each telescope is affected by artificial light.

REPETITIOUS A total of thirteen observatories are built on Arizona's Kitt Peak.
CONCISE Thirteen observatories are built on Arizona's Kitt Peak.

In writing direct quotations, many students tend to overwork forms of the verb *say.* Remember that many verbs besides *said* can introduce direct quotations. *Explained, pointed out, noted, continued, described,* and *observed* are only a few.

REPETITIOUS Our guide to the observatory said, "Be sure to bring a sweater to wear inside the building." He later said, "The building is kept cold to prevent the telescope's mirrors from warping."

BETTER Our guide to the observatory cautioned us, "Be sure to bring a sweater to wear inside the building." He later explained, "The building is kept cold to prevent the telescope's mirrors from warping."

Deduct 2 1/2 for each blank incorrectly filled and 2 1/2 for each incorrect revision.

Wordiness and Needless Repetition   Exercise 21–1

NAME _____ SCORE _____

DIRECTIONS   Cross out needless words in each of the following sentences. For each sentence needing only that revision, write *1* in the blank; for sentences that need additional changes, even changes in punctuation, write *2* in the blank and make the needed revision. There may be more than one way to revise some sentences.

EXAMPLES

~~It can be clearly seen that~~ ᴛ/he science fiction novel *Two Moons Over*

Tuvald is descended from the movie *Shane*.   __2__

Author John White has said that ~~the movie~~ *Shane* ~~it~~ was his favorite

movie as a child.   __1__

1. ~~The main reason why~~ *Shane* appealed to White ~~was~~ it~~s~~ por-   *mainly because*

   tray~~al of~~ *ed* a boy who learns the meaning of courage and honor.   __2__

2. White explained his long fascination with Shane: ~~by saying,~~

   "The boy has two role models, his father and Shane the gun-

   fighter. Both men are courageous and honorable, but they

   demonstrate these qualities in different ways. The boy has to

   learn that in essence the two men are alike."   __2__

3. A similar dilemma confronts the boy in *Two Moons Over Tu-*

   vald. In a pastoral setting ~~of green fields and rolling hills,~~ the

   boy grows up with Andrew, his father and a rancher, and

   Shane Cleaveland, a weary hired gun.   __1__

4. Like his namesake, Shane has built his life around his prowess

   with a gun, ~~(he is very good with it)~~ but at this point in his

   life he recognizes the limits of his power.   __2__

5. Shane knows that Andrew's quiet persistence eventually will
   prove stronger than any power based on guns~~ or weapons~~/ _____2_____

6. Andrew and the boy ~~together~~ have established a small ranch
   on Tuvald's First Moon where they raise Tuvaldian sheep. _____1_____

7. The boy finds Shane Cleaveland lying beside a creek‸ uncon-
   scious and ~~wounded—he has been~~ shot in the shoulder—and
   brings him home. _____2_____

8. At first the reticent Shane ~~who does not like to talk~~ reveals
   nothing of his past. _____1_____

9. But the perceptive boy ~~who notices everything~~ and his father
   realize that Shane's laser guns mark him as a gunfighter. _____1_____

10. ~~Disregarding Shane's past~~/ Andrew and the boy ask him no
    questions about his past and accept him as part of the family. _____1_____

11. On Tuvald the wealthy landowner Max Waters plans to force
    the sheepherders off the First Moon so he can continue to
    graze his vast herd of Tuvaldian musk-ox there. Water ~~is~~
    ~~in~~ agree*s*ment‸ with the ancient belief that sheep and musk-ox
    cannot share a range. _____2_____

12. Like most characters in the novel, Waters does not say much.
    He ~~says~~/ *believes that* "Talking ain't doing/" ~~And he goes on to say/~~ *and that* "You
    can't talk a sheepherder to death." _____2_____

Wordiness and Needless Repetition   Exercise 21–1 (continued)

13. Having given up on talk, Waters can only try force, so he

    sends two gangs of androids to attack Andrew, the boy, and

    Shane on the First Moon. The first gang ~~is to~~ kill the sheep.

    The second gang ~~is to~~ evict and/or kill all sheepherders.   2

14. Andrew confronts the androids and tries to reason with them.

    But they ~~have their orders and~~ attack.   2

15. ~~With regard to this scene~~ Shane feels as though he has lived

    through ~~it~~ *this scene* many times before.   2

16. He has enjoyed his peaceful months with Andrew and the boy,

    but now he must revert to his old way of life to save them. ~~and~~

    ~~to prevent their being hurt/~~   2

17. With laser guns ablaze he defeats the androids, *which* ~~and in doing~~

    ~~so he~~ confuses the boy.   2

18. The boy watched his father be defeated. ~~And~~ *J* then he watched

    Shane triumph. Now he is tempted to see his father as a

    failure.   2

19. Ironically, Max Waters helps clarify the issue. ~~He~~ *by* kidnap ~~s~~ *ping* the

    boy. ~~and~~ Andrew is the first to fight Max for the boy's life.   2

20. ~~Despite the fact that~~ *although* Shane has to step in again to save Andrew

    and the boy, the boy now understands that his father's cour-

    age and honor equal Shane's.   2

22

Do not omit a word or phrase necessary to the meaning of the sentence.

22a Be careful to include all necessary articles, pronouns, conjunctions, and prepositions. Revised omissions are indicated by a caret (∧) in the following examples.

(1) Do not omit a needed article before a noun or another adjective.

In general, Americans find astrology a silly diversion and ∧*an* unpleasant reminder of the superstitious past. [The article *a* precedes a word that begins with a consonant; *an* precedes a word that begins with a vowel.]

(2) Do not omit necessary prepositions or conjunctions.

The type ∧*of* observatory usually seen in this country is a large white dome. [*Type* is not an adjective here.]

Most Americans do not believe ∧*in* or care for astrology. [*Believe for* is not idiomatic phrasing.]

Do not omit *that* when it is needed as a subordinating conjunction.

We learned ∧*that* even the slightest distortion of the mirrors or lenses will ruin the telescope's performance. [*That* introduces the clause that functions as the complement of the sentence.]

The guide said ∧*that* Mt. Hopkins' newest observatory uses six large mirrors to capture light. [Here the conjunction *that* signals the beginning of an indirect quotation.]

That may be omitted when the meaning of the sentence would be clear at first reading without it.

We realized the observatory was another example of the benefits of computers.

22b Include necessary verbs and helping verbs.

been

For decades Arizona's Kitt Peak and Hawaii's Mauna Lea have ^ and will continue

to be the major observatory sites in the United States.   [*Have continued to be* is

an error in tense.]

22c Include all words necessary to complete a comparison.

as

Stargazing is as old ^ or older than any sport.

about those of

Most Americans know more about the features of Mars than ^ any other planet.

22d When used as intensifiers, *so, such,* and *too* should usually be followed by a completing phrase or clause.

There's **too** much going on in there for them [Saturn's rings] to have remained stable for 4.6 billion years.   —PETER GOLDREICH

On Venus, rocks become **so** hot that they melt.

Deduct 6 2/3 for each blank incorrectly filled.

Omission of Necessary Words   Exercise 22-1

NAME _____ SCORE _____

DIRECTIONS   In the following sentences, insert the words that are needed to make the meaning or the grammatical construction complete. In the blank, write the words that you have added.

EXAMPLE   *other*
Mars continues to fascinate us more than any ∧ planet.   *other*

1. The orbiters and landers of the 1970s and 1980s crushed any
   when
   hope of our finding life on Mars ∧ they revealed barren deserts

   swept by raging dust storms.   *when*
                                    may
2. Nevertheless, human visitors of the future ∧ find an abundant

   supply of water.   *may*

3. The geologists and atmospheric scientists who are analyzing
                                    that
   the data from the Mariner and Viking probes agree ∧ Mars is

   wet.   *that*
                beneath   *beneath*
4. Rivers may surge deep ∧ the planet's shifting sands.
                                    to
5. Mars may once have experienced flooding and ice ages similar ∧

   those that changed the face of Earth.   *to*

6. What evidence is there for a wetter age in Mars' past? If water
                        did it go
   was abundant, why did it disappear and where ∧?   *did it go*

7. Mars today has light ground frosts, thin clouds and hazes, and
   its
   ice on ∧ polar caps.   *its*
                                    the
8. But only a slight amount of water vapor can be found in ∧ atmo-

   sphere.   *the*

9. The frigid climate, −123 degrees at dawn and −24 *degrees* at mid-

   day, does not permit water to exist on the surface.   *degrees*

10. But the Martian surface is scarred *if* by glaciers and flooding.   *if*

11. Therefore, scientists believe *that* in the past the climate must have

    been warmer.   *that*

12. Scientists have for some time *believed* and continue to believe that a

    shift in Mars' relationship to the Sun could have altered the

    climate from warm to frigid.   *believed*

13. We now know that as Mars rotates on its axis, its tilt toward

    the Sun can vary as much *as* 20 degrees.   *as*

14. In contrast, Earth's tilt toward the Sun varies by no more than
    2 degrees
    ~~two~~.   *2 degrees*

15. Climatic changes on Earth occur over periods of tens of thou-

    sands of years, but they may occur much more rapidly on
    because
    Mars the change in the tilt toward the sun can be relatively

    quick and extreme.   *because*

SENTENCE UNITY   su 23

23

In a unified sentence, ideas within the sentence are clearly related; excessive detail, mixed metaphors, and mixed constructions do not obscure the ideas; and subjects and predicates fit together logically.

23a Establish a clear relationship between the clauses in a sentence; develop unrelated ideas in separate sentences.

When you write a compound sentence, you suggest that the ideas in the two main clauses are closely related. Similarly, when you write a complex sentence, you make your reader expect a relationship between the ideas in the main and subordinate clauses.

UNCLEAR   Nearby stars may contain other civilizations, and the star nearest to our Sun is 25 trillion miles away, too far for us to travel.

CLEAR   Although nearby stars may contain other civilizations, the star nearest to our Sun is 25 trillion miles away, too far for us to travel.

UNCLEAR   Scientists have pieced together a picture of the origin of life on Earth, and no living forms existed on our planet in its infancy.

CLEAR   Scientists have pieced together a picture of the origins of life on Earth. No living forms existed on our planet in its infancy.

23b Avoid excessive or poorly ordered detail.

Too much subordination or detail, even if relevant, will obscure the central focus of a sentence.

UNCLEAR   No concrete evidence exists for belief in UFOs, but if, in fact, some UFOs have originated beyond the Earth, science has something to say about them although they cannot have come from another planet circling our Sun, because no intelligent life exists in this solar system except on Earth, making us conclude that UFOs have come from other star systems.

CLEAR   No concrete evidence exists for belief in UFOs, but if, in fact, some UFOs have originated beyond the Earth, science has something to say about them. They cannot have come from another planet circling our Sun because no intelligent life exists in this solar system except on Earth. We must conclude that UFOs have come from other star systems.

23c Be aware of mixed metaphors and mixed constructions.

UNCLEAR   Immanuel Velikovsky, the author of *Worlds in Collision*, has been described as a grain of sand crying out in the forest.

CLEAR   Immanuel Velikovsky, the author of *Worlds in Collision*, has been described as a voice in the wilderness.

UNCLEAR   When Velikovsky hypothesized prehistoric collisions between planets in our solar system angered many other scientists.

CLEAR   When Velikovsky hypothesized prehistoric collisions between planets in our solar system, he angered many other scientists.

OR

Velikovsky's hypothesis of prehistoric collisions between planets in our solar system angered many other scientists.

23d Avoid faulty predication.

Make the subject and predicate of a sentence fit together grammatically and logically.

ILLOGICAL   UFOs are a serious controversy today.   [This sentence contains a mismatch between the plural subject, *UFOs*, and its singular complement, *controversy*. There is also a problem with logic: *UFOs* does not equal *controversy*, as the linking verb, *are*, suggests.]

LOGICAL   The existence of UFOs is often debated today.   [The *existence* of UFOs can be debated.]

ILLOGICAL   The source of much of the controversy is because no scientific proof supports their existence.   [*Source* does not equal *because*, as the linking verb, *is*, suggests. A *because* clause serves as a modifier, not as a basic sentence part.]

LOGICAL   Because no scientific proof of UFOs exists, their existence is often debated.

OR

The source of much of the controversy is the absence of scientific proof that UFOs exist.

ILLOGICAL   In the emotional debate over UFOs causes some scientists to lose sight of their major goal—knowledge.   [The writer has mistaken the object of a preposition, *debate*, for the subject of the sentence.]

LOGICAL   The emotional debate over UFOs causes some scientists to lose sight of their major goal—knowledge.   [Here *debate* is the subject.]

23e Define a word or an expression clearly and precisely.

The use of forms of the linking verb *be*—*is, are, was, can, be,* and so on—frequently leads to faulty predication, particularly when the linking verb is followed by *when* or *where*. By substituting a nonlinking verb such as *occur* or *is found*, you can often eliminate the error in unity or logic.

ILLOGICAL   An example of Velikovsky's theory is when the biblical Red Sea was parted by the gravitational pull of a passing comet.

LOGICAL   Velikovsky's theory explains the parting of the biblical Red Sea as the effect of a passing comet.

OR

An example of Velikovsky's theory is the parting of the biblical Red Sea by the gravitational pull of a passing comet.

Deduct 4 for each blank incorrectly filled and 4 for each incorrect revision. (Revisions will vary.)

Unity in Sentence Structure   Exercise 23–1

NAME _____ SCORE _____

DIRECTIONS   In the blanks, write *a*, *b*, *c*, *d*, or *e* to indicate whether the chief difficulty in each sentence is (a) an unclear relationship among ideas, (b) excessive detail and subordination, (c) mixed metaphors and mixed constructions, (d) an illogical combination of subject and predicate, or (e) unclear or imprecise definitions. Revise the sentences to make them effective.

EXAMPLE
Because some scientists suppressed Immanuel Velikovsky's work, ~~is~~

~~why~~ he lived many years in obscurity.   *e*

1. Recent major collisions between Saturn and Venus were al-

   leged in a popular book, *Worlds in Collision*, published in

   1950 by a psychiatrist named Immanuel Velikovsky. *He* ~~who~~ pro-

   posed that many ancient catastrophes could have resulted

   from the effects of a passing comet, the comet eventually com-

   ing to rest in an orbit around the Sun as the planet Venus.   *b*

2. Velikovsky's climb up the ladder of success was *interrupted* ~~nipped in the~~

   ~~bud.~~   *c*

3. Velikovsky explained the development of our solar system as

   resulting from a series of planetary collisions. ~~but~~ Venus and

   Jupiter have completely different chemical compositions, so

   Venus could not have once been a part of Jupiter.   *a*

4. Velikovsky argued that Venus somehow had been ejected from

   Jupiter to become a kind of billiard ball ricocheting around

   the solar system, but *that seems unlikely because* Jupiter is composed almost entirely of

   hydrogen.   *a*

5. When the comet Venus passed, stopped the Earth's rotation. _C_

   it (or the comet Venus's passing stopped....) [inserted above "stopped"]

6. Passing over the Earth, Venus caused a variety of natural phe-

   nomena, including extensive volcanism and flooding—and the

   parting of the Red Sea which allowed Moses to escape with

   the Israelites, and Edmund Halley first explained an historical   _b_

   was the person to [insertion]

   event as having been caused by a comet.

7. Halley argued that the cause of Noah's flood was when a large

   comet passed near the Earth.   _e_

   ing [insertion above "passed"]

8. Halley's theory, like Velikovsky's, is stimulating but which is

   unlikely.   _C_

9. One book I read about Velikovsky believes in planetary colli-

   The author of (or In one book... the author believes) [insertion]

   sions—but not in recent planetary collisions.   _d_

10. An example of why scientists do not believe Velikovsky or Hal-

    One   who es [insertions]

    ley is Carl Sagan.   _d_

11. But when Sagan discusses Velikovsky demonstrates Sagan's re-

    he   his [insertions]

    gard for free speech.   _d_

12. Sagan argues that because some scientists who disagreed with

    Velikovsky did not give them the right to suppress his views.   _d_

    have [insertion]

24

Use subordination to relate ideas concisely and effectively. Use coordination to give ideas equal emphasis.

Subordination is the method good writers most often use to extend their sentences and to vary the beginnings of sentences. (Subordinated additions to the sentence base are italicized in the following paragraph.)

> Isaac Newton concluded *that there was no future for the type of telescope used by Galileo. Called the refractor,* it relies on a series of lenses to collect and focus the incoming light. But the design of lenses is fraught with problems, and almost a century passed *after Newton's comment before optical technicians could build a large telescope of this type.*

As this example shows, grammatically subordinate structures may contain very important ideas.

The following sentences demonstrate *coordination*, which gives equal grammatical emphasis to two or more ideas. (See also **12a**, **12c**, and section **26**.)

> Bigger and sometimes better telescopes allowed astronomers to collect more and more light from objects farther and farther away, thereby extending our ability to see and to understand our surroundings.   [Coordination gives equal emphasis to each word in a pair—*bigger* and *better, more* and *more, farther* and *farther*— and to a pair of phrases—*to see* and *to understand.*]
>
> Scientists used the improved telescopes to see more of the universe, and they used calculus to analyze what they saw.   [Here, coordination gives equal emphasis to each of two main clauses—*scientists used telescopes* and *they used calculus.*]

24a Instead of writing a series of short, choppy sentences, choose one idea for the sentence base, or main clause, and subordinate other ideas.

Because it stands apart from other sentences in a paragraph, a short sentence is often used for emphasis (see section **29h**). But if the paragraph contains only short, choppy sentences, no single idea stands out, and the primary effect is monotony.

SHORT AND CHOPPY	Galileo invented a telescope. It is called a refractor. It used a series of lenses to collect and focus incoming light.
SUBORDINATION	Galileo's invention, the refractor telescope, used a series of lenses to collect and focus incoming light. [The subordinated part is an appositive.]
SHORT AND CHOPPY	Technicians in the seventeenth century could not build good large lenses. Newton decided to build a different type of telescope. His telescope used a large mirror to collect and focus light.

SUBORDINATION   Because technicians in the seventeenth century could not build good large lenses, Newton decided to build a different type of telescope that used a large mirror to collect and focus light. [The subordinated parts are an adverb clause and an adjective clause.]

24b Instead of linking sentences primarily with coordinating conjunctions such as *and, so,* or *but* or with conjunctive adverbs such as *however* and *therefore,* extend most sentences through subordination.

Coordination of main clauses is helpful in developing a varied style because it gives equal emphasis to separate ideas.

Newton's first reflector telescopes were not much more powerful than Galileo's refractors, but later in the century William Herschel of England was building reflectors with metal mirrors four feet in diameter.

But when ideas have a time, place, descriptive, or cause and effect relationship, use subordination to show the connection between clauses while emphasizing the main idea.

STRINGY   William Herschel could not afford a good telescope, so he decided to build his own.

RELATED   Because William Herschel could not afford a good telescope, he decided to build his own.   [shows cause and effect]

STRINGY   Herschel needed to avoid the technical difficulties of making glass lenses, so he replaced the glass lenses with metal mirrors.

RELATED   To avoid the technical difficulties of making glass lenses, Herschel replaced the glass lenses with metal mirrors.   [shows cause and effect]

24c Avoid faulty or excessive subordination. (See also 23a and b.)

If you overdo or overlap subordination, your reader will have difficulty deciding what the sentence base, or main clause, is.

UNCLEAR   On March 13, 1781, William Herschel, who like his peers had assumed that only six planets orbited the Sun, the six that are visible to the naked eye, but who now had the advantage of his large reflector telescope, discovered Uranus, the first planet discovered in modern times.

CLEAR   Like his peers, William Herschel had assumed that only the six planets visible to the naked eye orbited the Sun. But on March 13, 1781, while peering through his large reflector telescope, Herschel discovered Uranus, the first planet discovered in modern times.

ILLOGICAL   Because scientists were unable to predict Uranus's orbit, another as yet undiscovered planet was distorting its orbit.   [The undiscovered planet distorted the orbit and prevented prediction, not the other way around.]

LOGICAL   Because another as yet undiscovered planet was distorting Uranus's orbit, scientists were unable to predict its orbit.

Deduct 20 for each incorrect sentence. (Answers will vary.)

Subordination and Coordination for Effectiveness   Exercise 24–1

NAME _____ SCORE _____

DIRECTIONS   Combine each of the following groups of short, choppy sentences into one effective sentence. Express the most important idea in the main clause and put lesser ideas in subordinate clauses, phrases, or words. Use coordination when ideas should be given equal emphasis.

> EXAMPLE
> Asteroids are usually discovered photographically. Patrol cameras automatically scan the skies. Asteroids show up in the film as short bright streaks.
>
> *Patrol cameras that automatically scan the skies usually discover asteroids, which show up in the film as short bright streaks.*

1. On the night of January 1, 1801, Giuseppe Piazzi found a tiny planet. Piazzi was an Italian astronomer. The new planet was only 480 miles in diameter. Piazzi named the planet Ceres.

   On the night of January 1, 1801, the Italian astronomer Giuseppe Piazzi found a tiny, new planet only 480 miles in diameter which he named Ceres.

2. Ceres was the forerunner of a group of minor planets. They usually are called "asteroids" or "planetoids." *Planetoid* is a more accurate name than asteroid. *Planetoid* means "like a planet" and *asteroid* means "like a star."

   Ceres was the forerunner of a group of minor planets usually called "asteroids" or "planetoids," although planetoid (meaning "like a planet") is a more accurate name than asteroid (meaning "like a star").

3. The asteroids vary in size. Ceres is the largest, and others are the size of flying mountains.

   Ceres is the largest of the asteroids, which vary in size and often are the size of flying mountains.

4. A 200-pound man standing on Eros would weigh 6 ounces. Eros's surface area is about equal to that of Pennsylvania. Its gravitation is correspondingly weak.

   Eros's surface area is about equal to that of Pennsylvania, and its gravitation is correspondingly weak, which would cause a 200-pound man standing on Eros to weigh 6 ounces.

5. The asteroid Eros changes in brilliance over a period of time. Apparently it is an oval about 25 miles long. It tumbles over and over as it orbits the Sun. It is brighter when we see the long side.

   The asteroid Eros, apparently an oval about 25 miles long that tumbles and changes in brilliance as it orbits the Sun, becomes brighter when we see the long side.

Deduct 20 for each incorrect sentence. (Answers will vary.)

Subordination and Coordination for Effectiveness   Exercise 24–2

NAME _____ SCORE _____

DIRECTIONS   Rewrite each of the following stringy sentences to make one effective sentence. Express the most important idea in the main clause, and put lesser ideas in subordinate clauses, phrases, or words. Use coordination when ideas should be given equal emphasis.

EXAMPLE

The moon completes its cycle of phases during one trip around the Earth, and the trip takes about 27 days, and in that trip, the Moon makes one slow turn on its own axis, so the same face of the Moon is always turned toward the Earth.

The same face of the Moon is always turned toward the Earth because in the time that the Moon takes to complete its cycle of phases — one trip around the Earth of about 27 days — it only completes one turn on its own axis.

1. The Lunik III photographs seem crude in comparison to today's brilliantly clear television transmissions from space, and we are accustomed now to thinking about the Moon as explored terrain, but before October, 1959, the far side of the Moon was a mysterious, private place visited only by human imagination.

We are accustomed now to thinking about the Moon as an explored terrain and to viewing space through brilliantly clear television transmissions, but prior to October, 1959, and those Lunik III crude photographs, the far side of the moon was a mysterious, private place visited only by human imagination.

2. The Russians launched a space vehicle called Lunik III in October of 1959, and they timed the launch to arrive at the Moon during the new phase; during the new phase the Sun illuminates the far side of the Moon, so Lunik III could photograph the far side for the first time.

During the new phase of the Moon the Sun illuminates the Moon's far side, so the Russians timed the launch of Lunik III in October of 1959 to permit it to photograph the far side for the first time.

3. Devices built into Lunik III aimed the camera at the Moon, and at the proper instant the film was exposed, and other devices then processed and developed the film.

Devices built into Lunik III aimed the camera at the Moon, exposed the film at the proper instant, and then processed and developed the film.

4. Lunik III passed about 40,000 miles from the far side of the Moon, and during the flight about 89 percent of the far side was illuminated, so the photographs could have revealed much unknown landscape.

Because Lunik III passed about 40,000 miles from the Moon's far side, 89 percent of which was illuminated, the photographs could have revealed much unknown landscape.

5. Unfortunately, transmission to Earth lowered the quality of the photographs, so the resulting black and white images were coarse and sometimes blurred, but they showed the Moon's far side to be more rugged and mountainous than the side we see.

Although transmission to Earth lowered the quality of the photographs by coarsening and blurring them, they showed the Moon's far side to be more rugged and mountainous than the side we see.

Subordination and Coordination for Effectiveness   Exercise 24–3

NAME _____ SCORE _____

DIRECTIONS   Rewrite the following paragraph, using subordination to eliminate the short, choppy sentences and the stringy compound sentences. Use coordination when ideas should be emphasized equally. (Not every sentence must be changed.) You will notice the improvement in style that proper subordination and coordination achieve if you read aloud first the original version of the paragraph and then your revision.

¹The whole idea of changes in heavenly bodies is modern. ²Aristotle believed the heavens to be perfect and unchanging. ³Other Greek philosophers agreed with Aristotle. ⁴The only change, corruption, or decay occurred on Earth. ⁵This seemed only common sense. ⁶The Greeks looked at the Moon, and it never changed, and they looked at the stars, and they never changed. ⁷From generation to generation, from century to century, only the Earth changed. ⁸Of course, comets did appear and disappear. ⁹They seemed to come from nowhere and then they disappeared. ¹⁰Apparently they were a different sort of heavenly body. ¹¹Perhaps, the ancients reasoned, they were meant to be signs. ¹²Comets came to represent omens of evil or disaster. ¹³Aristotle tried to explain comets as belonging somehow to the atmosphere of Earth. ¹⁴They were not permanent heavenly bodies, so, he reasoned, they must be earthly in origin. ¹⁵Aristotle's view of comets prevailed for hundreds of years. ¹⁶Then, in 1577, Tycho Brahe discovered that comets lay far beyond the Moon. ¹⁷They did not belong to Earth's atmosphere. ¹⁸Brahe made his discoveries mathematically. ¹⁹These mathematics forced people to recognize change and imperfection in the heavens.

REVISION

REVISION (CONTINUED)

25

Place modifiers carefully to indicate clearly their relationships with the words they modify.

An adverb clause can usually be moved to various places in a sentence without affecting the meaning or clarity of the sentence.

> *When Einstein formulated the equation E = MC²*, there was no way to check the computations.
> There was no way to check the computations *when Einstein formulated the equation E = MC²*.
> There was no way, *when Einstein formulated the equation E = MC²*, to check the computations.

The movement of the adverb clause affects the punctuation of the sentence and the part of the sentence to be emphasized (see also section **29**). But the sentence has the same meaning and that meaning is clear whether the adverb clause is an introductory, interrupting, or concluding addition.

Other sentence parts may not be moved around as easily, as the following discussions of various modifiers will show.

25a Avoid needless separation of related parts of a sentence.

(1) In standard written English, adverbs such as *almost, only, just, hardly, nearly,* and *merely* are usually placed immediately before the words they modify.

MISPLACED	Einstein *nearly* devoted ten years of his life to developing the theory.
BETTER	Einstein devoted *nearly* ten years of his life to developing the theory.
MISPLACED	Special relativity *only* deals with measurements of time and space made by observers moving at uniform velocity.
BETTER	Special relativity deals *only* with measurements of time and space made by observers moving at uniform velocity.

(2) Prepositional phrases are almost always placed immediately after the words they modify.

MISPLACED	Grossman's help enabled Einstein to imagine the geometry of curved space *with the math problems of special relativity.*
CLEAR	Grossman's help *with the math problems of special relativity* enabled Einstein to imagine the geometry of curved space.

As long as no awkwardness results, a prepositional phrase can be moved to different places in a sentence for variety. (See also **30b**.)

Einstein completely changed, *with the geometry of curved space*, our concept of gravity. [The *with* phrase modifies *changed*.]

With the geometry of curved space, Einstein completely changed our concept of gravity.

Einstein completely changed our concept of gravity *with the geometry of curved space*.

(3) Adjective clauses should be placed near the words they modify.

Unlike the adverb clause, discussed at the beginning of this section, an adjective clause cannot be moved around freely in a sentence without changing the meaning or causing a lack of clarity.

CLEAR   Proving the theory of special relativity, *which proposes that energy and mass are interchangeable*, is possible with particle accelerators.

UNCLEAR   Proving, *which proposes that energy and mass are interchangeable*, the theory of special relativity is possible with particle accelerators. [The placement of the adjective clause now suggests that *proving proposes*.]

UNCLEAR   Proving the theory of special relativity is possible with particle accelerators, *which proposes that energy and mass are interchangeable*. [Here, *proving the theory with particle accelerators* seems to propose that energy and mass are interchangeable.]

For the sentence to make sense, the adjective clause must be placed immediately after the word it modifies. Other examples would be

MISPLACED   Einstein received help from Grossman, *who had needed Marcell Grossman's help to pass a math class as a student*, in formulating the math for special relativity.

CLEAR   Einstein, *who had needed Marcell Grossman's help to pass a math class as a student*, received help from Grossman in formulating the math for special relativity.

MISPLACED   A student seems unlikely to succeed as a physicist *who needs help with math*.

CLEAR   A student *who needs help with math* seems unlikely to succeed as a physicist.

(4) Avoid "squinting" constructions—modifiers that may refer to either a preceding or a following word.

SQUINTING   The physicist Arthur Eddington was asked *on May 29, 1919*, to study a solar eclipse. [The adverbial phrase can modify either *was asked* or *to study*.]

CLEAR   The physicist Arthur Eddington was asked to study a solar eclipse *on May 29, 1919*.

OR

The physicist Arthur Eddington was asked to study the *May 29, 1919*, solar eclipse.

(5) The parts of the sentence base should not be awkwardly separated, nor should an infinitive be awkwardly split.

AWKWARD   The theory of general relativity, *after its publication in 1916 as a supplement to the theory of special relativity,* **helped** to explain Einstein's new concept of gravity.   [The verb is awkwardly separated from its subject.]

BETTER   *After its publication in 1916 as a supplement to the theory of special relativity,* the theory of general relativity **helped** to explain Einstein's new concept of gravity.

AWKWARD   Einstein intended **to,** *with the theory of general relativity,* **eliminate** the concept of gravitation as a force.   [The prepositional phrase awkwardly splits the infinitive *to eliminate.*]

BETTER   *With the theory of general relativity* Einstein intended **to eliminate** the concept of gravitation as a force.

Although the awkward splitting of an infinitive should be avoided, sometimes an infinitive split by a single modifier is acceptable and sounds natural.

In 1919 scientists were able to *accurately* measure Mercury's orbit as a test of Einstein's ideas about curved space.

25b Avoid dangling modifiers.

Dangling modifiers are most often dangling verbal phrases that do not refer clearly and logically to a word or phrase in the sentence base. To correct a dangling modifier, either rearrange the words in the sentence base so that the modifier clearly refers to the right word, or add the missing words that will make the modifier clear and logical.

DANGLING   *Blotting out the Sun's rays,* the scientists were able to study the effect of the Sun's gravity on light rays from other stars.   [The verbal phrase illogically modifies *scientists.*]

CLEAR   *Blotting out the Sun's rays,* the eclipse enabled scientists to study the effect of the Sun's gravity on light rays from other stars.   [The verbal phrase logically modifies *eclipse.*]

DANGLING   *Thinking about light as if it had mass,* the theory of general relativity predicted that the Sun's gravitation would bend passing light rays. [The verbal phrase illogically modifies *theory.*]

CLEAR   *Thinking about light as if it had mass,* Einstein predicted in his theory of general relativity that the Sun's gravitation would bend passing light rays.   [The verbal phrase logically modifies *Einstein.*]

OR

Einstein, *thinking about light as if it had mass,* predicted in his theory of general relativity that the Sun's gravitation would bend passing light rays.

Deduct 5 1/2 for each blank incorrectly filled and for each incorrectly formed sentence. (Sentences will vary.)

Placement of Modifiers

Exercise 25-1

NAME _____ SCORE _____

DIRECTIONS   Below each of the following sentences is a word, phrase, or clause that, if inserted correctly in the sentence, could serve as a clear and logical modifier. Write *1* in the blank if the modifier can be inserted in only one place in the sentence and *2* if it can be inserted in two or more places. Then write the sentence with the modifier placed in all the positions where it will not cause an unclear or awkward sentence.

EXAMPLE
Einstein's equations pointed to an unstable universe.

which were published in 1917   *1*

Einstein's equations, which were published in 1917, pointed to an unstable universe.

1. Among other astronomers, the Dutch astronomer Willem de Sitter had already solved the equations.

   which indicated that the universe was either expanding or collapsing   *1*

   Among other astronomers, the Dutch astronomer... solved the equations which indicated ... collapsing.

2. Einstein wanted his equations to show the universe to be stable and unchanging.

   however   *2*

   However, Einstein... unchanging. Einstein wanted his equations, however... unchanging. Einstein, however, wanted... unchanging. Einstein wanted, however, ... unchanging.

3. There was one way out of his predicament.

   only   *1*

   There was only one way out of his predicament.

4. He altered his equations.

in order to make general relativity fit a stable model of the

universe   _2_

In order to make ... universe, he altered his equations.
He altered his equations in order to make ... universe.
He, in order ... universe, altered his equations.

5. He referred to his change in the equations as a "slight modifi-

cation."

adding a figure he called the cosmological constant   _2_

Adding a figure ... constant, he referred to ... "slight
   modification."
He referred to his change in the equations, adding a
   figure ... constant, as a "slight modification."

6. These "delta terms" were really unnecessary.

as they were called   _1_

These "delta terms," as they were called, were
really unnecessary.

7. A Russian mathematician, Alexander Friedman, solved Ein-

stein's equations both with and without the delta terms.

in 1922   _2_

A Russian ... delta terms in 1922.
In 1922, a Russian ... delta terms.
A Russian mathematician, Alexander Friedman in 1922
   solved ... delta terms.
A Russian mathematician, Alexander Friedman solved in
   1922 ... delta terms.
A Russian mathematician ... solved Einstein's equations in
   1922 ... delta terms.

8. Like Einstein's his solution with the delta terms produced a

static universe.

that remained the same forever   _1_

Like Einstein's, his solution ... produced a static universe
   that remained the same forever.

MISPLACED PARTS, DANGLING MODIFIERS

Deduct 10 for each incorrect sentence. (Answers will vary.)

Placement of Modifiers

Exercise 25–2

NAME _____ SCORE _____

DIRECTIONS   Rewrite each of the following sentence bases so that the modifier that follows it is clearly and logically related to a word or phrase in the sentence base. Or expand the modifier so that it is clear by itself when it is attached to the sentence base. (Include examples of both methods in your answers.) Be sure to capitalize and to punctuate the modifier correctly when you attach it to the sentence base (see **12b** and **12d**).

EXAMPLE

Friedman solved the equations and actually created two models of an expanding universe.

omitting the delta terms

After omitting the delta terms, Friedman solved the equations and actually created two models of an expanding universe. or
Because he omitted the delta terms, Friedman solved the equations and actually created two models of an expanding universe.

1. The first model describes an infinite universe that will expand forever.
   rejected by most scientists today

   The first model, which is rejected by most scientists today, describes an infinite universe that will expand forever.

2. In the second model the expansion of the universe will one day cease.
   approved by most modern cosmologists

   In the second model, which is approved by most modern cosmologists, the expansion of the universe will one day cease.

3. A balloon with spots on it can help you visualize an expanding universe.
   representing galaxies

   A balloon with spots on it, representing galaxies, can help you visualize an expanding universe.

4. The galaxies move apart from each other.
   blowing up the balloon

   As you blow up the balloon, the galaxies move apart from each other.

Copyright © 1990 by Harcourt Brace Jovanovich, Inc. All rights reserved.

241

5. That the universe is expanding was confirmed by Edwin Hubble by 1929. measuring distances between galaxies with a telescope

   By measuring distances between galaxies with a telescope, Edwin Hubble had confirmed by 1929 that the universe is expanding.

6. Physicists began tracing back in time the expansion of the universe. wanting to know what initiated the expansion

   Physicists who wanted to know what initiated the expansion began tracing back in time the expansion of the universe.

7. They were asking the question, "What happened at the very beginning of the universe?"
   being confronted

   They were confronting the question," What happened at the very beginning of the universe ?"

8. Two of the physicists, Stephen Hawking and Roger Penrose, intended to prove that the universe had started from a "singularity."
   a beginning in which all matter was concentrated in a single point

   Two of the physicists, Stephen Hawking and Roger Penrose, intended to prove that the universe had started from a "singularity," a beginning in which all matter was concentrated in a single point.

9. A star may also create a "singularity."
   collapsing in on itself

   By collapsing in on itself, a star may also create a "singularity." *or*
   A star may also create a "singularity" by collapsing in on itself.

10. Penrose and Hawking decided to investigate the singularity of a collapsed star.
    a star's singularity resembling the universe's singularity

    Because a star's singularity would resemble the universe's singularity, Penrose and Hawking decided to investigate the singularity of a collapsed star.

26

Use parallel structure to give grammatically balanced treatment to items in a list or series and to parts of a compound construction.

Parallel structure means that a grammatical form is repeated—that an adjective is balanced by another adjective, a verb phrase by another verb phrase, a subordinate clause by another subordinate clause, and so on. Although ineffective repetition results in poor style (see section **21**), repetition to create parallel structure can result in very effective writing. The repetition of a sentence construction makes ideas clear to the reader, emphasizes those ideas (see section **29**), and provides coherence between the sentences in a paragraph (see section **32**).

Connectives such as *and*, *but*, and *or* often indicate that the writer intends to use parallel structure to balance the items in a list or series or the parts of a compound construction.

> LIST OR SERIES   The mission of the NASA satellite International Cometary Explorer (ICE) has three stages: *study* of solar flares, *flight* through the tail of Comet Giacobini-Zinner, **and** *study* of the solar wind ahead of Halley's Comet.

> COMPOUND PARTS   The satellite *has studied* solar flares for nearly four years and *has* recently *completed* its flight through Comet Giacobini-Zinner's tail **but** *has* not *completed* its study of Comet Halley.

26a To achieve parallel structure, balance a verb with a verb, a prepositional phrase with a prepositional phrase, a subordinate clause with a subordinate clause, and so on.

The following examples are written in outline form to make the parallel structure, or lack of it, more noticeable. Correct parallel structure is indicated by vertical parallel lines, repeated words are printed in italics, and connectives are printed in boldface.

> AWKWARD   Some critics believe that the designers of the satellite's mission
>   seek publicity
> rather than
>   seeking valuable scientific knowledge.

> PARALLEL   Some critics believe that the designers of the satellite's mission seek
> ‖ *publicity*
> **rather than**
> ‖ valuable scientific *knowledge*.

> AWKWARD   Despite the value of the satellite's solar research, all that people
>   read about in newspapers,
>   hear about on radio,

and
> what they watch on television

are the satellite's encounters with Comet Giacobini-Zinner and Halley's Comet.

PARALLEL   Despite the value of the satellite's solar research, all that people
‖ *read* about in newspapers,
‖ *hear* about on radio,
and
‖ *watch* on television
are the satellite's encounters with Comet Giacobini-Zinner and Halley's Comet.

26b To make the parallel clear, repeat a preposition, an article, the *to* of the infinitive, or the introductory word of a long phrase or clause. (Repeated elements of this type are printed in italics.)

Certainly the satellite's mission has been saddled
‖ *with* providing information about one rather obscure comet
as well as
‖ *with* furnishing information about Comet Halley that will not interest the average person.

However, proponents of the mission describe the goals of the comet encounters as clearly scientific:
‖ *to* provide the first scientific study
   ‖ *of* a comet's tail
   and
   ‖ *of* the solar wind in front of a comet,
not
‖ *to* seek any publicity that attends the study of comets.

Proponents also point out
‖ *that the* entire mission is relatively inexpensive ($5 million)
and
‖ *that the* study of comets will provide information valuable to later, more expensive probes.

26c In addition to coordinating conjunctions, connectives like *both . . . and, either . . . or, neither . . . nor, not only . . . but also,* and *as well as*—and expressions like *not* and *rather than* which introduce negative phrasing—are used to connect parallel structure. (These connectives are printed in boldface below.)

The varied mission of the ICE satellite is the result
   not only
‖ of careful planning
   but also
‖ of luck.

Parallel Structure   Exercise 26–1

NAME _____ SCORE _____

DIRECTIONS   Make an outline, like the outlines used in this section, of the parallel parts
of each of the following sentences.

> EXAMPLE
> British Aerospace has designed an "aerospace plane" that not only will boost pay-
>
> loads into Earth orbits but also will cost far less than the American shuttle.
>
> *British Aerospace has designed an "aerospace plane" that*
> *   not only*
> * || will boost payloads into Earth orbits*
> *   but also*
> * || will cost far less than the American shuttle.*

1. The aerospace plane, called HOTOL (for Horizontal Takeoff and Landing),

   will be both a flying laboratory and a cargo launcher.

   The aerospace plane, called HOTOL (for Horizontal Takeoff
   *   and Landing), will be*
   *   both*
   * || a flying laboratory*
   *   and*
   * || a cargo launcher.*

2. One reason HOTOL will be less expensive to operate than the shuttle is that

   it uses a metal skin rather than fragile and expensive heat tiles.

   One reason HOTOL will be less expensive to operate than
   *   the shuttle is that it uses*
   * || a metal skin*
   *   rather than*
   * || fragile and expensive heat tiles.*

3. Because the craft will glide back to Earth slowly, its skin will become hot,

   but not so hot as to require special protection.

   Because the craft will glide back to Earth slowly, its
   *   skin will become*
   * || hot,*
   *   but not*
   * || so hot*
   *   as to require special protection.*

4. HOTOL's design also permits it to launch horizontally, not vertically.

HOTOL's design also permits it to launch
|| horizontally,
not
|| vertically.

5. A horizontal launch uses neither booster rockets nor a large, complex tower.

A horizontal launch uses
neither
|| booster rockets
nor
|| a large, complex tower.

6. The British shuttle will be used not only for commercial missions but also for military missions, so some details of its design are secret.

The British shuttle will be used
not only
|| for commercial missions
but also
|| for military missions,
so some details of its design are secret.

7. The design of the engine has not been completely publicized, and neither British Aerospace engineers nor independent analysts are willing to discuss it at length.

The design of the engine has not been completely
publicized, and
neither
|| British Aerospace engineers
nor
|| independent analysts
are willing to discuss it at length.

Deduct 10 for each incorrect rewrite.

Parallel Structure   Exercise 26–2

NAME _____ SCORE _____

DIRECTIONS   Rewrite the following sentences to restore the parallel structure.

EXAMPLE

The satellite had not so much a research mission but rather a military mission.

The satellite had not so much a research mission as a military mission.

1. Virtually all scientific research in the United States is both government funded and it is expensive.

   Virtually all scientific research in the United States is goverment funded and expensive.

2. Developed and named after Franz Waldo, the Waldo Institute is a think tank for physicists.

   Developed by and named after Franz Waldo, the Waldo Institute is a think tank for physicists.

3. Some scientists claim that the expense of launching a satellite by the shuttle now exceeds the expense of a single rocket.

   Some scientists claim that the expense of launching a satellite by the shuttle now exceeds the expense of launching by a single rocket.

4. The shuttle can be used to launch satellites; it also can be used to repair satellites and to conduct experiments.

   The shuttle can be used to launch satellites, to repair satellites, and to conduct experiments.

5. Unlike previous spaceships the shuttle is not so much a rocket but rather a converted airplane.

   Unlike previous spaceships the shuttle is not so much a rocket as a converted airplane.

6. Today the shuttle may seem more a luxury rather than a necessity.

   Today the shuttle may seem more a luxury than a necessity.

7. Critics insist that the shuttle program must do two things: establish a dependable schedule for missions and to become profitable.

   Critics insist that the shuttle program must do two things: establish a dependable schedule and became profitable.

8. Not only is NASA relying on American companies to support the shuttle but also on foreign investors.

   NASA is relying not only on American companies to support the shuttle but also on foreign investors.

9. Criticism of the shuttle program was increased after the destruction of Challenger and began to come from all segments of society.

   Criticism of the shuttle program increased after the destruction of Challenger and began to come from all segments of society.

10. The shuttle must prove itself as dependable and safe. It must also demonstrate that it is flexible.

    The shuttle must prove itself as dependable, safe, and flexible.

27

As much as possible, maintain consistent grammatical structure, tone or style, and viewpoint.

As you read the following paragraph, notice how many times you must refocus your attention because of an unnecessary shift in number, tense, voice, or discourse.

Thirty years ago Professor John von Neumann proved that it was possible to build a self-replicating, computer-controlled, voyaging robot. The robot would *number tense* weigh 100 tons or more but would be virtually indestructible. They are to be made in space from material that other robots would mine from small asteroids. Computer instructions built into each robot would direct any necessary repairs. And *number* *tense* *tense* each unit would reproduce themselves. One machine will make 10; 10 will make *voice/tense* 100; 1000 will be made by 100. Some scientists are now asking that they be al- *discourse* lowed to build an experimental model robot and can they be given federal funding *person* for the project. We want to know if the military is interested in robots that could colonize the galaxy.

27a Avoid needless shifts in tense, mood, or voice.

SHIFT   During the discussion of Frank's new science fiction novel, he *listened* carefully but *said* nothing while his wife *listens* carefully and loudly *applauds* every compliment for the novel.

CONSISTENT   During the discussion of Frank's new science fiction novel, he *listened* carefully but *said* nothing while his wife *listened* carefully and loudly *applauded* every compliment for the novel.

SHIFT   Some contemporary writers suggest that robots now *be shown* as possessing the best human traits and that man *is* the mindless destroyer.   [shift from subjunctive mood to indicative mood]

CONSISTENT   Some contemporary writers suggest that robots now *be shown* as possessing the best human traits and that man *be* the mindless destroyer.

SHIFT	Isaac Asimov *invented* the intricate robot R. Daniel Olivaw for his novels *The Caves of Steel* and *The Naked Sun;* the best aspects of the virtuous human being *are represented* by Olivaw. [shift from active voice to passive voice]
CONSISTENT	Isaac Asimov *created* the intricate robot R. Daniel Olivaw for his novels *The Caves of Steel* and *The Naked Sun;* Olivaw *represents* the best aspects of the virtuous human being.

Be especially careful in writing essays on literature or historical topics to maintain a consistent present tense while retelling a plot or an event.

SHIFT	In early science fiction, robots *are* often *characterized* as soulless monsters that dispassionately *destroyed* man. [shift from present tense to past tense]
CONSISTENT	In early science fiction, robots *are* often *characterized* as soulless monsters that dispassionately *destroy* man.

27b Avoid needless shifts in person and in number. (See also section **6**.)

SHIFT	When *we* read *The Caves of Steel*, *one* realizes that Daniel Olivaw has become more than a robotic tool. [shift from first person to third person]
CONSISTENT	When *we* read *The Caves of Steel*, *we* realize that Daniel Olivaw has become more than a robotic tool.
SHIFT	A *robot* like Olivaw acts as if *they* are driven by a conscience. [shift in number]
CONSISTENT	*Robots* like Olivaw act as if *they* are driven by a conscience.

27c Avoid needless shifts between indirect and direct discourse. (See also section **26**.)

SHIFT	Before acting, Olivaw would ask himself *if the act would harm* anyone and *is he doing* his duty. [shift from declarative word order to interrogative word order]
CONSISTENT	Before acting, Olivaw would ask himself *if the act would harm* anyone and *if he would be doing* his duty.

OR

Before acting, Olivaw would ask, "*Will this act harm* anyone? *Am I doing* my duty?"

27d Avoid needless shifts in tone or style.

SHIFT	Isaac Asimov has formulated a series of laws to govern the behavior of robots in his fiction: they will not injure a human being or allow one to be injured; they will obey orders; they will protect their existence; and they *will interface with humanity in a positive way.* [shift from formal style to doublespeak]

CONSISTENT . . . and they will not injure humanity or, through inaction, allow humanity to come to harm.

27e Avoid needless shifts in perspective or viewpoint.

SHIFT R_2D_2 looks like a can with a domed top; silicon chips and mazes of circuits make it capable of extremely sophisticated responses. [shift from external to internal perspective]

CONSISTENT R_2D_2 looks like a can with a domed top, but an interior of silicon chips and mazes of circuits makes it capable of extremely sophisticated responses.

Deduct 3 1/3 for each blank incorrectly filled and 3 1/3 for each incorrect revision. (Revisions will vary.)

Shifts   Exercise 27–1

NAME _____ SCORE _____

DIRECTIONS   Indicate the kind of shift in each of the following sentences by writing *a* (tense, mood, voice), *b* (person, number), *c* (discourse), or *d* (tone, style) in the blank. Then revise the sentence to eliminate the needless shift.

EXAMPLE
The strength of the gravitational attraction between two particular

objects of a given mass depends on the distance between ~~its~~ *their* cen-

ters.   *b*

1. For instance, when *you are* ~~one is~~ standing on Earth's surface, the

    strength of Earth's gravitational pull on you depends on your

    distance from Earth's center.   *b*

2. Not all of you, however, *is* ~~was~~ at the same distance from Earth's

    center.   *a*

3. Your feet are nearly two meters closer to the Earth's center

    than your ~~cranium~~ *head* is.   *d*

4. That means that your feet are more strongly attracted to the

    Earth because gravitational attraction increases as distance ~~is~~

    decreases ~~decreased~~.   *a*

5. This difference in the gravitational attraction between two

    ends of an object is called the tidal effect. ~~They also say that~~

    *U*nder ordinary circumstances tidal effects are not great.   *a*

6. Consider a man who is two meters tall and who weigh~~ed~~*s* 90

    kilograms.   *a*

7. If he is standing on the Earth at sea level in the United States, the center of the Earth ~~can be found~~ *is* 6,370,000 meters beneath his feet. _____a_____

8. The man's head is slightly farther from the Earth's center, so we need to ask whether the tidal effect is stronger on the feet or the head and ~~can we~~ *whether we can* measure the difference~~?~~. _____c_____

9. The tidal effect is stronger on the feet, of course; the pull on ~~your~~ *his* feet is 1.0000008 times greater than the pull on ~~the~~ *his* head. _____b_____

10. We can visualize this difference if ~~you~~ *we* imagine the weight of about four drops of water pulling on the feet but not on the head. _____b_____

11. The difference is so slight that we ~~have been unable~~ *are unable* to detect any effects of tidal pull on our bodies. _____a_____

12. When we examine the tidal effect of the Moon on the Earth, ~~one~~ *we* easily discover detectable influences. _____b_____

13. The solid ball of the Earth stretches by about a third of a meter, and the ocean ~~is~~ stretche*s* by just over a meter. _____a_____

14. Because of the Moon's pull, the Earth has two bulges, one on the side facing the Moon and one on the opposite side. As the Earth rotates, ~~their~~ *its* land surfaces rotate into the bulge and out again, then into the other bulge and out again. _____b_____

15. Now do you understand why the tides rise and fall and how ~~do~~ the land surfaces move into the bulging oceans? _____c_____

Deduct 5 for each shift incorrectly identified and 5 for each shift incorrectly revised.

Shifts   Exercise 27–2

NAME _____ SCORE _____

DIRECTIONS   The following paragraphs, which discuss tidal effects, contain ten needless shifts in tense, voice, person, number, and discourse. Correct each shift by marking through it and writing your revision above the line. Finally, if possible, read aloud the original version and your revision to compare the improvement in coherence when consistent tense, voice, person, number, and discourse are maintained.

Newton could not tell us what gravitation is, but simply what it does. It is an invisible force, like electricity and magnetism, and ~~you~~ *we* do not know what these last two forces are either. We know how all three forces operate, and we can make some use of ~~it~~ *them*, but that is all.

We know that the gravitational force *s* of the Moon and, to some extent, the Sun lift~~ed~~ the waters of Earth to create tides in the oceans. We also know that the solid substance of the Earth itself is distorted by these forces. Because of the Moon's nearness to the Earth, its tide-controlling effect~~s~~ ~~is~~ *s are* far greater than those of the Sun.

If the Earth were covered by one great ocean, the wave of the tides created by the Moon would move smoothly around the Earth. With the continents acting as barriers, however, the tides ~~have been~~ *are* less regular; but they ~~have followed~~ *do follow* the Moon to a large extent. Because the motion of the tides does not occur at the same speed as the motion of the Earth, its effect is to slow the rotation of the Earth, even though the tides move generally in the same direction as the Earth's rotation—from west to east.

The constant friction of the tides is slowing down the spin of the Earth, and ~~they are~~ *it is* making our days and nights longer. When scientists realized that tidal friction affected the Earth's rotation they immediately asked themselves whether

the slowing was constant and ~~could~~ *whether* they *could* measure it. They soon discovered that

the slowing is constant and measurable: the Earth's rotation slows down about

one second every 100,000 years.

28

Make each pronoun refer unmistakably to its antecedent.

A pronoun has no real meaning of its own; rather, it depends on its antecedent, the word it refers to, for its meaning. If a pronoun does not refer clearly and logically to another word, then your reader will not know what the pronoun means. And if a pronoun refers broadly to the general idea of the preceding sentence or sentences, the reader may have to reread a part or parts of the earlier material to try to determine the meaning of the pronoun.

> *They* claim that the brain of a genius differs from the brain of a person of ordinary intellect. *They* say *this* because *it* has been found to be fundamentally, structurally different from the brain of an ordinary intellect.

There are three main ways to correct an unclear reference of a pronoun: (1) rewrite the sentence or sentences to eliminate the pronoun; (2) provide a clear antecedent for the pronoun to refer to; or (3) substitute a noun for the pronoun or, as in the case of *this*, add a noun, making the pronoun an adjective.

> *Professor Marian Diamond and her co-workers at the University of California, Berkeley,* claim that the brain of a genius differs from the brain of a person of ordinary intellect. *They* make *this claim* because *they* have discovered fundamental, structural differences between the brain of a genius and the brain of an ordinary intellect.   [Note in the second sentence that *this* has become an adjective modifying the noun *claim*.]

28a   Avoid ambiguous reference.

AMBIGUOUS   Albert told Ashley that *he* was innately aggressive.

CLEAR   Albert told Ashley, "*You* are innately aggressive."

OR

Albert told Ashley, "*I* am innately aggressive."

28b Avoid remote or obscure reference.

A pronoun that is located too far from its antecedent, with too many intervening nouns, will not have a clear meaning; nor will a pronoun that refers to an antecedent in the possessive case.

REMOTE   Einstein wanted his brain preserved after his death. He hoped that future scientists might be able to learn something about his unique intellect. In accordance with his wishes, Dr. Thomas Harvey removed and preserved *it* during the autopsy.   [Readers might think that *it* refers to *intellect*.]

CLEAR   Einstein wanted his brain preserved after his death. He hoped that future scientists might be able to learn something about his unique intellect. In accordance with his wishes, Dr. Thomas Harvey removed and preserved the *brain* during the autopsy.

OBSCURE   When her father's car drove up, Anna was glad to see *him*.   [*Him* illogically refers to *car*.]

CLEAR   When her *father* drove up in his car, Anna was glad to see *him*.   [*Him* logically refers to *father*.]

28c In general, avoid broad reference.

Pronouns such as *this, it, that, which,* and *such* may sometimes be used effectively to refer to the general idea of a preceding sentence, or even of a preceding paragraph. But such broad reference is easily misused and should generally be avoided. Make sure that each pronoun you use has a clear reference.

BROAD   He was a good mathematician, and he used *this* to explain his ideas about the universe.

CLEAR   He was a good mathematician, and he used *his ability* to explain his ideas about the universe.

OR

He used his ability as a mathematician to explain his ideas about the universe.

28d Avoid using *it* in two different ways in the same sentence. Avoid using the pronouns *it* and *you* awkwardly.

CONFUSING   Although *it* was difficult for Einstein to pass math classes as a student, as an adult he was excellent at *it*.   [The first *it* is an expletive; the second *it* refers to *math*.]

CLEAR   Although *it* was difficult for Einstein to pass math classes as a student, as an adult he was excellent at *math*.

AWKWARD   In the article "Einstein's Brain," *it* discusses the physical composition of his brain.   [The pronoun *it* refers clumsily to *article*.]

CLEAR   The article "Einstein's Brain" discusses the physical composition of his brain.

AWKWARD   *One* may wonder what researchers discovered about Einstein's brain. It may surprise *you* to learn that researchers found Einstein's brain to be physically different from ordinary brains.

CLEAR   *One* may wonder. . . . It may surprise *one* to learn that researchers found Einstein's brain to be physically different from ordinary brains.

Note: Some grammarians feel that *you* is both natural and correct as long as the writer does not shift person in the sentence or the paragraph; other grammarians feel that *you* should be avoided in formal composition.

Deduct 4 1/6 for each blank incorrectly filled and 4 1/6 for each unsatisfactory revision. (Revisions will vary.)

Reference of Pronouns

Exercise 28-1

NAME _____ SCORE _____

DIRECTIONS   In the following sentences mark a capital *V* through each pronoun whose reference is vague or awkward and write that pronoun in the blank. Then revise the sentence or sentences to clarify the meaning.

EXAMPLE

is interesting

~~It is interesting to read~~ Montagu's article ^ because it demonstrates

Einstein's great compassion for humanity.   *It*

1. ~~In~~ Montagu's article ~~it~~ explains that Einstein began working

   for nuclear disarmament immediately after World War II.   *it*

2. Einstein and others tried to persuade President Truman not

   using a nuclear device

   to use the atomic bomb on Japan because ~~this~~ might start the

   world on a path to self-destruction.   *this*

3. Einstein believed that humans are innately aggressive and

   their aggression

   that ~~it~~ would prevent them from achieving world peace. *it*

4. Einstein suggested that parents ~~which~~ *who* discipline children with

   spankings are exhibiting the same kind of aggression that leads

   to war.   *which*

5. Montagu disagreed, arguing that ~~they~~ *humans* are not innately aggres-

   sive. In fact, Montagu argued, they are born with no instincts

   at all.   *they*

6. Montagu and Einstein also discussed the recognition Einstein

   received for his work. It was difficult, Einstein said, to under-

   the recognition

   stand what ~~it~~ was all about.   *it*

7. Einstein genuinely did not believe he had earned such fame. ~~This is~~ because he had found the work to be easy. _This_

8. Despite his accomplishments, Einstein occasionally was mistreated. Before he left Germany he attended a conference for physicists; during the conference one of ~~them~~ *the scientists* insulted him because he was a Jew. _them_

9. Later, during the McCarthy era, a writer in the magazine *American Mercury* falsely accused him of being a communist. Einstein reacted to both incidents similarly; he laughed and characterized both of ~~them~~ *the men* as acting out of ignorance. _them_

10. For years before he met Einstein, Montagu was interested in the principle of indeterminacy, or chance. Like Montagu, ~~he~~ *Einstein* was a determinist, one who believes that everything has an explicable cause. _he_

11. Both of them agreed that only people's ignorance prevented their understanding all of creation. No problem was insoluble to humans; ~~you simply~~ *they* had not yet learned enough to solve it. _you_

12. According to Montagu, Einstein also had a grand sense of humor. He delighted in stories ~~who~~ *that* revealed the average person's understanding of relativity. _who_

29

Arrange the parts of a sentence, and the sentences in a paragraph, to emphasize important ideas.

Emphatic word order, used at the proper time, is an effective way to emphasize ideas and add variety to your writing. But emphatic sentence patterns should be saved for ideas that deserve special stress; if you use unusual patterns too often, your style will appear stilted.

29a   Gain emphasis by placing important words at the beginning or the end of a sentence—especially at the end—and unimportant words in the middle.

UNEMPHATIC   Saturn is the most beautiful object in the sky, according to most observers.

EMPHATIC   Saturn, according to most observers, is the most beautiful object in the sky.

Note: The beginning and the end (again, especially the end) are also the two most effective places to put important ideas in a paragraph or an essay.

29b Gain emphasis by using periodic sentences. (This rule is an extension of **29a**.)

A sentence that holds the reader in suspense until the end is called *periodic;* one that makes a complete statement and then adds details is called *loose.* The loose sentence, which is more common, is usually easier to follow. But the periodic sentence, by reserving the main idea until the end, is more emphatic.

LOOSE   Saturn is a dull yellowish color and appears to move sluggishly when observed by the naked eye.

PERIODIC   When observed by the naked eye, Saturn is a dull yellowish color and appears to move sluggishly.

29c Gain emphasis by arranging ideas in the order of climax.

In a series, place ideas in order beginning with the least important one. Present the most important or most dramatic idea last.

UNEMPHATIC   Telescopic observation of Saturn reveals a brilliantly colored planet, a glorious ring system, and numerous satellites.

EMPHATIC   Telescopic observation of Saturn reveals a brilliantly colored planet, numerous satellites, and a glorious ring system.

29d Gain emphasis by using the active instead of the passive voice.

UNEMPHATIC   In 1659 the rings of Saturn were discovered by Christian Huygens.

EMPHATIC   In 1659 Christian Huygens discovered the rings of Saturn.

Gain emphasis also by using action verbs or linking verbs that are more forceful than a form of *have* or *be*.

UNEMPHATIC   Christian Huygens *was* the discoverer of the rings of Saturn.

EMPHATIC   Christian Huygens *discovered* the rings of Saturn.

Note: When the receiver of an action is more important than the doer, the passive voice will make the emphasis clear.

Huygens' explanation of the ring system was immediately accepted.

29e Gain emphasis by repeating important words.

Later astronomers gained fame not by discovering the ring system but by interpreting it. In 1676 G. D. Cassini interpreted a dark line in the system as a division between the rings, subsequently called the Cassini Division. In 1837 John Franz Encke interpreted a dark line in the system as another division between the rings, subsequently called the Encke Division. In 1850 G. P. Bond interpreted a dark line in the system not as a division between the rings but as a new ring, subsequently called the C Ring.

Caution: Repetition of a word produces only monotony unless the word is important enough to be emphasized. (See also **21c**.)

29f Gain emphasis by using inverted word order or by putting a word or phrase out of its usual order.

UNEMPHATIC   The large, orange satellite Titan interests scientists because its atmosphere is largely composed of nitrogen.

EMPHATIC   The satellite Titan, large and orange, interests scientists because its atmosphere is largely composed of nitrogen.

UNEMPHATIC   Perhaps signs of life could be found beneath the thick cloud cover.

EMPHATIC   Perhaps, beneath the thick cloud cover, could be found signs of life.

29g Gain emphasis by using balanced constructions. (See also section **26**.)

UNEMPHATIC   Perhaps life could exist on Titan, but Saturn is a dead planet.

EMPHATIC   Perhaps life could exist on Titan; on Saturn it could not.

29h Emphasize an important sentence in a paragraph by making it noticeably shorter than the others. (See also section **24**.)

    Saturn must have been known since very early times because, at its brightest, it outshines all stars except Sirius and Canopus. The first recorded observations of Saturn seem to have been made in Mesopotamia in the mid-seventh century B.C. About 650 B.C. there is a record that Saturn "entered the Moon," which is presumably a reference to an occultation of the planet. Until 1619 observations were made with the naked eye and perpetuated the ancient view of Saturn as a large, rather baleful object moving slowly across the sky. *In July of 1610 Galileo first turned a telescope toward Saturn.*

Emphasis   Exercise 29–1

NAME _____ SCORE _____

DIRECTIONS   Rewrite each of the following sentences in emphatic word order. Use the rule indicated in parentheses after the sentence to guide you in revising for emphasis.

EXAMPLE
There are many satellites around Saturn in addition to the fascinating Titan.

(29b)

In addition to the fascinating Titan, there are many satellites around Saturn.

1. Obscured by a bluish haze and methane clouds, Titan's surface remains a mystery.   **(29f)**

   Titan's surface, obscured by a bluish haze and methane clouds, remains a mystery.

2. Surface temperatures on Titan have been estimated by scientists to be cold enough to freeze methane.   **(29d)**

   Scientists estimate that surface temperatures on Titan are cold enough to freeze methane.

3. The extreme cold probably has prevented life from developing. The chemistry to support life, however, may not have been prevented from developing.   **(29e, 29g)**

   The extreme cold probably has prevented life from developing, but it may not have prevented the chemistry to support life from developing.

4. A future probe to Titan will analyze the atmosphere, search for signs of life, and land on the surface.   **(29c)**

   A future probe to Titan will analyze the atmosphere, land on the surface, and search for signs of life.

5. The photographs of Saturn from Voyager 1 and 2 are not soon to be forgotten.   (**29f**)

Not soon to be forgotten are the photographs of Saturn from Voyager 1 and Voyager 2.

6. Images of the rings, the satellites, and the great, gaseous globe appeared in living rooms around the world through the miracle of television.   (**29a**)

Through the miracle of television, images of the rings, the satellites, and the great, gaseous globe appeared in living rooms around the world.

7. The photographs verified much scientific speculation about the ring system, confirmed Saturn's reputation as the most beautiful object in the solar system, and gave us a tantalizing look at Titan.   (**29c**)

The photographs verified much scientific speculation about the ring system, gave us a tantalizing look at Titan, and confirmed Saturn's reputation as the most beautiful object in the solar system.

8. Hyperion, looking more like a potato than a sphere, has an irregular shape.   (**29a**)

Hyperion, with its irregular shape, looks more like a potato than a sphere.

9. The irregular shape of Hyperion may have been caused by a collision.   (**29d**)

A collision may have caused the irregular shape.

10. Eventually Hyperion will acquire a spherical shape because of Saturn's gravitational influence.   (**29b**)

Eventually, because of Saturn's gravitational influence, Hyperion will acquire a spherical shape.

Answers will vary.

Emphasis

NAME _____ SCORE _____

DIRECTIONS   Write a paragraph in which you try to emphasize certain ideas by using three or more of the techniques explained in section **29**. When you have finished, number the sentences in your paragraph and analyze what you have done to achieve emphasis by answering the questions on the next page.

SUGGESTED TOPICS

your favorite science-fiction movie or story

a defense of the U.S. space program

your opinion of UFOs

why you would like to go into space

PARAGRAPH

ANALYSIS

1. Did you use a short, abrupt sentence to emphasize an idea? If so, which sentence is used in this way? _____

   _____

2. Why did you emphasize this idea?

3. Which sentences in your paragraph have loose structure? _____

   _____

4. Which sentences have periodic structure? _____

5. Did you use any other techniques to achieve emphasis—for example, inverted word order, balanced structure, repetition of an important word or words? If so, list each technique used and the number of the sentence in which it appears.

30

Vary the length, structure, and beginning of your sentences to make your style pleasing.

On a few occasions, a series of short sentences that all begin with the subject is effective. In general, however, vary the length, structure, and beginnings of your sentences to achieve a fluid style.

30a Vary the length of sentences, using short sentences primarily for emphasis. (See also **29h**.)

> Recently scientists have obtained photographs of Pluto that enable them to estimate the planet's mass. The calculations, however, have led to other problems. The orbits of Pluto's neighbors, Uranus and Neptune, are affected by the gravitational attraction of nearby objects whose mass the scientists also can estimate. Pluto is not large enough to provide all of that gravitational force. *So a tenth planet may await discovery.*

30b Vary the beginnings of sentences.

Subordination is the key to a variation from subject-first word order.

(1) Begin with an adverb or an adverb phrase or clause.

ADVERB   *Finally,* scientists could calculate the mass of Pluto.

ADVERB PHRASE   *In 1978,* scientists could calculate the mass of Pluto.

ADVERB CLAUSE   *After scientists obtained high-quality photographs of Pluto,* they could calculate its orbit.

(2) Begin with a prepositional phrase or a verbal phrase.

PREPOSITIONAL PHRASE   *In the photographs,* scientists also discovered Pluto's moon Charon.

VERBAL PHRASE   *Studying the first high-quality photographs of Pluto,* scientists were elated to discover its moon Charon.

(3) Begin with a coordinating conjunction, a conjunctive adverb, or a transitional expression when such a word or phrase can be used to show the proper relation of one sentence to the sentence that precedes it.

COORDINATING   Because our knowledge of the universe has expanded so rapidly,
CONJUNCTION   we may think that little is left to discover about our solar system. *But* the discovery of Pluto's moon and the possibility of the existence of a tenth planet remind us that more such surprises probably await us.

CONJUNCTIVE ADVERB *Indeed*, as we study the universe we turn our minds outward from ourselves and our planet, probing the outer limits of existence and trying to trace our origins.

TRANSITIONAL EXPRESSION But studying the universe does not lead us only outward. *In fact*, an important breakthrough in our study of the universe came when we changed our focus from determining where stars and planets are to determining what they are. Inevitably, we began studying the stars by studying atoms. [Notice the emphasis gained by using the two short sentences.]

(4) Begin with an appositive, an absolute phrase, or an introductory series.

APPOSITIVE *A cold distant planet*, Pluto remains relatively unknown. [appositive referring to the subject]

ABSOLUTE PHRASE *Their imaginations unrestrained*, the researchers eagerly awaited the first clear photographs of Pluto.

INTRODUCTORY SERIES *Cold, distant, lifeless*—Pluto is well named after the mythological Greek god of the underworld.

30c Avoid loose, stringy compound sentences. (See also **24b**.)

To revise an ineffective compound sentence, try one of the following methods.

(1) Make a compound sentence complex.

COMPOUND The planet Pluto was named after the mythological Greek god of the underworld, so it was fitting to name Pluto's moon after Charon, the ferryman to the underworld.

COMPLEX Because the planet Pluto was named after the mythological Greek god of the underworld, it was fitting to name Pluto's moon after Charon, the ferryman to the underworld.

(2) Use a compound predicate in a simple sentence.

COMPOUND Pluto is extremely far from Earth, and it is only dimly lit by the Sun, but scientists can learn something of its composition by studying its reflected light.

SIMPLE Far from Earth, Pluto is only dimly lit by the Sun but reveals to scientists something of its composition in its reflected light.

(3) Use an appositive in a simple sentence.

COMPOUND The ability of atoms to absorb light is called "absorption," and it affects the spectrum.

SIMPLE The ability of atoms to absorb light, "absorption," affects the spectrum.

1

(4) Use a prepositional or verbal phrase in a simple sentence.

COMPOUND   Absorption is the removal of specific parts of a light ray, and it creates gaps or black bands in the spectrum.

SIMPLE   By removing specific parts of a light ray, absorption creates gaps or black bands in the spectrum.

30d Vary the conventional subject-verb sequence by occasionally separating the subject from the verb with words or phrases.

Each subject and verb below is italicized.

SUBJECT-VERB   An atom's absorption *spectrum is* unique, and *it serves* as a kind of "fingerprint" of the atom.   [compound sentence]

VARIED   An atom's absorption *spectrum*, its "fingerprint," *is* unique.   [simple sentence]

SUBJECT-VERB   A *scientist can analyze* a spectrum and *identify* the source of the light.

VARIED   A *scientist*, after analyzing a spectrum, *can identify* the source of the light.

30e Occasionally, use an interrogative, imperative, or exclamatory sentence instead of the more common declarative sentence.

How can anyone read a physicist's account of what happens when a star shines or a moon glows and still see any romance in either object? In this case, knowledge kills. —BOB HERRING   [a rhetorical question followed by a declarative statement]

Concentrate. Keep your eye on the little point of light. Follow it with your eyes until you catch it in your hand. —*"How to Catch a Falling Star"*   [three imperative sentences]

Deduct 10 for each incorrect answer.

Variety Exercise 30-1

NAME _____ SCORE _____

DIRECTIONS   Analyze the ways in which variety is achieved in the following paragraph by answering the questions on the next page.

[1]In perhaps his most famous experiment, Isaac Newton held a glass prism up to the light, breaking it into its constituent colors. [2]In modern times we say that Newton produced a "spectrum."

[3]For many years the spectrum was no more than an entertainment for children or a nuisance for telescope makers. [4]One of the main problems for lens makers was the tendency of lenses to bend light much like a prism, thereby distorting a telescopic image instead of clarifying it. [5]Then in 1802 William Hyde Hollaston, a relatively unknown scientist, found stripes in the spectrum where colors were missing. [6]By 1814 Joseph von Fraunhofer, after whom the black lines were named, made the first map of the lines. [7]But their origin remained a mystery. [8]Finally, however, in 1859 Gustav Kirchoff, working with Robert Bunsen at Heidelberg, showed that the lines were caused by the presence of certain familiar chemical elements in the sun's outer atmosphere. [9]This connection between the light emitted by a star and the types of atoms in it fascinated scientists and changed the practice of astronomy. [10]Scientists examined the structure and behavior of atoms and began discovering new ways of thinking about the universe. [11]For example, think about the popular conception of an atom. [12]At its center is a small, dense, positively charged nucleus. [13]The light electrons, all negatively charged, circle the nucleus. [14]In fact, we could say that an atom resembles our solar system. [15]As the electrons circle the nucleus and are held in place by the electrical field, they create a structure much like the solar system.

ANALYSIS

1. Which sentences are shorter than the others? _____ *7 and 13* _____

_____

2. What is the purpose of the short sentences? *emphasis*

3. How many simple sentences are there? *7 (Sentences 1,3,4,7,11,12 and 13)*
   How many compound sentences? *2 (Sentences 9 and 10)*
   How many complex sentences? *6 (Sentences 2,5,6,8,14, and 15)*

4. In which sentences is the subject preceded by an adverb? *5 and 8*

5. In which sentences is the subject preceded by an adverb phrase?
   1, 2, 3, 5, 6, 8, and 12

6. In which sentence is the subject preceded by an adverb clause? *15*

7. Which sentence begins with a coordinating conjunction? *7*

8. Which sentences begin with a transitional expression? *5, 8, 11, and 14*

9. Which sentences vary from Subject-Verb-Complement word order by inserting a word or words between the subject and verb? *4, 5, 6, 8, 9, 12, and 13*

10. Which sentence is not a declarative sentence? *11*

   What kind is it? *imperative*

Answers will vary.

Variety   Exercise 30–2

NAME _____ SCORE _____

DIRECTIONS   Write a paragraph in which you use at least three of the methods for achieving variety explained in section **30**. Because most people are more likely to use varied sentence patterns when they write on subjects that they feel strongly about, traditional views that they can question, or topics that they can treat humorously, you may find one of the five beginnings suggested below useful. After you have finished your paragraphs, number your sentences and analyze what you have done to achieve variety by answering the questions on the next page.

SUGGESTED BEGINNINGS

1. NASA officials conducted an exhaustive search to find students with good ideas for experiments to be conducted in space. My idea for an experiment was not chosen, but it should have been.

2. The *Bay Area Digest* recently carried an "eye-witness account" of two alien spacecraft flying over the city. Everyone who was quoted in the article commented on the beauty of the spacecraft and the speed with which they maneuvered. But no one even speculated about why they were here. I know why they were here.

3. The claims made about the benefits of space exploration are ridiculously exaggerated.

4. Meteor showers, solar or lunar eclipses, and visitations by comets have strange effects on people. I work in a hospital emergency room, and I know.

5. My favorite character in a science fiction movie (or television series or book) is Yoda (or . . .) because . . .

PARAGRAPH

275

PARAGRAPH CONTINUED

ANALYSIS

1. Have you used a sentence or two that is noticeably shorter than the other sentences in the paragraph? _____

2. What type of sentence structure have you mainly used: simple, compound, or complex? _____

3. Which sentences have you begun with something other than the subject?

   _____

4. Does any sentence have a word or words inserted between the subject and verb or the verb and complement? _____

5. Have you used any kind of sentence other than the declarative sentence?

   _____

LOGICAL THINKING   log 31

31

Base your writing on logical thinking. Avoid common fallacies.

Learning to reason clearly and logically and to judge the reasoning of other writers is an essential part of your preparation as a writer. This section will help you to understand inductive and deductive reasoning and to avoid common errors in reasoning called *fallacies*.

31a Learn how to use inductive reasoning in your writing.

> Ancient peoples watched the Sun and Moon rise and set each day and studied the progression of the stars against a night sky. The evidence showed, they thought, that the Earth was the center of the universe, and for thousands of years they held to that belief.

Inductive reasoning, as in the above example, is based on evidence: people observe or otherwise acquire facts—or what they believe to be facts—and then make a generalization based upon them. But, as the example of the Earth-centered universe demonstrates, our reasoning sometimes fails us. When we reason inductively, we must take certain precautions: we must

> make sure the evidence is sufficient;
> make sure the conclusion fits the facts;
> make sure we do not ignore evidence;
> make sure we do not present only evidence that supports our conclusion.

31b Learn how to use deductive reasoning in your writing.

> If you know that comets are the only celestial bodies that have visible, elongated, curved vapor tails and you see an object in the sky with such a tail, you are likely to conclude that you have seen a comet.

The kind of reasoning used in this example is based on a logical structure called a *syllogism*.

SYLLOGISM

Major Premise (usually a generalization): Comets are the only celestial bodies with visible, elongated, curved vapor tails.

Minor Premise (a specific fact): An object I saw last night in the sky had an elongated, curved vapor tail.

Conclusion: The object that I saw last night was a comet.

When the major premise and the minor premise are correctly related to form a conclusion, the syllogism is valid. Even if the reasoning is valid, however, the conclusion may be false if one of the premises is false. For instance, suppose that what you saw last night was a meteorite, not a celestial object (an object out among the stars). That makes your minor premise false; therefore, your conclusion is false. Based on the evidence that you had, your reasoning was valid, but your conclusion was false.

As you use deductive reasoning in your writing, particularly in argumentative papers, think very carefully about your premises to be sure your argument is sound—both true and valid. Also, consider your reader as you frame your premises: how difficult will it be for the reader to accept your premises?

Deduction   Exercise 31–1

NAME _____

DIRECTIONS   Prepare for a class discussion of the premises and conclusions in the following:

1. Major Premise: All angels are immaterial beings.

   Minor Premise: All immaterial beings are weightless.

   Conclusion: All angels are weightless.

2. Major Premise: One must choose between learning to use a computer and making costly errors.

   Minor Premise: Anna has learned to use a computer.

   Conclusion: Therefore, she will not make costly errors.

3. Major Premise: It's impossible to be both rich and unhappy.

   Minor Premise: Terry isn't rich.

   Conclusion: Therefore, he must be unhappy.

31c Avoid fallacies.

Fallacies are faults in reasoning. They may result from misusing or misrepresenting evidence, from relying on faulty premises or omitting a needed premise, or from distorting the issues.

(1) *Non sequitur:* A statement that does not follow logically from what has just been said—a conclusion that does not follow from the premises.

> FAULTY   Of course we'll travel some day at the speed of light; we broke the sound barrier, didn't we?   [Breaking the sound barrier does not prove that we can break the light barrier.]

(2) Hasty generalization: A generalization based on too little evidence or on exceptional or biased evidence.

> FAULTY   Astronauts are fearless.   [Undoubtedly some astronauts sometimes feel fear.]

(3) *Ad hominem:* Attacking the person who presents an issue rather than dealing logically with the issue itself.

> FAULTY   His arguments against a "Star Wars" defense may sound impressive, but why should we take such comments seriously from a man who isn't even a high-school graduate?   [The man's education does not necessarily invalidate his arguments.]

(4) Bandwagon: An argument saying, in effect, "Everyone's doing or saying or thinking this, so you (or we) should, too."

> FAULTY   Everyone else is dumping chemical wastes in the river, so why shouldn't we?   [That others do it does not make it right.]

(5) Red herring: Dodging the real issue by drawing attention to an irrelevant issue.

> FAULTY   Why worry about nuclear war in space when thousands of people are starving in Africa?   [Starving people in Africa have nothing to do with nuclear warfare in space.]

(6) *Either . . . or* fallacy: Stating that only two alternatives exist when in fact there are more than two.

> FAULTY   We have only two choices: colonize the Moon or die in a nuclear war on Earth.   [In fact, other possibilities exist.]

(7) False analogy: The assumption that because two things are alike in some ways, they must be alike in other ways.

> FAULTY   Since the satellites cost the same and are about the same size, one is probably as good as the other.   [The cost and size of the satellites cannot predict whether one is as good as the other.]

(8) Equivocation: An assertion that falsely relies on the use of a term in two different senses.

> FAULTY The United States has a right to defend itself, so it should do what is right and build satellite weaponry.   [The word *right* means both "a just claim" and "correct."]

(9) Slippery slope: The assumption that one thing will lead to another as the first step in a downward spiral.

> FAULTY The Challenger explosion shows that NASA does not have the technology to explore space.   [One accident does not mean that the technology is not advanced enough to support exploration.]

(10) Oversimplification: A statement that omits some important aspects of an issue.

> FAULTY Now that we've gone to the moon, we can go to Mars.   [The technology is similar, but the considerations are much more complicated.]

(11) Begging the question: An assertion that restates the point just made. Such an assertion is circular in that it draws as a conclusion a point stated in the premise.

> FAULTY Mars is dry because there is no water on the surface.   [Being dry and having no water are essentially the same thing.]

(12) False cause: The mistake of assuming that because one event follows another, the first must be the cause of the second. (Also called *post hoc, ergo propter hoc*, or "after this, so because of this.")

> FAULTY Priestley's Comet passed near Earth in the fall of 1961 and that winter we had the great flu epidemic.   [The assumption is that the comet caused the flu epidemic, an assumption unlikely to be true.]

Deduct 10 for each blank incorrectly filled.

Fallacies

NAME _____ SCORE _____

DIRECTIONS   Identify the fallacies in the following sentences.

1. We must either have weapons in space or be prepared to lose our freedom.   *either ... or*

2. I wish they'd stop sending up satellites; every time a new satellite is launched, my dog gets sick.   *false cause*

3. Several other nations are working toward a manned expedition to Mars. Obviously, we must not abandon our own efforts to get there.   *bandwagon*

4. Americans are sick of hearing excuses for our slow progress in space, but it is a sickness we can cure with more funding. Our national health requires it.   *equivocation*

5. Several of the rocket experts worked for the Nazis; why should we take seriously their argument that more funds are needed for the space program?   *ad hominem*

6. Though a manned mission to Mars is dangerous and costly, our forebears who explored the oceans and blazed the trails westward showed that such things can be done.   *false analogy*

7. The space program is too expensive because we just cannot spare the money for it.   *begging the question*

8. He's intelligent and physically fit; he'll make a fine astronaut.   *non sequitur*

9. Scientific progress always requires that we be willing to make personal sacrifices.   *hasty generalization*

10. Why should we listen to the islanders' objections to our putting a NASA base on their island? Remember how they opposed our efforts to protect their fisheries. Their food supply is what they should be worrying about. _red herring_

32

Write unified, coherent, and adequately developed paragraphs.

We recognize the beginning of a new paragraph by the indention of the first word—about one inch when handwritten or five spaces when typewritten. A paragraph may range in length from 50 to 250 words, with an average length of about 100 words. The indention and length of a paragraph are signals to a reader that this unit of discourse will coherently and adequately develop an idea. As we read a paragraph, we expect to learn the controlling idea and to understand the relationship that each of the sentences has to that idea. And, finally, we expect the sentences to flow smoothly, so that we do not have to mentally fill in any words or phrases or stop reading at any point to refocus our attention.

32a Construct unified paragraphs.

(1) Make sure each sentence is related to the central thought.

In the following paragraph the controlling idea appears in italics. The words in boldface echo the controlling idea and help to unify the discussion.

> 1 *Galileo's revolution consisted in elevating "induction" above deduction as the logical method of science.* Instead of building a **conclusion** on an assumed set of **generalizations**, the **inductive method** starts with **observations** and derives **generalizations** (axioms, if you will) from them. Of course, even the Greeks obtained their **axioms** from **generalizations**; Euclid's axiom that a straight line is the shortest distance between two points was an **intuitive judgment** based on experience. But whereas the Greek philosopher minimized the role played by **induction,** the modern scientist looks on **induction** as the essential process of gaining knowledge, the only way of justifying **generalizations.** Moreover, the scientist realizes that no **generalization** can be allowed to stand unless it is repeatedly tested by newer and still newer experiments—the continuing test of further **induction.**
> —ISAAC ASIMOV, *Asimov's New Guide to Science*

Asimov explains that Galileo's greatest gift to science was to elevate inductive reasoning (see **31a**) to the status of "the logical method of science." Every sentence in the paragraph relates clearly and directly to that controlling idea. The reader never has to fill in gaps in the ideas or suffer the momentary confusion caused by a sentence that does not continue to develop the main idea.

(2) State the main idea of the paragraph in a clearly constructed topic sentence.

A topic sentence embodies the central thought of a paragraph. Notice how the first sentence of paragraph 2 clearly signals the idea to be developed; obviously the paragraph will define "exobiology."

2 Exobiology is quite different from other branches of astronomy in that much of it is experimental. Planetary atmospheres are simulated in the laboratory to see whether various organisms can survive in them, or perhaps even evolve naturally. Rocks are dated, fossils are examined, and radio telescopes are pointed toward potential candidates listening for signals that might mean another civilization. Many different branches of science (biology, chemistry, geology) are involved in the study.

—BARRY R. PARKER, *Concepts of the Cosmos*

Often the main idea of a paragraph is stated at the beginning, as in paragraphs 1 and 2, but it may ocur anywhere in the paragraph. In paragraph 3 the topic sentence is the third sentence.

3 Until the middle of the nineteenth century the main emphasis of astronomy was on identifying where objects were in the heavens. Scientists from Ptolemy to Newton were always interested in discovering where an object would be at a certain time and what forces caused its motion. But in the middle of the nineteenth century, when the art of spectroscopy was developed, it became possible for astronomers to study not only where an object was, but what it was. By observing the light emitted by distant stars, or by seeing what was absorbed when light passed through dust clouds in the galaxy, astronomers could discover what sort of atoms were in those stars or dust clouds. The connection between atoms and light permitted astronomers to discover the structure and composition of celestial bodies. Because the emphasis is on the physics of the objects being studied, this new field was named "astrophysics"—the physics of the stars.

When a paragraph progresses from particulars to a generalization, the topic sentence is likely to occur at the end, as in paragraph 4.

4 In 1967 a new radio telescope was erected at the Mullard Radio Astronomy Observatory, Cambridge, designed to investigate the scintillation of compact radio sources. When systematic observation commenced in November 1967, a radio source was discovered from the early records which was emitting a pulsed signal, the pulses each lasting about one third of a second and occurring with great regularity at intervals of $1\frac{1}{3}$ sec. Three more similar sources were discovered within a short time. These "pulsating radio sources" soon became popularly known as *pulsars.*

—GILBERT E. SATTERWAITE, *Encyclopedia of Astronomy*

A single topic sentence may serve for a sequence of two or more paragraphs. The second sentence in paragraph 6 unites paragraphs 5 and 6.

5 In our journey through the universe we have seen an amazing array of astronomical objects: stars in a profusion of types, spinning wheels of stars—galaxies, tiny stellar lighthouses called pulsars, quasars still enigmatic after twenty years, awe-inspiring black holes, and bleak but sometimes colorful planets and moons. Strangely, even though we have perhaps gained an appreciation for the size and numbers involved we are still no closer to being able to truly comprehend them.

6 The universe is gigantic beyond imagination; no matter how we try to visualize distances such as a million light years, times such as a billion years, or the immense explosion—the Big Bang—that gave us our universe, we cannot: they are beyond

human comprehension. But reflecting on them, and other aspects of what we have learned about the universe, can help us toward a recognition of our place in the cosmos, a better understanding of nature in general, and perhaps more importantly, an appreciation of our own planet. For we now know that, despite the size of the universe and the incredible number of objects in it, there is strong evidence that worlds such as ours are rare. We are privileged to live on a planet that is immensely fertile and rich in resources. And, perhaps, we have gained a vital insight: our resources are not limitless and our ecology is fragile, so, if we are to preserve our existence, we must protect and conserve what we have.

—BARRY R. PARKER, *Concepts of the Cosmos*

Occasionally no topic sentence is necessary because the details clearly imply the controlling idea.

7   During the Mesozoic era dinosaurs walked the Earth. *Tyrannosaurus rex*, the dominant example of the species, was the largest carnivorous land animal in Earth history. Other dinosaurs and large reptiles inhabited a lush, heavily vegetated landscape filled with smaller creatures that made easy prey. At the end of the Mesozoic era a large object collided with the Earth. Enormous clouds of dust erupted into the stratosphere. A long, frigid night fell over the world and photosynthesis ceased. The next era, the Cenozoic, did not contain dinosaurs. We refer to it as the age of mammals.

32b Make paragraphs coherent by arranging ideas in a clear, logical order and by providing appropriate transitions.

(1) Arrange ideas in a clear, logical order.

The paragraphs below illustrate several ways to arrange ideas in a paragraph. The choice depends on the context of the writing and on the writer's purpose.

TIME ORDER

8   As the solar system began to take on the structure that we know today, large objects, some even larger than the Moon, were hurled about among the developing planets. Objects collided repeatedly with each other or with the planets until some were finally destroyed. Others were catapulted out of the solar system; the gravitational forces of an immense planet such as Jupiter could capture debris and fling it great distances. Finally, after a long period of chaotic crashing about, the solar system was cleared of the largest debris. The planets assumed their regular orbits, but each planet wore a heavily cratered surface—a record of the system's violent formation.

Paragraph 9 demonstrates space order, an arrangement particularly useful for descriptions.

SPACE ORDER

9   The first visitors to the scene of the Tonguska Event, the apparent collision of a comet with Earth, discovered the effects of the release of awesome power. The

scene made a rough circle that covered over 2,000 square kilometers. Within that circle an entire forest was destroyed. Tree trunks that had been snapped off at ground level lay like spokes on a wheel, pointing silently away from the point of impact. The center of the circle was burned bare. The impact and explosion incinerated trees and soil. Farther out from the center, beyond the fallen trees, rivers showed the effects. The blasts that downed the forest had also sent waves rushing up streams. And the vast clouds of dust and ash that were stirred up by the impact had settled and left a fine gray film over everything.

ORDER OF IMPORTANCE

10   Ninety-seven percent of a satellite's stored fuel is used to resist the gravitational influence of the Sun and Moon on the satellite's orbit. But two other factors require compensation as well. The second most important influence on the satellite's orbit is the Earth's shape: it is not a perfect sphere. The various bulges of the Earth's shape distort the gravitational field, which then pulls unevenly on the satellite. The last important factor is the solar wind, which also varies in strength and which the satellite occasionally has to fire its small rockets to resist.

Sometimes the movement within the paragraph is from general to specific or from specific to general—as paragraphs 11 and 12 demonstrate.

GENERAL TO SPECIFIC; SPECIFIC TO GENERAL

11   The development of photography led to the greatest step forward in observational astronomy since the invention of the telescope; it has now virtually superseded visual observation in many branches of the subject, especially those involving the use of large telescopes. All studies of galaxies, nebulae and clusters are made with the aid of photographs, using long exposures which permit detail to be recorded which would be quite beyond the range of visual observers. In fields in which visual observation still plays a major part, e.g., observation of the surface features of the Sun, Moon, and planets, photography is also used a great deal as well. Spectroscopic investigations are normally carried out by means of photographs of the spectra concerned.

—GILBERT E. SATTERWAITE, *Encyclopedia of Astronomy*

12   Objective spectral analysis reveals that the dark brown object reflects a smaller amount of light than the orange object under a given level of illumination—because of its molecular structure. Generally, however, both objects reflect the same mix of light wavelengths. Yet they are obviously different colors. Compare a dimly lit orange and a brightly lit chocolate and they will look the same.

One common form of the general-specific pattern is topic-restriction-illustration. The writer announces the topic, restricts or qualifies it, and then illustrates it.

TOPIC-RESTRICTION-ILLUSTRATION

13   Unexpected circumstances have occasionally forced scientists to change their plans for a satellite's mission. The Mariner 9 probe to Mars, for example, was pro-

grammed to orbit Mars and photograph the planet's surface. But because sand-storms obscured the surface, scientists sent new commands to the satellite to train its cameras on Mars's satellites. They were surprised to discover that the satellites are not spheres at all; in fact, they look more like a mass of baking potatoes—replete with craters for eyes—methodically orbiting the red planet.

In the problem-solution pattern, the first sentence states a problem and the solution follows.

PROBLEM-SOLUTION

14 Kary Jensky, a young engineer at Bell Laboratories, was intrigued by the static that always accompanied radio reception. Instead of dismissing it as an inescapable nuisance, he began studying it. By 1933, he discovered that the radio waves were coming from the Milky Way, and further research demonstrated that they were coming from a source at the galaxy's center. With these first experiments Jensky established a new field of study—radio astronomy.

In the question-answer pattern, the topic sentence asks a question and the supporting sentences answer it.

QUESTION-ANSWER

15 What do cosmologists do? First, they create a theory about the structure of the universe and the processes occurring within it. Then, on the basis of that theory, they formulate a model of the universe. They test and continually refine the model by comparing it to observed data.

Many types of development exist, and you will have occasion to create types that combine or modify those represented in the preceding paragraphs. Remember, however, that your goal as a writer is to make your sequence of thought clear.

(2) Provide appropriate transitions.

Transitional devices such as pronouns, repetition of key words or ideas, appropriate conjunctions and other transitional expressions, and parallel structures help create a coherent paragraph. Paragraph 16 exhibits several transitional devices.

16 **They** came. Out of the sky, riding on the polar winds, across the seas and the land, over the burning snow, and under it and through it, **they** came. The shape-shifters drifted across the fields of white, and the sky-walkers fell down like leaves; trumpets sounded over the wastes, and the chariots of the snow thundered forward, light leaping like spears from their burnished sides; cloaks of fur afire, white plumes of massively breathed air trailing above and behind **them**, golden-gauntleted and sun-eyed, clanking and skidding, rushing and whirling, **they** came, in bright bal-dric, wer-mask, fire-scarf, devil-shoe, frost-greaves and power-helm, **they** came; and across the world that lay at **their** back, there was rejoicing in the Temples, with much singing and the making of offerings, and processions and prayers, sacrifices and dispensations, pageantry and color. For the much-feared goddess was to be wed with Death, and it was hoped that this would serve to soften both their dispositions. A festive spirit had also infected Heaven, and with the gathering of the gods, and the demigods, the heroes and the nobles, the high priests and the favored rajahs and high-ranking Brahmins, this spirit obtained force and momentum and spun like an all-colored whirlwind, thundering in the heads of the First and latest alike.

—ROGER ZELAZNY, *Lord of Light*

In this wonderfully imagined scene Roger Zelazny uses several devices to achieve coherence.

PRONOUN REFERENCE   Repetition of *they* and *them*.

REPETITION OF KEY WORDS OR IDEAS   The repeated statement *they came*.

PARALLEL STRUCTURE   Much of the energy of the paragraph is generated by the repetition of participial phrases (*riding on the polar winds, clanking and skidding, rushing and whirling*) and the clusters of other single words and prepositional phrases used as modifiers. A cluster of modifiers precedes the subject-verb unit or one of the verbs in a compound verb construction.

Zelazny could have used conjunctions and other transitional expressions to link sentences, but he did not need them. Notice, however, the transitional devices within the long sentences.

You may find the following list of connectives useful:

1. *Alternative and addition:* or, nor, and, and then, moreover, further, furthermore, besides, likewise, also, too, again, in addition, even more important, next, first, second, third, in the first place, in the second place, finally, last.
2. *Comparison:* similarly, likewise, in like manner.
3. *Contrast:* but, yet, or, and yet, however, still, nevertheless, on the other hand, on the contrary, conversely, even so, notwithstanding, for all that, in contrast, at the same time, although this may be true, otherwise, nonetheless.
4. *Place:* here, beyond, nearby, opposite to, adjacent to, on the opposite side.
5. *Purpose:* to this end, for this purpose, with this object.
6. *Cause, result:* so, for, hence, therefore, accordingly, consequently, thus, thereupon, as a result, then.
7. *Summary, repetition, exemplification, intensification:* to sum up, in brief, on the whole, in sum, in short, as I have said, in other words, that is, to be sure, as has been noted, for example, for instance, in fact, indeed, to tell the truth, in any event.
8. *Time:* meanwhile, at length, soon, after a few days, in the meantime, afterward, later, now, then, in the past.

Clear writing demands clear transitions between paragraphs as well as between sentences. Notice the transitional devices used in the following paragraphs.

17   Like many other amateurs I devoted many long, cold hours to trying to see Halley's Comet before it really was visible. That first venture as an astronomer taught me—more concretely than any amount of reading could have—just what frustrations astronomers must experience.

First, I had to deal with the clutter of lights from my city. Although I live in a fairly secluded area next to a large farm, I still had to contend with the neighbors' outside lights, occasional street lights, and even the beacon light at the local airport. Any one of those lights was able to wash out the features of the night sky.

Second, I was still unfamiliar with my telescope. Simply pointing it at the right celestial object was difficult enough. When I finally focused on an object, I usually lost sight of it when I locked my telescope in position. The motion of the locking screw was sufficient to disrupt the field of vision.

And third, I didn't know where to look for a given object. On one particularly memorable night I devoted 15 minutes to showing my younger daughter Sarah the Little Dipper constellation. We were enjoying ourselves immensely until my older daughter Anna pointed out that we were not looking at the Little Dipper. We were looking at the Pleiades, a fuzzy cluster of stars that the Cherokees called "The seven women who ate onions."

The transitional expressions—*first, second, third*—effectively signal the relationships between the paragraphs; the content of the paragraphs bears out the signal. Other similarly useful expressions are

First . . . Then . . . Next . . . Finally . . .
Then . . . Now . . . Soon . . . Later . . .
One . . . Another . . . Still another . . .
Some . . . Others . . . Still others . . .
A few . . . Many . . . More . . . Most . . .
Just as significant . . . More important . . . Most important of all . . .

32c Develop the paragraph adequately.

Sometimes very brief paragraphs, even paragraphs of one sentence, are appropriate. But most very brief paragraphs are brief because their topics are not developed or because they are not paragraphs at all—they are fragments of paragraphs which actually belong elsewhere in the writing. Analyze the paragraphs below to decide how they are inadequately developed and what revision would improve them.

18   A number of factors have affected the development of life on Earth: the composition of the Earth's atmosphere, the distance of the Earth from the Sun and the resulting change of temperatures experienced on the Earth, the chemical nature of the Earth's crust, the presence of a high percentage of water both on the Earth surface and its atmosphere, etc.

19   The inclination of the Earth's axis and the obliquity of its orbit give rise to seasonal variations in temperature and general climatic conditions; life-forms have adapted to these, and also to local circumstances dependent upon location on the Earth's surface—e.g., the life-forms which survive in polar regions are quite different from those flourishing in the tropics.

20   The development of certain life-forms is in itself a factor governing the environmental adaptation of other life-forms; thus the development of certain forms of vegetable life has stimulated the development of fauna adapted to the use of such vegetation as food; similarly the development of some forms of animal and insect life has been followed by the development of other species to prey upon them.

—GILBERT E. SATTERWAITE, *Encyclopedia of Astronomy*

These three paragraphs are paragraphs only insofar as indention denotes a paragraph. Together, however, they form a complete discussion of the idea stated in the first sentence. If you have difficulty developing paragraphs, study carefully the methods of development discussed in **32d**.

(1) Use relevant details to develop the controlling idea.

You always need to know the details that support the idea you are writing about. Occasionally you may not use those details, but knowing them will make it possible for you to write about the idea with confidence. All the types of development discussed in **32d** require that you know and use relevant details.

In the following paragraph the author explains the problem of space debris, the collection of man-made refuse that orbits the Earth. Although the United States has contributed to the problem, the Soviet Union, he says, is more responsible.

21   Scientists now keep track of nearly 3,000 objects in orbit. Fragments of satellites that have broken apart or that have exploded make up a large percentage of the debris. American scientists know of 87 explosions that have destroyed satellites and, sometimes, their booster rockets; 64 of those explosions involved Russian rockets. And nearly 600 other large pieces of debris are attributable to Soviet experiments that have ended, or were abandoned, or simply never worked. Nearly three-fourths, then, of the 3,000 objects being tracked belong to the Russians. Why such a large percentage? It is because the Russians launch so many more rockets than anyone else—about 100 per year, which is roughly five times more than all other countries combined. Apparently they have come to expect their launches to fail at a relatively high rate. Instead of refining their technology and launching procedures, they simply send up more rockets.

By presenting the details about space debris first, the writer raises certain questions in the reader's mind: What caused the debris? Who is responsible? The writer even asks one of the questions for the reader: "Why such a large percentage?" The controlling idea answers that question.

(2) Illustrate a generalization using several closely related examples or one striking example.

22   The world of physicists puzzles most of us; we can neither define the term "physics" nor explain what a physicist does. And when we read about physicists we immediately encounter equations and numbers so confusing that we stop reading and return to looking at the pictures in our familiar, even if prosaic, *People* magazine. But physics is not all dull, lifeless numbers. Consider, for example, the "quark." Quarks are hypothetical particles, smaller than atoms, that are proposed as the fundamental units of matter. The idea of quarks came to the American physicist Murray Gell-Mann in 1964. Gell-Mann thought of the existence of quarks as a possible explanation for the results of some experiments he was conducting. In order to complete an explanation of some of his findings, he needed three subatomic particles. He named them quarks because the need for three reminded him of a line from James Joyce's *Finnegan's Wake:* "Three quarks for Muster Mark." Gell-Mann continued to demonstrate his flair for the imaginative by naming the quarks the "up-quark," the "down-quark" and the "strangeness-quark." Since Gell-Mann's original work, other physicists have postulated new quarks and have given them equally silly names: "charm-quark," "u-quark," "d-quark," "anti-u-quark," "anti-d-quark," "top-quark," and "bottom-quark."

32d Learn to use various methods of paragraph development.

Writers do not often write paragraphs that perfectly exemplify a single method of development. Most paragraphs combine two or more of the methods as the writer adapts them to a particular audience and purpose. The models that are presented below will help you, however, to learn the characteristics of each type of development. By studying and imitating the models you are not simply restricting yourself for the moment to a particular type of writing; instead, you are learning to use that type of writing to make yourself a more flexible and confident writer. You will have that type of development in mind the next time you write and will almost unconsciously use it in paragraphs or parts of paragraphs because you know it fits your purpose, audience, and content.

(1) Narrate a series of events.

The writer of paragraph 23 recounts a series of events in chronological order to illustrate a change in people's opinions about meteors.

23   Serious interest in meteors did not begin until well into the nineteenth century. Early in the century two young scientists reported having seen an elaborate shower of stones coming from the sky. President Thomas Jefferson gave the typical response when he scoffed at the idea of "stones from the heavens." Then, in November of 1833, a meteor shower of the type that we now call the Leonids hit the United States. Accounts of the shower describe it as a sensational Fourth of July celebration; the entire night sky was lighted for several hours. Although there are no reports of any rocks having been found after the shower, the scientific community and the general public began to take the study of meteors more seriously.

(2) Describe by presenting an orderly sequence of sensory details.

Paragraph 24 contains one astronomer's view as the Earth passed through the tail of Halley's Comet in the early morning hours of May 19, 1910. She watched the passage from atop the New York Times Tower and her account was printed in the May 20 edition. Notice the details, the narrative structure, and the obvious attempt to help readers visualize the experience.

24   . . . At 2:30 o'clock the Moon, ruddy in hue, was low down in the western sky. Looking again in the direction of the eastern horizon, a white mist could be seen

drifting over the bridge, and reaching upward beneath the Square of Pegasus. A soft glow of grayish hue now became plainly visible, spreading from Pegasus as far as Cassiopeia's Chair. The light of the Moon no longer interfering made this observation possible. At 2:34 o'clock this soft glow of grayish hue extended in the northeastern sky to over the left of the Queensboro Bridge, as seen by the observers in the tower. . . . At 4:25 o'clock red streaks made their appearance in the eastern sky, and Venus paled as rosy-fingered dawn drew aside the curtain of day.

—MARY PROCTOR

(3) Explain a process.

The writer of paragraph 25 explains how black holes could cannibalize the universe.

25 Let us see what will happen if the universe does expand forever. In this case all galaxies will continue to expand away from any observer. Within each of the galaxies, stellar evolution will go on until all the available fuel is used up. The number of tiny red dwarfs will gradually increase; the number of black holes will also increase, and as time goes on the black holes will continue to grow as they cannibalize everything nearby, until they are exceedingly massive. Many of them will collide and coalesce. And finally most of the matter of the universe will be tied up in supermassive black holes.

—BARRY R. PARKER, *Concepts of the Cosmos*

(4) Show cause and effect.

A paragraph of this type asserts a causal relationship; it must explain why one thing caused another and must do so convincingly. The first sentence of paragraph 26 states the causal relationship. The remaining sentences explain it.

26 Without water Venus is doomed to a searing, lifeless environment. Water in Earth's atmosphere combines with carbon dioxide to make a mild acid rain. This rain then leaches minerals from the rocks on which it falls and flows to the ocean to form limestone and other carbonate rocks. Thus, over the eons, water has scrubbed out a lot of our primordial CO_2. But on water-poor Venus so much carbon dioxide still fills the air that it creates an intense greenhouse effect. Like a blanket, the CO_2 holds in the solar energy that falls on Venus, making its surface hot enough to melt lead. Earth, by contrast, maintains just enough carbon dioxide to stay moderately warm in the deep freeze of space.

(5) Compare or contrast to develop a main idea.

Paragraph 27 demonstrates the analysis necessary for comparison and contrast. Notice that the discussion focuses on Venus, then on Earth, then on both, and finally on Venus again. The writer could have focused entirely on one planet and then entirely on the other—or the discussion could have been blended throughout the paragraph.

27 Venus is very comparable to the Earth in both size and mass; it has a deep cloudy atmosphere which may also contain dust particles. Certainly the atmosphere is very opaque, and absorbs much of the solar radiation falling upon it, thus preventing it

from reaching the solid surface of the planet; the surface temperatures are therefore probably much more similar to those on Earth than we might conclude from the proximity of Venus to the Sun. It has been suggested from theoretical considerations that there should be a considerable amount of water on Venus, but no spectroscopic evidence of water vapor in the atmosphere has been obtained; neither is there any evidence of oxygen. The principal constituent of the Cytherean atmosphere seems to be carbon dioxide. The Earth's vegetation lives by means of a process which involves its absorbing carbon dioxide, from which to draw its energy, and then emitting oxygen; the high proportion of oxygen in the Earth's atmosphere is probably due to the action of its abundant vegetation. It is to be expected that any planet with a constitution similar to Venus or the Earth would have an atmosphere containing a high proportion of carbon dioxide during the period following the formation of its crust; if we assume that, being closer to the Sun, the crust of Venus formed more recently than that of the Earth, we might expect to find a greater amount of carbon dioxide; this, coupled with the lack of oxygen, might be regarded as suggesting that Venus has not yet developed a comparable amount of vegetation. Such a deduction would be rather dangerous, however, as a comparable portion of oxygen may in fact be present on Venus but its presence may be masked by the impenetrable atmosphere.

(6) Use classification and division to relate ideas.

Classification and division require grouping ideas or elements into categories. In paragraph 28 the author explains various theories for the origin of the Moon.

28   Theories concerning the origin of the moon fall into three general classes. In fission theories, the moon is torn from the body of the Earth. In capture theories, the moon originates elsewhere and is drawn into its present orbit by the gravitational attraction of the planet. In simultaneous creation theories, the moon and Earth form near each other in space. In this latter case, the two bodies probably grew up together by attracting and sharing the same local material within the large nebula that gave rise to the other protoplanets and the sun itself..

—JAMES T. TREFIL, *Space, Time, Infinity*

(7) Formulate a definition.

The writer of paragraph 29 defines the term "accretion." Notice that the topic sentence is actually the last clause of the paragraph.

29   It has long been recognized that "space" is not empty, but contains molecules of "interstellar gas" (largely hydrogen) at a very low density. A star passing through this tenuous medium will gather some of these molecules to itself by its gravitational attraction, and thus increase in mass; this process is known as accretion.

—GILBERT E. SATTERWAITE, *Encyclopedia of Astronomy*

(8) Use a combination of methods to develop the main idea.

Combining methods of development, the authors of the following paragraphs serve their readers well by writing clear, complete, and appropriate discussions. Notice how difficult it is to separate the methods of development in these paragraphs.

30   Between the early 1960s and into the 1980s, Sir Fred Hyole and his colleague N. C. Wickramasinghe, an authority on interstellar dust, developed the hypothesis that comets carry the seeds of life, ready to evolve whenever cometary materials fall into a fertile environment. They argued, in effect, that our most distant ancestors arrived inside one or more comets and that virus particles in meteors—cometary debris falling into the atmosphere—could be responsible for outbreaks of disease against which we have no resistance, such as the global epidemic, or pandemic, of influenza that cost millions of lives in 1918. The wavelengths of infrared heat radiation from interstellar dust, they said, appear "uncannily similar" to those from the cellulose in bacterial cell walls, plant stems, and tree trunks. Comets sweep up such dust grains and, they believe, sometimes deliver them to Earth.

—RICHARD FLASTE ET AL., *The New York Times Guide to the Return of Halley's Comet*

31   Before we talk about antimatter, we must explain what it is. We saw in Chapter 15 that to each type of particle (e.g., an electron) there corresponds an antiparticle (an anti-electron, or positron). When the two collide, they both disappear and are replaced by one or more photons.

Antimatter is of considerable interest to scientists, and there are still many unanswered questions about it. We do not even know, for example, whether matter and antimatter attract or repel one another. It might seem that we could merely project a beam of antimatter along the surface of the earth (which is made of matter) and observe whether it is deflected upward or downward. It turns out, though, that the lifetime of antimatter is too short for such an attempt.

Another interesting question related to antimatter is how much there is in the universe. It seems reasonable that there should be half matter and half antimatter, but most astronomers do not believe that this is the case. Current evidence indicates that matter predominates.   —BARRY R. PARKER, *Concepts of the Cosmos*

Deduct 12 1/2 for each incorrect response.

Unity, Coherence, and Development

Exercise 32–1

NAME _____ SCORE _____

DIRECTIONS   Discuss the unity, coherence, and development of the following paragraphs by answering the questions that follow them.

PARAGRAPH ONE

[1]The idea of manned missions to the heavenly bodies is dormant, but it is not yet dead. While NASA officials plan a space station, other space enthusiasts are pushing to put people on other planets. [2]In July 1984 a contingent of them met to discuss the logistics of colonizing Mars—crew sizes, designs of the mother ships, how to get water, and other essential topics. [3]Scientists from university research faculties, government agencies, NASA, and the Jet Propulsion Laboratory led the discussions. [4]As they planned the Mars trip the scientists intended to take advantage of the "enabling technologies" that have been developed to support the space shuttle. [5]These support programs already have developed long-term life support systems, radiation shielding, advanced space-suit design, and the construction of modular habitats. [6]While the officials do not expect manned missions to Mars to occur in the near future, they do plan to see to it that the United States makes them a goal for the future.

QUESTIONS

1. Which sentence states the controlling idea? __1__

2. What are the key words in the controlling idea? _idea,_
   manned missions, dormant, dead

3. What transitional expressions help achieve coherence? _"while...,"_
   "as...," repetition of "manned missions"

4. What is the main method used to develop the controlling idea? _____
   narration, relevant details

PARAGRAPH TWO

¹Compared to humans, however, stars live an exceedingly long time. ²Even short-lived stars live for millions of years, and average stars, like our sun, live for billions. ³This being the case, we cannot, of course, follow their life cycles by watching them; the human life span, even the entire time that man has been on earth, is but the blink of an eye on the cosmic scale of time. ⁴However, although we cannot see stars change (with few exceptions), we can learn from the billions of stars we can see that are at various stages of their lives; we have "still" pictures of them, and we are like a person looking at such stills outside a theater and trying to determine the plot of the movie from them. ⁵With only a few pictures this would, no doubt, be quite difficult, but as you looked at more and more, the likelihood of being correct would increase.

—BARRY R. PARKER, *Concepts of the Cosmos*

QUESTIONS

1. Which sentence states the controlling idea? ___*1*___

2. What transitional devices are used in sentences 3 and 4? *"this being the case," "however"*

3. What devices for achieving coherence are used in sentence 4? ___ *repetition of idea of lives, life cycles*

4. What is the main method used to develop the controlling idea? ___ *comparison/contrast*

Answers will vary.

Paragraph Practice: Details   Exercise 32–2

NAME _____ SCORE _____

DIRECTIONS   Using *details* as the method of development (see **32c(1)**), write a paragraph on one of the subjects listed below or on one of your own or your instructor's
choosing. First, plan the paragraph, writing out a controlling idea and making a list of
three or more details that will develop the controlling idea. Then compose the sentences
in your paragraph. You may use details from this book (rephrased in your own words,
of course), details from your own knowledge, or, if your instructor permits, details gathered from research.

SUBJECTS

1. a meteor shower you saw
2. your view of Comet Halley
3. your favorite episode of *Star Trek*
4. a description of an extraterrestrial being
5. a description of the surface of Mars

CONTROLLING IDEA

DEVELOPMENT

1.

2.

3.

4.

5.

PARAGRAPH

Answers will vary.
Paragraph Practice: Examples   Exercise 32–3

NAME _____ SCORE _____

DIRECTIONS   Using several closely related *examples* or one striking *example* as the
method of development (see **32c(2)**), write a paragraph on one of the subjects listed
below or one of your own or your instructor's choosing. First, plan the paragraph, writing out the controlling idea and making a list of three or more examples that will develop
the controlling idea. Then compose the sentences in your paragraph. You may use examples from this book (rephrased in your own words, of course), examples from your own
knowledge, or, if your instructor permits, examples gathered from research.

SUBJECTS

1. some of the good results of space exploration
2. some of the bad results of space exploration
3. great discoveries made by amateur astronomers
4. great discoveries made by Galileo
5. successful Soviet space missions

CONTROLLING IDEA

DEVELOPMENT

1.

2.

3.

4.

5.

PARAGRAPH

Answers will vary.
Paragraph Practice: Process Analysis   Exercise 32–4

NAME _____ SCORE _____

DIRECTIONS   Using *process analysis* as the method of development (see **32d(3)**), write a paragraph on one of the subjects listed below or one of your own or your instructor's choosing. First, plan the paragraph, writing out the controlling idea and making a list of three or more details that will develop the controlling idea. Then compose the sentences in your paragraph. You may use details from this book (rephrased in your own words, of course), details from your own knowledge, or, if your instructor permits, details gathered from research.

SUBJECTS

1. how to make a telescope
2. how to make a camera
3. how the sun affects a comet
4. how entering the Earth's atmosphere affects a meteor
5. how a moon colony could survive

CONTROLLING IDEA

DEVELOPMENT

1.

2.

3.

4.

5.

PARAGRAPH

Answers will vary.

Paragraph Practice: Cause and Effect

NAME _____ SCORE _____

DIRECTIONS   Using *cause or effect* as the method of development (see **32d(4)**), write a paragraph on one of the subjects listed below or one of your own or your instructor's choosing. First, plan the paragraph, writing out the controlling idea and making a list of three or more points that will develop the controlling idea. Then compose the sentences in your paragraph. You may use facts from this book (rephrased in your own words, of course), facts from your own knowledge, or, if your instructor permits, facts gathered from research.

SUBJECTS

1. the effects of the Moon's gravity on Earth
2. why comets have large elliptical orbits
3. why the Sun's heat does not destroy the Earth
4. the effects of solar flares on Earth
5. why space exploration is important

CONTROLLING IDEA

DEVELOPMENT

1.

2.

3.

4.

5.

PARAGRAPH

Answers will vary.

Paragraph Practice: Comparison or Contrast   Exercise 32–6

NAME _____ SCORE _____

DIRECTIONS   Using *comparison or contrast* as the method of development (see **32d(5)**), write a paragraph on one of the subjects listed below or one of your own or your instructor's choosing. First, plan the paragraph, writing out the controlling idea and making a list of three or more points that will develop the controlling idea. Then compose the sentences in your paragraph. You may use facts from this book (rephrased in your own words, of course), facts from your own knowledge, or, if your instructor permits, facts gathered from research.

SUBJECTS

1. manned and unmanned spacecraft
2. astrology and astronomy
3. old and modern science-fiction movies
4. the myths and realities of comets
5. old versus modern telescopes

CONTROLLING IDEA

DEVELOPMENT

1.

2.

3.

4.

5.

PARAGRAPH

Answers will vary.

Paragraph Practice: Classification

Exercise 32–7

NAME _____ SCORE _____

DIRECTIONS   Using *classification* as the method of development (see **32d(6)**), write a paragraph on one of the subjects listed below or one of your own or your instructor's choosing. First, plan the paragraph, writing out the controlling idea and making a list of three or more categories that will develop the controlling idea. Then compose the sentences in your paragraph. You may use facts from this book (rephrased in your own words, of course), facts from your own knowledge, or, if your instructor permits, facts gathered from research.

SUBJECTS

1. the functions of NASA
2. the parts of the space shuttle
3. types of unmanned spacecraft
4. types of heavenly bodies orbiting the Sun
5. types of suns

CONTROLLING IDEA

DEVELOPMENT

1.

2.

3.

4.

5.

PARAGRAPH

Answers will vary.

Paragraph Practice: Definition   Exercise 32–8

NAME _____ SCORE _____

DIRECTIONS   Using *extended definition* as the method of development (see **32d(7)**), write a paragraph on one of the subjects listed below or one of your own or your instructor's choosing. First, plan the paragraph, writing out the controlling idea and making a list of three or more points that will develop the controlling idea. Then compose the sentences in your paragraph. You may use facts from this book (rephrased in your own words, of course), facts from your own knowledge, or, if your instructor permits, facts gathered from research.

SUBJECTS

1. black holes
2. the Big Bang theory
3. radio astronomy
4. the Copernican universe
5. gravity

CONTROLLING IDEA

DEVELOPMENT

1.

2.

3.

4.

5.

PARAGRAPH

Answers will vary.

Paragraph Practice: Combination of Methods   Exercise 32–9

NAME _____ SCORE _____

DIRECTIONS   Write a paragraph on one of the subjects listed below. First, plan the paragraph, writing out a controlling idea and making a list of three or more points that will develop the controlling idea. Then compose the sentences of the paragraph. When you have finished writing the paragraph, list in the margin the type or types of development you have used. Underline the controlling idea of your paragraph, and make a list of the transitional devices you have used to achieve coherence.

SUBJECTS

1. books or television programs that have changed the way you think about the universe
2. the achievements of Stephen Hawking
3. the chance that life exists elsewhere in the universe
4. the industrial value of space exploration
5. the military value of space exploration

CONTROLLING IDEA

DEVELOPMENT

1.

2.

3.

313

4.

5.

PARAGRAPH

TRANSITIONAL DEVICES

33

Learn to plan, draft, and revise your compositions effectively.

The principles that you studied for writing effective paragraphs—unity, coherence, and adequate development—are equally important for writing a whole composition. But even more than for a paragraph, the writing of an essay requires a complex of activities—planning, drafting, and revising—that is seldom linear or neat. Usually composing will require you to engage in the three activities several times as you discover, develop, and create the final form of a composition. Whatever repetition or messiness you experience, you must learn to be patient with yourself at the same time you work to improve. The more aware you become of the conventions of writing and of what works well for you, the better and easier your writing will become.

33a Consider the purpose and audience of your composition.

PURPOSE

Although it is sometimes difficult to identify, writing always has a purpose. Once you know what a given composition is supposed to accomplish, the composing process will begin to proceed smoothly.

The purposes of nonfiction writing may be classified as *expressive, informative,* and *persuasive.* Very seldom will you write an extended composition that has only one of these purposes, but the terms will help you describe what you wish to write or analyze what you have written.

Expressive writing emphasizes a writer's feelings and reactions to the world. If you keep a diary or journal or write personal letters in which you recount your responses to your experience, you are engaging in expressive writing.

Informative writing focuses a reader's attention on the objective world, not on the writer's responses to that world. This textbook is a good example of informative writing as it leads you to think about the ideas and actions that help you learn to write. News articles, encyclopedia articles, science reports, and other technical writing that transmits information to a specific audience—all are good examples of informative writing.

Persuasive writing attempts to affect a reader's opinions and/or actions. It relies specifically on evidence and logical reasoning. And, as you attempt to persuade, you are likely to employ expressive and informative writing. Whatever final purpose you decide on, you must have a clear picture in your mind of what you intend to accomplish. Only then can you begin to control your writing.

AUDIENCE

In recent years many authors have written books that make challenging scientific subjects available to the general public—Carl Sagan's *Cosmos* and Lewis Thomas's *Lives of a Cell* come to mind. Sagan and Thomas are highly trained scientists who can write very specialized articles or books for equally specialized audiences. They are comfortable with the *jargon* or technical vocabulary that is appropriate for their subject and audience. Fortunately for us, however, they are also comfortable writing for readers who understand little about such technical training and subjects. When they write to us—a general audience—they simply assume that we are curious, interested, attentive readers. They either omit the jargon or translate it into diction we can understand; they explain ideas in terms that we know.

Sagan and Thomas are particularly good at infusing dry, technical information with a human element. Thomas describes a parasite in a human body in terms that make it seem almost demonic. Sagan recounts an experiment designed to test whether life from Earth could survive on Mars: in a "Mars jar" he recreated a Martian atmosphere and injected microbes into it. Some of the microbes, he tells us, "froze to death . . . and were never heard from again"; others "gasped and perished from lack of oxygen"; still others "fried under the ultraviolet light." A few microbes, however, survived by "closing up shop," or by "hiding . . . under pebbles . . . or sand."

Sagan and Thomas succeed as writers—in large part—because they know their audiences. They bring us information in a language that we find vivid and accessible; as a result we as general readers get to see and know what they see and know.

33b Find an appropriate subject.

In a college setting, an "appropriate subject" is one that meets the needs of the writing assignment. Sometimes your instructor assigns a topic, in which case you can immediately begin considering the needs of the audience (**33a**), what aspects of the topic you want to emphasize (**33c**), and how the composition should be organized (**33d**). Many times, however, you will be allowed to choose a topic; for some students this freedom feels more like an obstacle to successful writing than an opportunity. In this case, your personal experience, knowledge, and interests are a good place to start looking for subject matter. You can write an interesting, stimulating paper on almost anything you care about.

Sometimes you will need to choose a topic outside your own experience. For example, a history professor who asks you to write a composition on some aspect of nineteenth-century France will want you to demonstrate your command of certain information rather than your personal experience or feelings. But, again, you can write a better paper if you find an aspect of the topic that interests you.

And, of course, two other vital practical considerations are time and length. If you have to write a paper in a few hours, choose a subject you already know about—not one that requires research. If you have to write a paper of 500–600 words on Napoleon, do not choose "Napoleon's Military Career" as your subject. Choose "Why Napoleon Lost at Waterloo" or "Napoleon's Final Years in Exile." Find a subject appropriate to the amount of time you have and the length the instructor has asked for.

33c Explore and focus the subject.

(1) Explore the subject.

Once you have a general subject in mind, the following methods, used singly or in combination, will help you explore it.

Listing   Write down everything that comes to mind. Disregard grammar, spelling, and diction—just write. Here is a typical list one student made as he thought about a very broad subject: the Moon.

> over Miami
> pie
> Craig McDaniel
> various meanings of the term "moon"
> where the word came from
> how the word has changed in meaning
> how man's relationship to the Moon has changed
> role of the Moon in superstition, romance
> first Moon landing
> effect it had on our view of the Moon
> effect it had on Neil Armstrong
> can I find information about the effect of the Moon landings on astronauts?
> Buzz Aldrin, John Young—two I recall
> how changed they must have been—this is the question

The list demonstrates the student's discovery of a possible subject—the answer to the question "How did the first lunar landings affect the astronauts?"

Questioning   Journalists typically ask *who? what? when? where? how?* and *why?* Answering those questions about a topic may help you find your subject. Look at the preceding list and consider the benefit of asking these questions about Neil Armstrong or lunar landings. Simply asking why Armstrong became an astronaut or why the United States sponsored lunar landings will stimulate ideas.

Strategies for Development   Think about Neil Armstrong or the lunar landings from three different approaches—static, dynamic, and relative. A *static* approach focuses on what a lunar landing is or who Neil Armstrong is. A *dynamic* perspective focuses on action and change: What did Armstrong do? How did he change? Did lunar landing change? A *relative* perspective examines relationships within a system. Think of lunar landings as part of a larger system—as part of

America's impulse to explore, to be forever young, to know; or perhaps as part of America's need to control and even dominate.

The development strategies discussed in **32d** suggest ways of thinking about a topic. For example,

Narration   What happened during the first lunar landing?

Process   What training did astronauts have?

Cause and Effect   How did the landing affect the astronauts?

Description   What did the Moon's surface look like? What did the Earth look like from the Moon?

Definition   What is a lunar lander? a lunar river? a command module?

Classification and Division   Who benefitted from the landings—business, military, pure science?

Example   What were some benefits?

Comparison and Contrast   How were the lunar missions different from current shuttle missions? How different would life on the Moon be from life on Earth?

(2) Limit and focus the subject.

During the previous discussions of exploring the subject, we also have examined limiting and finally focusing the subject—getting a clear idea of what you want to accomplish for a certain audience in a paper of a certain length. Suppose, for example, we move from the very broad topic, the Moon, to topics that are more and more limited:

the Moon→lunar landings→astronauts who made lunar landings→effects of lunar landings on astronauts

The last topic—What effects did lunar landings have on astronauts?—focuses the subject. You now know the limits of your discussion, and you know what kind of information you must research.

33d Construct a focused, specific thesis statement containing a single main idea.

In **33c** we suggested a variety of ways to limit and focus a subject. We finally narrowed the broad subject, the Moon, into a single specific question: *What effects did lunar landings have on astronauts?* The question demonstrates a limited, focused subject. The paper we write will answer the question for ourselves and our reader. At some point in the composing process we need to condense that answer into a single statement that clearly suggests the thesis of the composition—the idea that binds together the discussion. For example,

VAGUE THESIS   Astronauts found lunar landings to be unforgettable.

IMPROVED THESIS   After walking on the Moon astronauts reported having a strong sense of the universe's vastness combined with a comforting sense of their being a part of it.

The vague thesis statement is as true as the improved one, but it helps neither the writer nor the reader. The word "unforgettable" expresses no clear focus for the writer; therefore, the reader is not sure what to expect. The improved thesis statement focuses by explaining "unforgettable": after walking on the Moon, astronauts' perceptions of their place in the universe changed; they saw its vastness, yet they felt a sense of belonging to it.

The thesis statement helps a writer decide how to construct the essay. For example, a series of brief case studies of astronauts' explanations of their reactions could be used to develop the two ideas of (1) the strong sense of the vastness of creation and (2) the comforting sense of one's place in it. And, of course, a reader will interpret a thesis statement as an indication of the form and content of the discussion.

Depending on the method of development, the thesis statement may occur anywhere in the essay. Or it may not need to be stated at all. For the reader's benefit, however, the thesis statement usually appears at or near the beginning of the essay. At other points in the discussion the writer may repeat the thesis entirely—although in different terms—or in part. The repetition helps to guide the writing and reading processes.

33e Choose an appropriate method or combination of methods of development for arranging ideas, and prepare a working plan.

The strategies for developing paragraphs and possible essay topics also work very well for developing longer pieces of writing. Exemplification, narration, process, cause and effect, classification, definition, description, analysis, and comparison and contrast—one of these or a combination of them can be used for organizing your paper effectively. Review **32d**.

Eventually every writer develops a working plan; if you intend to write successfully, you must find one that works well for you and master it. Some writers use a very *informal* plan; perhaps a list (see **33c**) is sufficient for them. They jot down ideas, cross out some, move others to another location in the list, draw lines to suggest connections or overlap. They are comfortable with this relatively imprecise kind of plan, knowing that they will write, revise, write some more, and finally clarify what to say and how to say it. The plan remains extremely flexible.

An informal plan may begin with a list and evolve into an informal outline. The earlier list about the Moon could evolve into this informal outline.

Informal Outline

Thesis statement: After walking on the Moon astronauts reported having a strange sense of the universe's vastness combined with a comforting sense of their being a part of it.

1. How Armstrong reported his first step on the Moon
2. Armstrong's later descriptions of the experience
3. Contrast Aldrin's experience as second man
4. How Armstrong coped with the experience and his fame
5. Contrast Aldrin's handling of the experience and fame
6. Other astronauts' experiences and how they handled them

A *formal* outline uses indention and numbers to indicate levels of subordination.

Formal Sentence Outline

Thesis statement: After walking on the Moon astronauts reported having a strange sense of the universe's vastness combined with a comforting sense of their being a part of it.

I.   Neil Armstrong becomes the first person to walk on the Moon.
    A.   Armstrong plans a formal, public statement to communicate his first step on the Moon.
    B.   Armstrong's later comments explain his personal response.
II.   Buzz Aldrin becomes the second person to walk on the Moon.
    A.   Aldrin's response is less formal.
    B.   Aldrin seems more obviously moved by the experience.
III.   Armstrong and Aldrin leave the space program.
    A.   Armstrong remains a private, quiet professional who seldom discusses his walk on the Moon.
    B.   Aldrin has serious problems adjusting to life on Earth after his lunar experience. He is haunted by what he has seen and felt.
IV.   Subsequent astronauts have similar responses.
    A.   Their transmissions to Earth during lunar walks demonstrate the awe they feel.
    B.   In more meditative moments they express the deep emotional quality of the experience—often in religious terms.
    C.   Some have adjustment problems.

Formal Topic Outline

Thesis statement: After walking on the Moon astronauts reported having a strange sense of the universe's vastness combined with a comforting sense of their being a part of it.

I.   Armstrong first on Moon
    A.   Armstrong's planned, formal first statement
    B.   Later, more personal remarks
II.   Aldrin second on Moon—less pressure on him
    A.   Never as formal as Armstrong
    B.   Obviously moved, sometimes overwhelmed
III.   Armstrong and Aldrin after the space program
    A.   Armstrong as private, quiet
    B.   Aldrin with serious adjustment problems

IV. Subsequent astronauts
    A. Commentary becomes more personal, less inhibited, more revealing
    B. Religious element
    C. Adjustment problems for a few

33f Write the first draft.

Writers often handicap themselves by assuming that they should write a composition in a certain order—that they should write the first word of the composition first and the last word last. Those writers mistake the order of the words in the completed composition (a product) for the order of the words as they come out in the actual writing (a process). Writing—including all the preliminary steps that we have discussed—usually is anything but straightforward and linear. So the best advice you can give yourself as you begin writing is to begin anywhere you can. Only after you get words on the page can you begin making decisions about revision and altering the content or form of the composition as you wish.

(1) Write effective introductions and conclusions.

Introductions and conclusions occupy strategic locations in a composition and strongly affect a reader's reaction to the composition. In general they are also harder to write because they differ in function from the rest of the composition. An introduction is the point of entry that arouses a reader's interest and indicates the subject and strategy of the composition. A conclusion satisfactorily completes the essay; it may summarize, restate certain ideas, contain the conclusion of an argument, or point to the other subjects that could be discussed.

    The introductory paragraph below grabs the reader's attention and indicates the content, and to some extent the tone (the writer's attitude toward the subject) of the discussion that will follow.

> Ask a scientist about certain subjects—extrasensory perception, flying saucers, faith healing—and you're likely to get a scornful sneer. Ask an astrologer about the science establishment, and the reply will probably refer to closed minds.
> —MICHAEL LEMONICK, *"Science at the Fringe"*

    In the body of the essay, author Lemonick discusses the efforts of the American Association for the Advancement of Science to explore these areas that lie outside of, but have some relationship to, traditional science. He concludes the discussion with a quotation from Rolf Sinclair, president of the AAAS.

> "Scientists have to remember," [Sinclair] says, "that the edges of science shift with time. What is on the fringe today may be beyond legitimate discussion in fifty years—or it may be in the mainstream. In physics, much of what we're working on wasn't even known about ten years ago."

    This conclusion states the thesis of Lemonick's essay and for the first time uses the phrase "on the fringe" which apparently inspired the title. The thesis of the essay has been clear throughout, but this final quoted statement by such an authoritative figure validates the entire discussion.

In the following introductory paragraph the author states his thesis directly and concisely. But the concluding paragraph does not refer to the thesis at all. Because the author has already established that idea and discussed its implications, he turns to the idea of building hotels in space to be served by newly developed spaceships.

INTRODUCTION   We are going to need an easier and less costly way of flying into space if we are to exploit fully the potential of a manned space station. . . .

CONCLUSION   The next step would be to build . . . hotels and sell them to an orbiting public as time-shared condominiums. Our future in space will then involve more than computers and rockets and dispassionate scientists. It will include planeloads of tourists aiming their cameras and flashing their credit cards.

—T. A. HEPPENHEINER, *"Star Raker: Jetlines of the Space Age"*

The purpose of Heppenheiner's essay is to persuade. By stating his thesis at the beginning, he establishes his point of view immediately. And the conclusion indicates that he believes he has made his point and now looks toward the benefits that would accrue if an easier, cheaper method of space flight were created.

As you read essays in magazines, textbooks, or newspapers, look carefully at the introductory and concluding paragraphs. Examine the strategy involved in writing them and try to discover methods that you are comfortable using.

Caution: Avoid using clichés in your introductions. Also avoid unnecessary definitions, such as "Webster's defines a quasar as. . . ." Finally, do not apologize in either your introduction or your conclusion ("Although I'm no expert on this subject, I . . ."). Apologies undermine the effectiveness of your paper.

(2) Develop a good title.

Good titles help establish good first impressions. But they can do much more. They can indicate the tone and content of a composition, and they can pique a reader's interest. The introductory and concluding paragraphs in **33f(1)** give one particularly good example. Lemonick's essay is titled "Science at the Fringe." The introductory paragraph presents first the responses of traditional scientists to the "fringe" subjects and then the responses of those outside traditional science to the "fringe" subjects. The title and introductory paragraph work well together to focus the reader's attention. A less skilled writer might have been tempted to title the essay "Nontraditional Sciences" or "The Changing Dynamic of Science." Lemonick's title has a sharper focus and prepares the reader for the opening sentences of the essay. The concluding paragraph brings the discussion full circle to the title again as Lemonick uses a quotation containing the phrase "on the fringe." The reader recognizes the relationship of the title to the thesis of the essay and is pleased by the symmetry of the discussion.

33g Revise and edit the composition.

Do not think of revision as simply the last stage of composing. Revision plays an important part in every stage of composition—from the first vague notions about the subject to the last proofreading. During the composing process you will often pause to rethink or to see in a different way some aspect of the paper; each of these acts is a part of revision.

There is, however, some danger of being overly conscious of the need to revise as you write. Some writers become so impressed with the inadequacy of what they have written or are about to write that they freeze up, fall victim to a writer's block, and cannot continue. The best advice to give yourself is to write, to get words on the page that you and your instructor can assess. Until you get the words out of your head and onto a piece of paper, there is very little anyone can do to help you improve as a writer.

Below is a list of questions that you will find useful as you revise your papers. Apply them systematically to the final draft of the paper before you submit it for grading. Use the questions on the essay as a whole and on individual paragraphs to help you assess your writing during composition.

REVISER'S CHECKLIST

The essay as a whole

1. Does the whole essay stick to the purpose (see **33a**) and the subject (see **33b**)?
2. Have you kept your audience clearly in mind? Is the tone appropriate and consistent? See **33a**. Do any terms require definition?
3. Is the focus consistent (**33c**)? Do the ideas in the essay show clear relationships to the central idea, or thesis?
4. Is the central idea or thesis sharply conceived? Does your thesis statement (if one is appropriate) clearly suggest the position and approach you are taking? See **33d**.
5. Have you chosen an effective method or combination of methods of development? See **33e**.
6. Is the essay logically sound both as a whole and in individual paragraphs and sentences? See **31**.
7. Will the introduction arouse the reader's interest? Does it indicate what the paper is about? See **33f**.
8. Does the essay come to a satisfying close? See **33f**.

Paragraphs

1. Are all the paragraphs unified? Are there any ideas in any paragraph that do not belong? See **32a**.

2. Is each paragraph coherent? Are sentences within each paragraph in a natural and effective order? Are the sentences connected by repetition of key words or ideas, by pronoun reference, by parallel structure, or by transitional expressions? See **32b**.
3. Is the progression between paragraphs easy and natural? Are there clear transitions where needed? See **32b**.
4. Is each paragraph adequately developed? See **32c**.

Sentences and diction

1. Have you used subordination and coordination to relate ideas effectively? See **24**.
2. Are there misplaced sentence parts or dangling modifiers? See **25**.
3. Do you find any faulty parallelism? See **26**.
4. Are there any needless shifts in grammatical structures, in tone or style, or in viewpoint? See **27**.
5. Does each pronoun refer clearly to its antecedent? See **28**.
6. Are ideas given appropriate emphasis within the sentence? See **29**.
7. Are the sentences varied in length? in type? See **30**.
8. Are there any fragments? comma splices or fused sentences? See **2** and **3**.
9. Do all verbs agree with their subjects? pronouns with their antecedents? See **6**.
10. Have you used the appropriate form of the verb? See **7**.
11. Are any words overused? used imprecisely? vague? See **20**.
12. Have all unnecessary words and phrases been eliminated? See **21**. Have any necessary words been omitted? See **22**.

EDITING CHECKLIST

Punctuation, spelling, mechanics

1. Are commas (see **12**) and semicolons (see **14**) used where required by the sentence structure? Have superfluous commas been removed (see **13**)?
2. Is any end punctuation omitted? See **17**.
3. Are apostrophes (see **15**) and quotation marks (see **16**) placed correctly?
4. Are all words spelled correctly? See **18**.
5. Are capitalization (see **9**), italics (see **10**), and abbreviations used correctly?
6. Is your manuscript in an acceptable form? Have all words been divided correctly at the ends of lines? See **8**.

33h Write well-organized answers to essay tests; write effective in-class essays.

(1) Write clear, concise, well-organized answers on essay tests.

The best preparation for an essay test is to ask yourself questions that might be on the test and then to formulate responses to those questions. You may want to write out these responses before you take the test to make sure that they are unified, coherent, and clear.

If you get in the habit of identifying potential test questions before you take tests, you will improve not only as an essay test writer but as a student in general. You will become better at identifying what is important and you will get good practice at formulating essential concepts.

Before you begin writing, plan how you intend to spend the time in prewriting, writing, and revising. Just a few moments of planning will probably prevent your being caught at the end of class furiously trying to scribble one last paragraph.

Be sure you read the instructions and questions on the test carefully. And as you write, be sure you carefully follow the guidelines that are stated or implied in the instructions or questions.

(2) Write well-organized, clear in-class essays.

In-class essays require you to use time well. Plan your time: jot down a brief outline of your essay; then quickly decide how much time you will need to allow to prewriting, to writing, and to revision.

If you have in mind the essentials of the Reviser's Checklist (**33g**), you can use them to help you analyze your writing as you write and after you finish.

Limiting a Topic

NAME _____

DIRECTIONS   Point out the problems that you might have in writing about the following topics. Evaluate each topic on the basis of its suitability for an essay of 300–500 words written for readers like those in your English class.

TOPICS

1. our Earth

2. meteorites that have hit Philadelphia

3. the mineral content of Asteroid 7

4. why women should not be allowed to be astronauts

DIRECTIONS   Choose one of the general topics listed below and plan a limited essay of 300–500 words. Consider your classmates as the audience for your essay. To limit the general topic that you choose, use one of the techniques discussed in **32a** or some other technique that you have found useful. Save the work that you do in limiting the topic because your notes will be useful in future exercises.

TOPICS

1. the Moon	6. Albert Einstein
2. Sun spots	7. Isaac Newton
3. women in space	8. Tycho Brahe
4. astronomy	9. Russia's space program
5. telescopes	10. funding America's space program

PLAN

PLAN CONTINUED

Planning the Composition: The Thesis   Exercise 33–2

NAME _____

DIRECTIONS   Point out the weaknesses of the following thesis statements. Then use the space below to write your own thesis statement for the limited topic that you chose in Exercise 33–1 or on another topic that your instructor approves.

THESIS STATEMENTS

1. We should colonize the Moon for three main reasons.

2. Space exploration is important to the American way of life.

3. The main idea is to explain why Russia is getting ahead of the U.S. in space

   research.

4. People who do not like astronomy are a bunch of jerks.

THESIS STATEMENT

Planning the Composition: The Outline

NAME _____

DIRECTIONS   Read the following essay carefully and make a topic outline of it.

If you were fascinated by television programs like Carl Sagan's *Cosmos* or by the recent appearances of Comet Halley, Comet Kahoutek, and Comet West, you may be considering making astronomy a hobby. Before you invest any money in equipment, however, take this advice: start simply.

A good pair of binoculars or a spotting scope will allow you to see more than you might think. The moons of Jupiter, the rings of Saturn, the craters of the Moon, and many deep sky objects will be visible. Eventually, though, you will want to buy an astronomical telescope. The two main types on the market are reflectors and refractors; or, for a little more money, you can get a small Schmidt-Cassegrain. The advertising pages of magazines such as *Astronomy* or *Sky and Telescope* will give you a good idea of what you can get for your money. You may also want to visit some of your local department stores; many now carry astronomical telescopes.

The feature of the telescope that is most important for determining what you will see is the size of the objective (the mirror in a reflector; the large lens in a refractor). The larger the objective, the more light the telescope will gather and the better your view will be (assuming the oculars themselves are of high quality). Don't be misled by claims of high power—it's the size of the objective that counts.

Inch for inch, refractors cost more than reflectors; this is one reason why most amateurs use reflectors. A 6-inch reflector is a good starting instrument; it is, in fact, unwise to select anything smaller than about 4 inches in a reflector or 2.5 inches in a refractor.

After you have decided on a size, look carefully at the instrument's stability. If it jiggles easily or seems nonrigid in any way, don't buy it. At the high powers you will be using, these jiggles will be considerably magnified—and very frustrating. Look at how well the telescope is built and how easy it is to use. Do the slow-motion controls work smoothly? Do the clamps hold the telescope rigidly? Check each of these items carefully, as large telescopes (particularly reflectors) are difficult to move from position to position and must be held solidly in place. Their unwieldiness is one of the reasons why small, compact Schmidt-Cassegrain telescopes have become so popular in recent years. Schmidt-Cassegrains are expensive but, because they are easy to use, many people find them worth the money.

A clock drive is a desirable, but not an essential, feature. The Earth is in continual motion and any object you are viewing will move across the field of vision in a minute or so (depending on the power you are using). Frequent adjustments are disruptive and frustrating but a clock drive on your telescope will do away with them once the telescope is equatorially mounted. Finally, you will want to buy at least two eyepieces—one of low power and one of moderate power. If you can afford it, a third, high-power eyepiece is useful, but you will find later on that you use it less than the other two.

Set up your telescope in the darkest part of your yard, well away from the glare of streetlights, on a rigid (preferably concrete) base. You are almost ready to enjoy the magnificent sights of deep space. But in order to find most of them you will need a good star atlas. *Norton's Star Atlas* is an excellent standard guide that has been used by amateurs for years. Another useful atlas—although more expensive—is the larger, more impressive *Skalnate Pleso Star Atlas*. You may want it later on.

The first objects you will no doubt want to look at are the planets. Their locations are given in astronomy magazines such as *Astronomy* or *Sky and Telescope*. The Messier objects are another group that have challenged amateurs for decades. Details on how to find them are given in most observer handbooks (for example, *Burnham's Celestial Handbook*, published by Dover Press).

As you become increasingly involved in amateur astronomy you may wish to turn to astrophotography. With patience, excellent photographs can be obtained

Planning the Composition: The Outline   Exercise 33–3 (continued)

with even a relatively small telescope. A 35-mm camera is perhaps the easiest to use; you can buy an adapter that will allow you to attach the camera body directly to your telescope's eyepiece. Although almost any type of film can be used, there is a good selection on the market of both color and black-and-white, 400 ASA film. It is best to use fast film such as this because it will allow shorter exposure times.

Before you begin, you must mount your telescope equatorially (that is, align the telescope's axis with the Earth's axis). Details on how to do this are given in most books on astrophotography (or see the August 1982 issue of *Astronomy*). With your telescope equatorially mounted and the clock drive running, the Earth's rotation will be compensated for and you will be able to take short exposures; with practice you will be able to get excellent photographs of the Moon and the planets. Photographs of deep-space objects (for example, galaxies) will need longer exposures and, consequently, additional guiding. Because of turbulence in the atmosphere, objects do not remain centered for long, even with the clock drive running. It is essential, therefore, that you be able to speed up or slow down the telescope; this is accomplished with a guiding system (again, see the advertising section of one of the astronomy magazines). Your first deep sky photos may be disappointing, but they will improve steadily as you master the techniques. Very soon you will be producing excellent photos.

OUTLINE

Writing the Composition:
Introductions and Conclusions   Exercise 33–4

NAME _____

DIRECTIONS   Using the outline that you completed for Exercise 33–3 as a guide, make notes for a new introduction and conclusion to the essay. Write the new introduction and conclusion in the space below.

INTRODUCTION

CONCLUSION

Writing the Composition Exercise 33–5

NAME _____

DIRECTIONS   Write an outline for an essay of 300–500 words on the limited topic you selected earlier or on a topic that your instructor approves. Remember that your outline is only a guide and that you can change it, add to it, or subtract from it whenever you have reason to do so. When you have finished the outline write a rough draft and evaluate your composition using the checklist below. Make any changes that are needed. Then make a final neat copy of your work. Be sure to give your essay a title that is suitable to the contents of your essay and that will make your audience want to read it.

CHECKLIST FOR A COMPOSITION

1. Is the title both provocative and appropriate?
2. Does the introduction include the thesis statement or a sentence that suggests the thesis? Is the rest of the introduction appropriate, and does it lead smoothly into the statement or the suggestion of the thesis?
3. Is the relationship of each paragraph to the thesis clear?
4. Is each controlling idea in the paragraph developed fully enough?
5. Is the essay coherent—that is, does each paragraph flow smoothly into the one that follows it? (Compare the first sentence of a paragraph with the last sentence of the preceding paragraph.)
6. Does the conclusion make you feel that the composition is complete, that the essay has ended where it began, with a restatement of the thesis?
7. Are both the grammar and the punctuation of the composition correct? (Proofread the paper at least once for any error that you tend to make frequently.)
8. Are all the words spelled correctly?
9. Is there any wordiness that needs to be eliminated?
10. Does the style seem fluid and clear?

COMPOSITION

COMPOSITION CONTINUED

Writing the Composition

Exercise 33–5 (continued)

COMPOSITION CONTINUED

COMPOSITION CONTINUED

Parts of Speech	Uses in the Sentence	Examples
1. **Verbs**	Indicators of action or state of being (often link subjects and complements)	Tom *hit* the curve. Mary *was* tired. He *is* a senator.
2. **Nouns**	Subjects, objects, complements	*Kay* gave *Ron* the *book* of *poems*. *Jane* is a *student*.
3. **Pronouns**	Substitutes for nouns	*He* will return *it* to *her* later.
4. **Adjectives**	Modifiers of nouns and pronouns	The *long* poem is *the best*.
5. **Adverbs**	Modifiers of verbs, adjectives, adverbs, or whole clauses	sang *loudly* a *very* sad song *entirely too* fast *Indeed*, we will.
6. **Prepositions**	Words used before nouns and pronouns to relate them to other words in the sentence	*to* the lake *in* a hurry *with* no thought *beside* her
7. **Conjunctions**	Words that connect words, phrases, or clauses; may be either coordinating or subordinating	win *or* lose in the morning *and* at night We won today, *but* we lost last week. Come *as* you are.
8. **Interjections**	Expressions of emotion (unrelated grammatically to the rest of the sentence)	*Woe* is me! *Ouch!* *Imagine!*

Common auxiliaries (helping verbs)

am	do	might
am (is, are, *etc.*)	does	must
going to *or*	had	ought to
about to	had to	shall
are	has	should
be	has to	used to
been	have	was
can	have to	were
could	is	will
did	may	would

Forms of the verb to be

am	have been	will *or*
are	is	shall be
had been	was	will *or*
has been	were	shall have been

Common indefinite pronouns

another	everybody	nothing
anybody	everyone	one
anyone	everything	somebody
anything	neither	something
each	nobody	
either	no one	

[Usually considered singular]

all	more	none
any	most	some

[May be considered singular or plural]

Relative pronouns

that	who	whomever
what	whoever	whose
which	whom	

Subordinating conjunctions (or subordinators)

after	if	until
although	in order that	when
as	since	whenever
as if	so that	where
as though	that	wherever
because	though	while
before	unless	

Common prepositions

across	for	over
after	from	through
as	in	to
at	in front of	under
because of	in regard to	until
before	like	up
beside	near	with
between	of	
by	on	

Conjunctive adverbs

accordingly	hence	moreover
also	henceforth	nevertheless
anyhow	however	otherwise
besides	indeed	still
consequently	instead	then
first, second, third, *etc.*	likewise	therefore
furthermore	meanwhile	thus

Common transitional phrases

as a result	in addition	on the contrary
at the same time	in fact	on the other hand
for example	in other words	that is
for instance		

Principal Parts of Some Troublesome Verbs

Present	*Past*	*Past Participle*
begin	began	begun
blow	blew	blown
burst	burst	burst
choose	chose	chosen
draw	drew	drawn
drink	drank	drunk
drive	drove	driven
eat	ate	eaten
fly	flew	flown
freeze	froze	frozen
give	gave	given
lay	laid	laid
lie	lay	lain
raise	raised	raised
ring	rang	rung
rise	rose	risen
speak	spoke	spoken
steal	stole	stolen
swim	swam	swum
take	took	taken
wear	wore	worn

Individual Spelling List

Write in this list every word that you misspell—in spelling tests, in themes, or in any other written work. Add pages as needed.

NO.	WORD (CORRECTLY SPELLED)	WORD (SPELLED BY SYLLABLES) WITH TROUBLE SPOT CIRCLED	REASON FOR ERROR *
	considerable	*con·sid´·(er)·able*	*a*

* See pages 177–93 for a discussion of the chief reasons for misspelling. Indicate the reason for your misspelling by writing *a, b, c, d, e, f,* or *g* in this column.

a = Mispronunciation
b = Confusion of words similar in sound and/or spelling
c = Error in adding prefixes or suffixes

d = Confusion of *ei* and *ie*
e = Error in forming the plural
f = Error in using hyphens
g = Any other reason for misspelling

Individual Spelling List (cont.)

NO.	WORD (CORRECTLY SPELLED)	WORD (SPELLED BY SYLLABLES) WITH TROUBLE SPOT CIRCLED	REASON FOR ERROR

Individual Spelling List (cont.)

NO.	WORD (CORRECTLY SPELLED)	WORD (SPELLED BY SYLLABLES) WITH TROUBLE SPOT CIRCLED	REASON FOR ERROR

A 9
B 0
C 1
D 2
E 3
F 4
G 5
H 6
I 7
J 8